Early Beth Shan (Strata XIX-XIII):
G. M. FitzGerald's Deep Cut on the Tell

Tell Beth Shan, Spring 1990.

University Museum Monograph 121

Early Beth Shan (Strata XIX-XIII): G. M. FitzGerald's Deep Cut on the Tell

Eliot Braun

UNIVERSITY OF PENNSYLVANIA MUSEUM
of Archaeology and Anthropology

Philadelphia

Copyright © 2004
By the University of Pennsylvania Museum
of Archaeology and Anthropology
3260 South Street
Philadelphia, PA 19104

All rights Reserved
First Edition

Library of Congress Cataloging-in-Publication Data

Braun, Eliot.
   Early Beth Shan (strata XIX-XIII) : G.M. Fitzgerald's deep cut on the tell / Eliot Braun.-- 1st ed.
     p. cm. -- (University Museum monograph ; 121)
   Includes bibliographical references and index.
   ISBN 1-931707-62-6 (alk. paper)
   1. Bet She'an (Israel)--Antiquities. 2. Excavations (Archaeology)--Israel--Bet She'an. 3. FitzGerald, G. M. (Gerald Milnes), b. 1883--Archives. 4. University of Pennsylvania. Museum of Archaeology and Anthropology--Archives. 5. Archaeologists--United States. I. Title. II. Series.
   DS110.B393B73 2004
   933--dc22
                                          2004012822

Eliot Braun joined the Israel Department of Antiquities and Museums in 1977 and continues to work for its successor institution, the Israel Antiquities Authority. He has excavated extensively in Israel, specializing in rescue and salvage projects. His expertise is in the late prehistory of the southern Levant with particular emphasis on the Early Bronze I period. His published works include excavation reports and numerous contributions on all major aspects of the archaeology of the Neolithic through Early Bronze Ages of the southern Levant.

Printed in the United States of America on acid-free paper

In Loving Memory of My Parents

Contents

Illustrations viii

Preface and Acknowledgments xiii

1 THE DEEP CUT AND THE EXCAVATION REPORT 1

2 STRATIGRAPHY AND ARCHITECTURE 7

3 POTTERY FROM THE DEEP CUT AT BETH SHAN 30

4 SMALL FINDS: METAL, STONE, AND FLINT OBJECTS 56

5 FITZGERALD'S DEEP CUT: A SUMMARY STATEMENT 61

Appendix 1 New Data on Some Cultivated Plants and Weeds of the Early Bronze Age
            in Palestine, *Naomi Feinbrun* 66

Appendix 2 Room List 68

Bibliography 72

Figures 79

Index 192

Illustrations

Frontispiece: Tell Beth Shan, Spring 1990.

FIGURES

1.1	Letter from G. M. FitzGerald to Director of Museum, 1933	81
1.2	Topographic plan of Tell Beth Shan with excavation areas	83
1.3	Northwest Area of Level XII	84
1.4	Page 252 from FitzGerald's 1933 field diary	85
1.5	The expedition's permanent camp ca. 1924	86
1.6	Staff of the 1933 season	87
2.1	Plan of Stratum XIX	88
2.2	Close-up view of Pit 19-2	89
2.3	Close-up view of Pit 19-3	89
2.4	FitzGerald's Plan of Level XVIII	90
2.5	Annotated Plan of Stratum XVIII b-a	91
2.6	View of structures of Stratum XVIII	92
2.7	View of Strata XVIII with the partially excavated pits of Stratum XIX	92
2.8	Close-up of Room 1897	93
2.9	FitzGerald's Plan of Level XVII	94
2.10	Annotated Plan of Stratum XVII, phases c-a	95
2.11	Detail of Stratum XVII	96
2.12	Detail of Room 1893	96
2.13	"Plano-convex" bricks from Stratum XVII	97
2.14	Detail of Wall 1704	97
2.15	FitzGerald's Plan of Level XVI	98
2.16	Annotated Plan of Stratum XVI, phases b-a	99
2.17	Detail of Room 1882	100
2.18	Detail of Rooms 1885 and 1886	100
2.19	View of the curvilinear house of Stratum XVI	101
2.20	Potsherd floor in Room 1887	101
2.21	Detail of Room 1890	102
2.22	Detail of Walls 1618 and 1619	102
2.23	FitzGerald's Plan of Level XV	103
2.24	Annotated Plan of Stratum XV, phases b-a	104
2.25	Detail of Room 1874	105
2.26	The north end of Stratum XV	105
2.27	Northeast end of the Deep Cut in Stratum XV	106
2.28	Stratum XV	106
2.29	FitzGerald's Plan of Level XIV	107
2.30	Annotated Plan of Stratum XIV, phase b	108
2.31	Annotated Plan of Stratum XIV, phase a	109
2.32	View of Level XIV	110

2.33	Detail of the rooms of Level XIV at the south end of the Deep Cut	110
2.34	View of Rooms 1866 and 1867	111
2.35	View of Stratum XIV	111
2.36	FitzGerald's Plan of Level XIII	112
2.37	Annotated Plan of Stratum XIII, phases b-c	113
2.38	Annotated Plan of Stratum XIII, phase a	114
2.39	Detail of Room 1846	115
2.40	Northern building in Stratum XIII	115
2.41	Mudbricks from Room 1848	116
2.42	Detail of a stone-paved bin in Room 1857	116
2.43	Detail of pottery *in situ* on the floor of Room 1848	117
2.44	East-west lane in the northern precinct of Stratum XIII	117
2.45	Room 1856	118
2.46	View of buildings in the southeast precinct of Stratum XIII	118
2.47	View of buildings in the southeast precinct of Stratum XIII	119
3.1	Pottery of Stratum XIX	120
3.2	Pottery of Stratum XVIII	122
3.3	Pottery of Stratum XVIII	124
3.4	Pottery of Stratum XVII	126
3.5	Pottery of Stratum XVII	128
3.6	Pottery of Stratum XVII	130
3.7	Pithoi fragments from Yiftah'el II	132
3.8	Selected Early EB I Pithoi fragments from Strata XVII-XVI	133
3.9	Pottery of Stratum XVII	134
3.10	Pottery of Stratum XVI	136
3.11	Pottery of Stratum XVI	138
3.12	Pottery of Stratum XVI	140
3.13	Pottery of Stratum XV	142
3.14	Pottery of Stratum XV	144
3.15	Pottery of Stratum XV	146
3.16	Pottery of Stratum XIV	148
3.17	Pottery of Stratum XIV	150
3.18	Pottery of Stratum XIV	152
3.19	Pottery of Stratum XIV	154
3.20	Pottery of Stratum XIII	156
3.21	Pottery of Stratum XIII	158
3.22	Pottery of Stratum XIII	160
3.23	Base with vestigial ring, typical of Chalcolithic workmanship	162
3.24	Base of a string-cut bowl, typical of Chalcolithic workmanship	162
3.25	Wheel-made, Chalcolithic bowl with typical base, internal view	163
3.26	Wheel-made, Chalcolithic bowl with typical base, external view	163
3.27	Late EB I storage jar, possibly of Egyptianized morphology, *in situ* in Room 1866	164
3.28	FitzGerald's photo of selected ceramics from the pits below Level XVIII (Stratum XIX)	164
3.29	FitzGerald's photo of selected ceramics from Level XVIII	165

ILLUSTRATIONS

3.30 FitzGerald's photo of selected ceramics from Level XVII 165
3.31 FitzGerald's photo of selected ceramics from Level XVII 166
3.32 FitzGerald's photo of selected ceramics from Level XVI 166
3.33 FitzGerald's photo of selected ceramic handles from Levels XVI and XV 167
3.34 FitzGerald's photo of selected ceramics from Level XV 167
3.35 FitzGerald's photo of selected ceramics from Levels XIV and XIII 168
3.36 FitzGerald's photo of selected ceramics from Levels XIV and XIII 168
3.37 Small jar of Stratum XIV 169
3.38 FitzGerald's photo of selected ceramics from Level XIV 169
3.39 FitzGerald's photo of selected handles from Level XIII 170

The Original Plates Reproduced from FitzGerald's (1935) Preliminary Report

I   Assorted ceramic, Levels XVI, XVII, XVIII 171
II   Assorted ceramic, Levels XVI, XVII, XVIII 172
III   Assorted ceramic, Levels XVI, XVII, XVIII 173
IV   Assorted ceramic, Levels XIII, XIV, XV 174
V   Assorted ceramic, Levels XIII, XIV, XV 175
VI   Assorted ceramic, Levels XIII, XIV, XV 176

4.1   Metal (copper?) objects from Stratum XVI 177
4.2   EB I Basalt Bowls 177
4.3   Large fragment of an unfinished, EB I Type III basalt bowl 179
4.4   Type EB I basalt bowl from Stratum V 180
4.5   Photos of bowl in Figure 4.4 181
4.6   Large fragment of an EB I basalt bowl from Room 1897 182
4.7   Example of 4-handled basalt bowls from an unknown, looted context 183
4.8   Small stone objects 184
4.9   Small stone objects 185
4.10 Assorted flint tools from Below Level XVIII 186
4.11 Assorted flint tools from Level XVIII 186
4.12 Assorted flint tools from Level XVIII 187
4.13 Assorted flint tools from Level XVII 187
4.14 Assorted flint tools from Level XVI 188
4.15 Assorted flint tools from Level XV 188
4.16 Assorted flint tools from Level XIV 189
4.17 Assorted flint tools from Level XIII 189
4.18 Assorted flint tools from Level XIII 190
4.19 Assorted flint tools from Level XIII 190

A1.1 Seed of Beth Shan lentils 191
A1.2 Seed of Beth Shan common beans 191

TABLES

2.1   Pits of Stratum XIXb 9
2.2   Walls of Stratum XIX 10

2.3	Walls of Stratum XVIIIb	11
2.4	Walls of Stratum XVIIIa	12
2.5	Dimensions of Plano-convex Bricks of Stratum XVII	13
2.6	Walls of Stratum XVII North	13
2.7	Walls of Stratum XVII South	15
2.8	Walls of Stratum XVI	17
2.9	Walls of Stratum XVb	18
2.10	Walls of Stratum XVa	19
2.11	Walls of Stratum XIVb	21
2.12	Walls of Stratum XIVa	22
2.13	Walls of Stratum XIIIc	24
2.14	Walls of Strata XIIIb and XIIIa	25
2.15	Walls of Stratum XIIIa only	27
5.1	Sequence of Chrono-cultural Periods in the Deep Cut	62
A2.1	Rooms of Level XVIII	68
A2.2	Rooms of Level XVII	68
A2.3	Rooms of Level XVI	69
A2.4	Rooms of Level XV	69
A2.5	Rooms of Level XIV	70
A2.6	Rooms of Level XIII	71

Semitic Place Names

Original transliteration	As it appears in the text
ʻAfula	Afula
Munḥatta	Munhatta
Naḥal	Nahal
Ḥarod	Harod
Ḥorvat	Horvat
Taḥtit	Tahtit
Palmaḥim	Palmahim
Iṣtaba	Istaba
Meṣer	Meser
ʻEn Shadud	En Shadud

Preface and Acknowledgments

Beth Shan is one of the major tells of the southern Levant and also one of the first to have yielded up its secrets on early pottery cultures of the region. Although often cited by scholars on the basis of two severely limited, preliminary publications, the full significance of the early levels at Beth Shan has remained largely obscure for want of a thorough treatment. Accordingly, I have endeavored, with the help of numerous individuals cited below, to produce a report that will adequately present the results of G. M. FitzGerald's last season on the high tell in which he probed the deposits from these early periods.

My special interest in Beth Shan began more than two decades ago when I excavated some late remains in the 6th century monastery just to the north of the tell. I was (and remain) much more interested in the earlier periods buried there, and every chance I had I would wander over the tell, exploring its steep, barren slopes, while hunting for evidence of the earliest levels in the potsherds and other artifacts eroding out of them.

Some years later, while researching the Early Bronze and Neolithic periods on other sites, I came to realize just how potentially important Beth Shan was and how inadequate were FitzGerald's preliminary reports for representing the early levels. I often thought what a great opportunity it would be to sink my own probe into the site and so add information to what FitzGerald had written. While such a project was not in the cards for me, I was able to do something equally exciting. Becoming the Robert H. Dyson Fellow at the University of Pennsylvania Museum of Archaeology and Anthropology allowed me the chance to reveal some of the mound's earliest secrets that had lain buried in FitzGerald's field notes in the Museum's archives since 1933.

The report I offer here to the reading public was researched mostly during my 10-month tenure as Dyson Fellow at the Museum in 1998. That proved to be not quite enough to finish a publishable manuscript, and so I have continued to work on it on a spare-time basis, between my other duties. As is self-evident, a report of this type was not produced single handedly, but rather assisted by numerous individuals whom I wish to thank.

I am grateful to the committee that chose me as the Dyson Fellow, allowing me the financial freedom and resources to pursue this research. Professor Jeremy A. Sabloff, the Williams Director of the Museum, has been particularly supportive and helpful in finding the means for allowing this research to come to fruition in the present publication. During my stay in Philadelphia I was privileged to have the support and help of the entire Museum staff and wish to express my thanks to them here. In particular, Richard Zettler, Curator in Charge of the Near East Section, and Bruce Routledge, James B. Pritchard Assistant Curator, went out of their way to make me welcome and encouraged me to publish this work. Shannon White, Fowler-Van Santvoord Keeper, shared her limited work space with me for 10 months, all the while retaining her pleasant ways and helping me access the Deep Cut collection and its database. Later, her considerable help also extended over long distances through the media of e-mail and telephones and gracious hosting during a couple of flying visits to the Museum.

I also wish to express thanks to the editorial staff of Museum Publications under the direction of Walda Metcalf, whose energy has helped me to produce a viable ms. for publication. Jim Mathieu, the editor who has nursed along the final phases of this work, has been extraordinarily helpful in putting the ultimate version together and particularly tolerant of late revisions and additions. I am extremely grateful to him for his help and his infinite patience.

The skills of Alex Pezzati, the Museum's archivist, eased my way into FitzGerald's field diaries and notes, making the task of organizing them far less daunting than it would otherwise have been. Thanks are also due Charles Kline, photo archivist, for helping me with the photographic archives. Carole Linderman undertook the laborious task of rendering the bulk of the pottery from the Philadelphia collection of ceramics and small finds for the new illustrations. Kim Leaman drew several basalt bowls in the Philadelphia collection. I am grateful to these skilled draftswomen for doing it in my absence. I am also indebted to Carmen Hersch (Jerusalem) who drew several objects in the Jerusalem collection. The consumate skills of Francine Sarin and Jennifer Chiappardi made new prints of FitzGerald's photographs from badly decayed negatives, as well as new photos of the basalt bowls. Michael Danti, Brad Hafford, Matthew Manieri, and Flint Dibble were extremely helpful in the digitization process of the line drawings, and I am grateful to them for doing it in a timely manner with no assistance from me.

Thanks are due Vadim Cohen, for helping me understand some aspects of the chipped stone collection while we were both in Philadelphia. I have also benefited from conversations with Catherine Commenge (Centre

PREFACE AND ACKNOWLEDGMENTS

Nationale de Recherche Scientifique, France), Ram Gophna (University of Tel Aviv), and Vladimir Zbenovich (Israel Antiquities Authority).

The botanical report (Appendix 1) of the late Naomi Feinbrun (The Hebrew University of Jerusalem) was brought to my attention by Mordechai Kislev (Bar Ilan University), to whom I am grateful. Thanks are also due Uriel Safriel, executor of Professor Feinbrun's scientific estate, for allowing and encouraging reproduction of the report. I can only hope that this re-publication in a tome devoted to archaeology will allow the wider archaeological community to appreciate it.

This final excavation report, on the earliest levels of the high tell of Beth Shan encountered to date, was limited to a sounding at its eastern perimeter the excavator nicknamed the "Deep Cut." Thirty-three days were sufficient for G. M. FitzGerald's workmen to clear ca. 5 m depth of debris. A brief review of the history of the season and methods of fieldwork and recording is followed by detailed accounts of the principal discoveries, including architecture and small finds (i.e., pottery, ground stone, chipped stone, and metal artifacts). Descriptions are complemented by interpretations of the data and synthetic studies of the major features of the site.

The final report is constructed so as to integrate it with the original, preliminary publications that for more than seven decades were the only public sources of information available on the earliest levels of the site. By including copious illustrations (field photos and documents) this work attempts to recreate for the reader an aura of having visited the excavation of 1933 and made acquaintance with Beth Shan as its deepest levels were probed. Appendices offer one of the earliest archaeo-botanical studies in the Near East and raw data derived from FitzGerald's field notes.

1

The Deep Cut and the Excavation Report

The Beisân Expedition and FitzGerald's Deep Cut

The era between the world wars was one in which extravagant plans for total exposure of archaeological sites, especially mounds of multi-period occupation, were considered not only feasible, but also desirable projects. In British Mandate Palestine the extraordinarily low cost and availability of local labor allowed for two such grandiose expeditions to be initiated–the Oriental Institute's work at the site of biblical Megiddo (Tell el Mutesellim) and the University Museum's long-term Beisân Expedition at (Tell el-Husn), biblical Beth Shan in the Jordan Valley. The expedition incorporated the modern Arabic name for the small village to the southeast of the mound (Rowe 1930:1, pl. 2). Happily, neither project succeeded in its original intent, although initial attempts at stripping these mounds of their uppermost strata succeeded in entirely denuding them of their latest occupations.

The Beisân Expedition,* begun in 1921, carried out lengthy and large-scale field seasons every year until 1932, when work was discontinued. By then, the enormity and virtual impossibility of the original task had become obvious, while economic parameters so deteriorated, the Museum could not afford to field the expedition that year. Although autumn 1933, at the height of the Great Depression, saw a resumption of fieldwork, it was with a realistic assessment of future prospects that G. M. FitzGerald, then director of the Beisân Expedition, must have planned his field strategy to include a "Deep Cut" (FitzGerald 1933a) into the earliest levels of the mound. In an end-of-season letter to Horace H. F. Jayne, then Director of the University Museum, he wrote: "I imagine that you are not at present making any plans for the resumption of digging next year" (FitzGerald 1933b; Figure 1.1).† As it turned out, FitzGerald's statement was as prophetic as it was realistic. Nineteen thirty-three was actually the ultimate season of fieldwork at the site for the Beisân Expedition.

Probably because FitzGerald did not expect to resume work, the 1933 season on the high tell of Beth Shan was designed with a twofold purpose, to continue exploration of Level VI and more importantly, to explore unknown levels. As FitzGerald (1933d:1; 1934:123) stated: "secondly, *the main work of the season* [was] to go down below Level XI on the South side of the Tell in a very restricted area and if possible to reach the surface of virgin soil, which is believed to be about 11 metres below the last level uncovered in the excavations of 1931" (emphasis added). Although FitzGerald set his workmen a formidable commission, this task proved to be considerably less onerous than originally estimated.

---

* The expedition incorporated the modern Arabic name for the small village to the southeast of the mound (Rowe 1930:1, pl. 2). The name is a transliteration from the Hebrew and is written in several variant forms, e.g., Beth Shean, Beth She'an, Bet She'an, Beth Shan, and Bet Shan. The Arabic form is Beisân.

† The early part of the season included a period of financial embarrassment when funds were not forthcoming, either heightened or brought about by the devaluation of the U.S. dollar (FitzGerald 1933c).

Between October 5 and November 13, in a total of only 33 work days, a zigzag-shaped pit (Figures 1.2 and 1.3) with inwardly sloping walls was carved out of more than 5 m of occupation debris, down to a level of what may be virgin soil. Bedrock, FitzGerald's ultimate goal in this sounding, was never reached, although an attempt at probing for it was made by driving a crowbar into the bottom of a pit in subsoil below the latest occupation level (1933a). This sounding, identified by FitzGerald as the "Deep Cut" in the field notebook, is today an area visible as a badly eroded, large, deep depression at the side of the mound, passed by those hardy tourists who make the effort to ascend a steep flight of steps that offers ascent to the summit.

One may especially appreciate FitzGerald's desire to probe these early levels and sympathize with what is clearly a sense of excitement and urgency underlying the formal language of his communications to Jayne. This was 1933 and, although W. F. M. Petrie's (1891) basic principles for sequence dating pottery had long been accepted, really very little was known of late prehistoric periods despite the fact that much excavation had been done in Palestine up to this time. The sole attempt to produce an early ceramic sequence for the region then available in print was Duncan's *Corpus of Dated Palestinian Pottery* (1930), in which anything earlier than Egypt's XIIIth Dynasty was relegated to a category known as "Neolithic Period: Cavedweller Ware—Prior to 1500 B.C. [sic!]" (Duncan 1930: 11-16).

FitzGerald in a sense was a pioneer at a time when the first major publications dealing with an early ceramic sequence for the southern Levant had not yet appeared (e.g., Engberg and Shipton 1934; Ben-Dor 1936; Wright 1937). He was obviously acutely aware of this lack of information on early ceramic traditions as represented in Duncan's work and was interested in obtaining a sequence and rushing the material into publication to help fill the lacuna. He seems to have been convinced that Beth Shan could supply the missing data and purposefully set out to obtain a sequence. His keen interest in the subject may be seen in a correspondence he carried on with George Ernest Wright, and his own subsequent publications (e.g., FitzGerald 1935; 1936; 1939b). Fitzgerald sent a letter to Wright with a copy of his Jericho pottery report (FitzGerald 1936) that prompted a reply. Preserved in the Museum's Beth Shan archives are several of Wright's replies (dated 1937) in which he discusses details of an early ceramic chronology. These early works, often overlooked by later scholars, indicate FitzGerald's ability to make thoughtful, sound contributions to the study of pottery of late prehistoric periods in the southern Levant. It is against this background that FitzGerald's contemporary notation, on the importance of rapidly publishing the material recovered from the Deep Cut is noted here in a letter to the Museum Director:

> It has occurred to me that, as our finds are of so novel a character and of so much importance for the history of early pottery in this country, it would be advisable to get these published as soon as possible. I would therefore ask you to consider whether you could give me the opportunity of writing an article for the Museum Journal on the pottery and objects found in the Early and Middle Bronze Age levels. Detailed description of the levels themselves, involving photographic illustrations, would of course stand over till the final publication, but the finds ought to be adequately illustrated by line drawings, and I should be much obliged if you could let me know how many plates of that sort you could allot to the subject, assuming that the idea of such a publication is agreeable to you. (FitzGerald 1933c)

Indeed, FitzGerald's (1934; 1935) initiative and industry, coupled with the encouragement of Horace H. F. Jayne, gave us some of our earliest glimpses of prehistoric pottery in a sequence from the southern Levant, together with basic information about the early levels of Beth Shan. However, almost 7 decades on, these brief reports remain the sole published sources for work on the "Deep Cut"; the promise of a "final publication" remained unfulfilled until the opportunity was provided to me, as a Robert H. Dyson Fellow of the Museum, to complement FitzGerald's work. The present report is my attempt, after such a "decent interval," at producing a "final publication" of the sort that one hopes G. M. FitzGerald envisaged and would have approved.

The Site

Beth Shan is a large site straddling Nahal Harod (Arabic: *Jâlûd*), a perennial stream at the eastern edge of the Harod Valley (Orni and Efrat 1980: 92) near its juncture with the Jordan Valley (map ref. 1977/2124, Israel Grid). It is a region with hot summers, mild winters, and abundant rainfall. The mound, occupied in many periods (Mazar 1993), lies well within the perimeter of a major town of Classical and later periods (FitzGerald 1939a; Foerster 1993). The tell is situated on a high hill, well above the surrounding topography on the north bank of the stream. Even its earliest occupations, well below the present, artificially truncated summit of the mound, command a view to the east of the broad Jordan Valley and the mountains of Gilead beyond. Westward, the narrow Harod Valley is framed by Mt. Gilboa to the south and the Heights of Issachar to the north.

Sources for the Final Report

The primary sources for work on the Deep Cut available for this study include FitzGerald's diaries, a field journal, his letters to the Museum Director, a preliminary report, his publications on Beth Shan, a set of stratigraphic plans, hand-written, annotated index cards with or without line drawings of pottery and other small artifacts, photographs taken in the field and collections of portable artifacts recovered in the excavations. These last are found in two repositories, the University Museum in Philadelphia and the Israel Antiquities Authority in Jerusalem.

Written and Pictorial Sources

G. M. FitzGerald's original notes, reports, correspondence and illustrative materials (sketches, line drawings and photographs), on file in the Archives of the Museum of Anthropology and Archaeology of the University of Pennsylvania, are the primary accounts of the excavation on which this report is based. They comprise a field journal that contains entries, apparently made on an almost daily basis, giving brief accounts of where the excavation took place and how it proceeded and, occasionally, detailed information on architecture and artifacts recovered.

Additional notes on index cards, describing pottery and other small objects, some bearing scale pencil drawings (also apparently prepared in the field either at the time of excavation or shortly thereafter by FitzGerald's team of draftsmen), offer some idea of the time when material was removed from the field. In addition to documenting artifacts that were published and/or retained for permanent collections, they also document other objects that were discarded. Some of these last are indicated by drawings of objects, others by mere written notations. Numerous cards also carry hand-written addenda of the late Frances James made during her tenure of research at the Museum. Although these notes are unsigned, comparing handwriting samples from them with specimens from James's letters allowed me to make this identification.

Architectural features are preserved in crude sketches (not to scale) in the field diary (e.g. Figure 1.4) and in a series of schematic blueprints drawn to scale by a skilled draftsman. Additional information is available in the small collection of field photographs and in specialized notebooks, called "Level Books," that sporadically recorded elevations of structures.

The recording system was not highly developed and the provenience of most objects is less precise than one would hope for. Indeed most of the small objects are derived from large excavation units termed "rooms" rather than small, well defined, discrete units (loci and baskets), as is the custom nowadays (e.g., Braun 1997: 15-16).

FitzGerald used architectural features as means for identifying locations within the excavated area and indicating provenience of objects. Walls on the sketch plans in the field diary that, to a greater or lesser extent, enclosed spaces, were designated as "rooms" and uniquely numbered, more or less with regard to their stratification. These rooms are the closest equivalent to my concept of locus, a three-dimensional excavation unit defined by the excavator. However, not all of FitzGerald's rooms directly relate to fill or debris that they purport to enclose. Sometimes the enclosure is merely a two-dimensional, horizontal designation for locating a deposit that is categorically indicated as below the architectural feature used to identify it. Accordingly, some objects belong to earlier horizons that have nothing to do with the rooms with which they were associated.

Incomplete Sources and Problems in Reconstructing Stratigraphy

While the archive concerned with the Deep Cut at Beth Shan is of considerable size, we lack many types of detailed data that are usually documented in modern excavations. The kinds of data that are now almost universally recorded on excavations were omitted from the Beisân Expedition's database. There is no information on digging and recovery procedures, nor, in most cases are precise data on the provenience of artifacts available. Absolute elevations of excavation units were not recorded nor is it likely they were taken. All references were to "rooms," but plans are somewhat schematic, and details, especially elevations of foundation courses that are essential for understanding stratigraphic ascriptions, are often not available. In addition, I have been unable to find evidence of any sections drawn for the Deep Cut and must conclude that none were drawn.

The lack of elevations, especially for wall foundations, hampers attempts at investigating associations between structures, at least in their periods of initial use. In addition, most objects recovered can, at best, be located only somewhere within a room in fill between the upper and lower elevations of its walls. The parameters of the fill are only rarely available when elevations for wall foundations and superstructures are indicated in the level book; most may be understood as relative to earlier and later deposits. Only occasionally is material noted as deriving from a floor or below it and so may be relegated to an alternate phase or even stratum. Often there is no way of determining whether fill within any particular room was recovered in deep or shallow deposits, or precisely where particular objects might have been recovered and their relationship to each other and the structures to which they are presumed to have been associated. In certain instances the depth of fill could be over 1.0 m or more, and beyond the existence of architectural phases, there is virtually no evidence for sub-phasing, even within well-preserved buildings.

Two sets of plans for the Deep Cut are offered for the reader's perusal. FitzGerald's original stratigraphic sequence includes Level XVIII through Level XIII, representing his interpretation, more or less as he understood it at the end of the excavation. In addition, in another set of plans I have suggested a slightly expanded stratigraphy that attempts to indicate sequential phasing within the levels. To distinguish this stratigraphy from FitzGerald's the term "stratum" replaces his use of "level." These new proposals, however, are of equivocal validity because of imprecision in recording work in the Deep Cut. Nevertheless, it is an attempt to provide a rational, stratigraphic sequence of the architecture that may be related, at least circumstantially, to an accompanying ceramic sequence that is basically FitzGerald's.

I did this by using available plans and elevations to relate the diverse structures to each other and to find spots for artifacts that could then be associated or dissociated with extant buildings. These associations suggest likely cultural horizons for the different strata represented in the Deep Cut. The reader is invited to judge the validity of these new stratigraphic proposals.

Artifact Assemblages

Objects from the Deep Cut include a modicum of artifacts now in two museum collections. The division of this material is the result of a policy instituted by the Department of Antiquities of the British Mandate of Palestine. It was customary for the Department to divide the finds more or less equally with foreign expeditions, but to retain artifacts that were unique or deemed especially important. One portion was allotted to the Department, while the other was retained by FitzGerald to become the property of the University Museum. The former collection, now belonging to the State of Israel, is presently administered by the Israel Antiquities Authority (IAA) and housed in its facilities in the Rockefeller Museum, Jerusalem. This collection is now considerably the smaller of the two, although whether as the result of a selective process of curation or unequal division of the spoils is unknown. By far the lion's share of artifacts presently available for study from the Deep Cut is the property of the University Museum that houses and curates it.

Unfortunately, there are no records as to the size of the complete artifact assemblage derived from the Deep Cut, but what is certain is that FitzGerald (ND) was selective in his retention of material. An index card file contains pencil drawings of sherds and flints noted as having been discarded, while there is additional, albeit circumstantial, evidence for selective retention by him of recovered pottery. F. Vitto (personal communication), during her excavations at Tel Naharon for the Israel Department of Antiquities and Museums (ca. 1 km to the west of the tell; Figure 1.5), encountered a major dump of what she believes to be FitzGerald's discarded potsherds deposited above an occupation of the Byzantine period. Vitto notes that many of these sherds could be dated to the Early Bronze Age, and she believes the dump to be adjacent to the Beisân Expedition camp. I assume that at least some of the discarded material was derived from the Deep Cut. Because of the obvious selective nature of the assemblage available for study, and since nothing more is known of the entire assemblage, no statistical inferences should be drawn from the material presented in this report.

FitzGerald's perspicacity in his understanding of pottery and a need for developing a reliable ceramic sequence allows me to assume the ceramic assemblage retained (presumably the sum of the Museum and IAA collections) and presently available for study is representative of the Deep Cut. FitzGerald had an eye for objects of importance and was interested in obtaining them for his employers. Such objects included not only what others might consider to be museum pieces, but also hitherto unknown types of ceramic artifacts, the worth of which he well understood as his letter to Museum Director Jayne, dated 31 December 1933, indicates:

On the whole I do not think we have any cause for complaint, and I hope that you will consider the objects we are sending to you a satisfactory addition to the Museum, bearing in mind that the season's work has been very instructive and that we could not hope for anything very decorative from the early levels. In fact, before we started I had a horrid fear that a series of "ledge handles" would be almost our only contribution to your collections. (FitzGerald 1933c)

In fact, the assemblage is indeed a great deal more than ledge handles, although it is composed of artifacts that are virtually all fragmentary.

The Excavator and His Methods

The reader will note that very often I am severely critical of the excavation and recording methods of FitzGerald and his team. However, to do justice to these pioneers we must remember that for the 1933 milieu in which they worked, they were neither unusual nor could they be considered less than competent (Figure 1.6). FitzGerald came to the Beisân Expedition from Egypt as an experienced excavator in a tradition of large-scale operations. He worked as an assistant at Beth Shan before he became field director. In keeping with the demands of the job, he worked and kept records in the accepted manner of two decades of predecessors at the site. In addition, it should be noted that the Deep Cut was only a part of a much larger operation, an unusually hurried sounding of limited size, intended to supply the maximum information in what was essentially a "go for broke" situation.

With these mitigating factors in mind, and with benefit of seven decades of hindsight, I suggest that FitzGerald did indeed achieve his basic aims. He dug intelligently and had reasonable control over what happened in the field, even if he did not always record the progress of work in the manner we would have wished him to. He was able to set forth in his publication a stratigraphic ceramic sequence for the site and to leave us, in archival form, the legacy of a skeletal architectural sequence to which it may be associated. His critical faculties, a good eye for differences in pottery, and what appear to be basically sound stratigraphic observations enabled him to roughly present several major chrono-stratigraphic delineations that more or less reflect the early occupational profile of the site—all this in a period when such a sequence was unknown.

The present work seeks to build on FitzGerald's structure and add appropriate nuances so we may better integrate the early levels of Beth Shan into our understanding of the late prehistory of the southern Levant.

Observations on the Ceramic Assemblage

Pottery makes up the bulk of the artifacts available for study from the Deep Cut and is the most reliable source for relative dating of the strata encountered within it. However, because of the limitations of FitzGerald's data, one must take a rather great leap of faith when uncritically accepting associations between find spots of particular artifacts and stratified structures in his preliminary publication (FitzGerald 1935).

A detailed examination of the whole Deep Cut ceramic assemblage indicates that some of FitzGerald's stratigraphic observations are highly problematic and in some cases misleading. Tell sites with multiple, superimposed occupations often produce large admixtures of chronologically varied ceramic materials in fills, and Beth Shan is no exception. FitzGerald was unable to perceive the non-homogeneous nature of such deposits as we now are capable of discerning. His comment on ledge handles, now known to be an essentially late feature in the Beth Shan sequence, must be understood as derived from basic ignorance of pottery of the Neolithic and Chalcolithic horizons. Thus, his early reports contain distinct references to associations of what we now know to be Early Bronze (henceforth EB) and Neolithic pot types he thought to be contemporary because they were found together. Lest we be too critical of FitzGerald's early work, we should remember that he had virtually no body of scholarly literature to consult,* and therefore no way of making distinctions between chronological disparities in what he believed to be discrete stratigraphic assemblages. In analyzing the material from the Deep Cut he was charting virgin territory.

Pottery is the most chronologically sensitive of diagnostic objects from the Deep Cut and forms the basis for most of the chrono-cultural ascriptions suggested in this work. The limitations of such an approach are obvious, especially when complete objects are few and far between, and the bulk of the assemblage is actually made up of quite fragmentary sherds likely to have been recovered in non-primary deposition. I have attempted to deal with the problem of non-homogeneous, stratigraphic assemblages in the

---

* There is archival evidence of his consultations by correspondence with G. E. Wright who was then working on his dissertation (1937), which was to become the first reliable synthetic work on pottery for early periods.

present study by culling what I believe to be almost certainly earlier residual and later intrusive objects from the bulk of material available for study. Although such arbitrary assumptions are derived from reliable ceramic sequences from nearby sites where data offer more complete assemblages, they are no assurance that definitions of what was intrusive and what was not are correct, and it remains for the reader to judge the validity of my chrono-stratigraphic associations. For several of the earlier levels it was also possible to correlate the ceramic horizons with architectural traditions and confirm the dating suggested by the bulk of the pottery. The result leaves us with a reasonably secure if not very detailed stratigraphic sequence tied in with chrono-cultural horizons of the late prehistory of the southern Levant.

Stratigraphy and Architecture

The deep sounding on the high tell of Beth Shan, although limited in area (ca. 660 m²), uncovered a series of superimposed deposits that are the basis for a stratified sequence of "Levels" (when capitalized, FitzGerald's stratagraphic nomenclature) suggested by the excavator and published by him only in two preliminary reports (FitzGerald 1934; 1935). The Deep Cut unearthed portions of Levels XIII down through pits cut into soil below Level XVIII. The present study recognizes the basic reliability of FitzGerald's fieldwork and, with the aid of available data, original field notes, and not a little hindsight, attempts to build upon and elaborate it. The result is a slightly expanded sequence of stratigraphic units that also identifies a number of sub-strata or structural phases not explicit in the early reports.

These additional phases of construction are quite obvious in FitzGerald's hitherto unpublished plans and did not go unnoticed by him. In his second and more detailed preliminary report, FitzGerald stated (1935:6): "so it will be sufficient to record here that we dug to a depth of 8.50 meters in an area measuring about 24 by 16 meters [the plans indicate a significantly larger area] through eight definite levels (numbered XI to XVIII) representing perhaps twelve separate periods of rebuilding, and finally came upon the pit dwellings dug in virgin soil by the earliest inhabitants of the site."

Thus, the present discussion considers the stratigraphy of Levels XIII through the pits in the lowest excavated level, taking into account the additional phases. It follows a chronological order, from the earliest deposits to the latest and is organized so as to present an overview of the significant, non-portable features of each stratum. Separate discussions (see below) deal with associated artifacts.

All stratigraphic observations noted here are in terms of architectural features and the fill encompassed by them because, with the exception of the basal layer of virgin soil, the records are silent on non-manmade deposits on the tell. Neither do they address the question of the re-deposition of building materials, the obvious result of generations of quarrying, building and rebuilding with mudbrick, and the fact of its decomposition by natural and unnatural means. This is not to imply that FitzGerald (1934: 124) was not aware of these processes. He did note there was no evidence for any appreciable soil deposition between his levels, which suggested to him that occupation on this part of the mound was continuous. He merely did not get around to address the question directly, although he must have done so at least indirectly when he proposed his stratigraphic ascriptions.

Stratigraphic Nomenclature

FitzGerald used the term "level" to indicate more or less horizontal, stratigraphic deposits representing successive occupations on the tell he apparently assigned to cultural horizons. My research suggests a considerably altered scheme, and I have replaced his term "level" with "stratum" so as to allow the reader to distinguish between FitzGerald's interpretation and my emended stratified sequence of deposits described below. Accordingly I have produced an altered set of annotated plans based on FitzGerald's unpublished, un-annotated originals that is marked with all strata and phases I have recognized. When these are substantially at variance with FitzGerald's stratigraphy and implied interpretations, I have reproduced his original plans (marked as Levels) so as to allow the reader to associate them with his preliminary reports.

In my scheme Stratum XIX is a new designation for FitzGerald's "Below Level XVIII," while I have also introduced phases that are obvious evidence of sequential, structural changes within the life span of buildings or associated open spaces. All such stratigraphic subunits of strata are designated in the descending order in which they were unearthed. Thus, Stratum XIIIa (the latest phase within the Deep Cut) is later than Stratum XIIIb and so forth.

Annotations on the newly organized plans indicate FitzGerald's "room" designations, but I have replaced the term "room" with "locus" (i.e., "L") because room numbers were never added to FitzGerald's formal plans. In reality they better represent excavation units that were very often not architectural features, but space between them. They do, however, appear on his schematic field plans in the diary (e.g. Figure 1.4), and occasionally they are found on small signs in the photographs. They are the basic excavation units described in the field diary. The terms "room" and "locus" are used interchangeably in the text.

I have attempted to reconstruct a stratigraphic sequence that is somewhat at variance with that indicated by FitzGerald. For the sake of clarity, I have assigned four-digit numbers to all constructed features (i.e., walls). The first two digits indicate the stratum to which the wall is assigned, while the latter two are arbitrary designations for the purpose of identification. Tables indicate their locations and, when available, their elevations in absolute terms.

The Architecture

Below Stratum XIX: FitzGerald (1934:125) described the matrix into which features of Stratum XIX were dug or laid, as a layer of reddish colored, virgin soil, the surface of which was "remarkably flat." However, the dissociation with human artifacts he suggests is somewhat contravened by his notation that the expedition "dug in Virgin Soil, in which a little pottery appeared" (FitzGerald 1933: 275). He attributed this level surface to "gradual human intervention," although it is not certain what his reasons for such a pronouncement were other than that he seems to have considered its flat aspect unnatural. It should be noted that the horizontality of this layer was relieved by at least two considerable depressions in this soil surface, one east of Locus 1899 (FitzGerald 1933:279) and the other south of Locus 1900. FitzGerald did not recognize this latter depression. This depression became obvious to me only after extensive study of the artifacts revealed that a number of apparently contemporaneous buildings found at more or less the same elevations could be shown to belong to two widely disparate cultural horizons (see below).

Although FitzGerald's avowed purpose was to reach bedrock within the Deep Cut, he was forced to abandon the effort after soundings below the lowest level of occupation (i.e., Stratum XIX) indicated that it lay too deeply buried to be reached. In a final effort to probe for bedrock he had workmen sink a crowbar through the bottom of Pit 19-1 (FitzGerald 1933: fig. XIX) into a layer of reddish soil. The absolute elevation of the bottom of the pit was noted as 78.85 and the crowbar reached a depth of 76.18, with negative results. Thereafter, FitzGerald, obviously convinced that the soil below Stratum XIX was a natural deposit free of artifacts and evidence for human activity and that bedrock lay somewhere below, abandoned excavation in this area of the tell.

Stratum XIX (Pits and Structural Features Below Level XVIII)

The primary units associated with this stratum are several pits filled with gray soil that contrasted with the reddish matrix into which they cut, and two constructed features with which these cavities may be associated (Figures 2.1, 2.2, 2.3). Fills within them represent the deepest deposits containing man-made material in which FitzGerald found archaeological artifacts. Although additional excavations have been conducted on the tell adjacent to the Deep Cut, nowhere has the soil at this great depth otherwise been probed, nor has bedrock been anywhere encountered (Mazar 1994 and personal communication 2001) and so we do not know definitively that the earliest artifacts from the Deep Cut represent primary human utilization of the site.

Pits

The pits fall within two size ranges that may, but need not necessarily, reflect their intended functions (if indeed there were any)(Figures 2.2, 2.3). The irregular aspects of these cavities, of whatever size, suggest that at least several, or possibly all, may have been the result of one or perhaps a combination of natural and man-

Table 2.1 Pits of Stratum XIXb

Pit #	SQ	SQ	SQ	SQ	Upper Elevations	Lower Elevations
19-1	J 22	K 22	K 21		79.07	78.85
19-2	J 22	K 22	J 23	K 23		
19-3	K 23	L 23	K 24	L 24		77.65
19-4	L 25					78.72
19-5	L 26					78.63
19-6	L 26				79.32	78.82
19-7	L 27					78.90
19-8	L 23					79.46

made agencies such as wind and water erosion and deliberate quarrying.

For purposes of identification I have designated each pit with an ordinal number preceded by the Arabic number of the Stratum. Pits 19-1, 19-2, 19-3, and 19-6 belong to the larger range and were supposed by FitzGerald (1934: 125) to have been used for habitation. He further hypothesized that they were roofed with "some form of matting or brushwood construction," although no definitive evidence for this seems to have been recovered. It is possible that FitzGerald considered "decayed vegetable matter" (to which he attributed the gray coloration of the fill within these pits) to be associated with roofing, although the notion is nowhere expressly stated in his notes.

Architectural Features

Two walls and perhaps several contour lines that appear on FitzGerald's plan are apparently the sole, definitively man-made features in this stratum (Figure 2.1). It is possible these were associated with one or more surfaces from which one or another of the pits may have been dug, although we cannot be certain of this.

The plans do not indicate precise features of individual walls. General observations in the field notes (FitzGerald 1934:125) explain that the walls of Level XVIII were mostly of small, plano-convex bricks or small stones and so the latter may also characterize this construction, even if they are not indicated on the plan.

Wall 1901 is an irregularly curved affair, probably fashioned of mudbricks (FitzGerald 1933: 275), that appears to be part of a small storage facility, only half of which is preserved. Wall 1902 is represented by a small, single line of stones (Figure 2.1) that seems to continue what may be contour lines in the soil layer, possibly representative of some structured shaping of the surface to the east of Pit 19-6. Elevations were taken at two points along this contour, although none is available for the adjacent surface. Although the nature of this juxtaposition of structure and minor topographical feature remains obscure, as do their functions, the stratigraphic relationship between them nevertheless seems clear.

In retrospect, FitzGerald's characterization of the function of the pits in Stratum XIX seems unjustified. Given the era in which he worked, I propose that FitzGerald may well have been influenced by beliefs that seem to have been common then. Apparently, preliterate societies of the southern Levant were conceived as exhibiting a "primitive" state of social development that might be understood as commensurate with utilization of such flimsily roofed cavities as semi-subterranean dwellings. It should be noted that the degree of sophistication of house construction we now know to date from as early as the Epipaleolithic period (Perrot 1993), and major discoveries at Neolithic sites in the region all lay in the future. It is now possible to better evaluate the function of these larger pits in light of a growing body of literature dealing with similar phenomena.

From a practical point of view it is obvious that the pits recorded by FitzGerald would have been wholly inadequate as dwellings. They are rather deep and provide no easy access to the interior, and their irregularly sloping walls suggest no care was taken in their quarrying. Although the covered pits could have provided shade and some shelter in the dry season, in winter they would have served as collection points for runoff rain. Thus, a domiciliary function for them seems virtually impossible.

So-called pit dwellings or semi-subterranean structures are indeed associated with Neolithic occupations (see below) and this is a period represented in the artifact assemblage from the early strata at Beth Shan.

Table 2.2 Walls of Stratum XIX

Wall #	SQ	SQ	Upper Elevations	Lower Elevations
1901	K 23		79.35	79.35
1902	L 26	M 26		79.25

However, those pits for which a domiciliary function is indicated at other sites are considerably more structured than are the amorphous cavities of Stratum XIX.

Neolithic "pit dwellings" in the southern Levant are virtually defined by their tendency toward regular aspects and associated appurtenances. They include such features as circumference walls, earthen or plastered floors, clay or gypsum-lined walls, ovens, fire pits, constructed installations, and sometimes explicit evidence of roofing (de Vaux 1961: 560-561; Kenyon 1960: 102-3; Anati et al. 1973: 79, figs. 60-61; Lovell, Kafafi, and Dollfus 1997: 362-364; Bourke 1997: 405; Tsuneki and Miyake 1998: 29-30). None of these man-made features is apparently associated with the pits of Beth Shan XIX.

If indeed these pits were man-made cavities, then I suggest they were created for the alternate function of soil quarrying (Lovell, Kafafi and Dollfus 1997: 362) and eventually, whether by design or otherwise, became depositories of refuse. If this is so, it would explain the lack of man-made features and the presence of the portable artifacts recovered from them, many of which are fragmentary (discarded) ceramic vessels. This latter function could as well be fulfilled by cavities of natural origin.

The smaller pits (19-4, 19-5, 19-7, and 19-8), almost circular depressions, are clearly too minute to have functioned as habitations. Their more regular aspects suggest a possibility of deliberate excavation. They may have been excavated to serve as installations, perhaps for storage. At some later date they also became repositories of rubbish and soil replete with organic detritus, although whether by design or default is unclear. Judging by the large accumulation of artifacts, especially the numerous handles of ceramic vessels, I suggest that a deliberate pattern of human behavior seems likely. Contrary to FitzGerald's observation that "as the ware was poorly baked, and the bulk of the vessels had doubtless disintegrated, while only the more solidly formed handles remained", (1934: 125) the pottery from these pits is actually quite well made. The fabrics are relatively hard and well fired and do not crumble and disintegrate. Thus, it is obvious that these handles were deposited there in their present state, as fragments, rather than as remainders of complete of vessels. Whether this was in some way associated with a primary function for some or all of these pits, or with a later utilization of preexisting features, remains unclear.

The date or dates of the creation of the pits remain obscure because there is no good evidence for human intervention in the process. If natural forces were at work to gouge them out of the layer of reddish soil, then they obviously precede human utilization of the site and are of themselves of little archaeological interest. However, were the pits provably quarried by humans, then this is most likely to have happened in the Neolithic period (see above). If for the moment we assume that some human agency were indeed responsible for their creation, then it must have been associated with a surface from which the pits were dug. Were it possible to date such a surface, then that would indicate the likely dating for the excavation of the pits and also for the construction of walls 1901 and 1902. Such a surface would have been immediately external to the pits, and FitzGerald's workmen would probably have collected materials from it together with materials from adjacent loci (rooms) attributed to Stratum XVIII. Since there is no way of stratigraphically separating material within these loci, we cannot utilize these artifacts to date the creation of these pits.

There is a possibility that some material associated with Stratum XVIII could be pertinent to this discussion. That would attest to the earliest human utilization of the site encountered in the excavations. Potentially, evidence of even earlier activity could be found beneath the layer of "virgin" (archaeologically sterile) soil below Stratum XIX, which, as noted above, was actually not totally devoid of evidence for material culture. However, lack of data does not permit me to suggest any dates for the creation of these pits with any confidence.

Stratum XVIII

Few walls and constructed features are ascribed to Stratum XVIII (Figure 2.4). Only several of them are

Table 2.3 Walls of Stratum XVIIIb

Wall #	SQ	SQ	SQ	SQ	Upper Elevations	Lower Elevations
1801	L 27	L 28	M 27	M 28	80.16	79.52
1802	K 24	L 24	K 25	L 25	79.66	79.18
1803	J 24	K 24				79.53?/79.61?
1804	J 23	J 24			80.05/80.21	79.72/79.98
1805	J 22	K 22			79.94	78.72
1806	J 22					
1807	J 23				70.76	
1808	L 24					
1809	K 24				79.46	
1810	L 24	M 24			79.46	79.26
1811	L 26	L 27				
1812	L 24				79.70	

so juxtaposed as to suggest coherency and mutual association. Structural features superimposed on earlier structures and relative elevations suggest two phases respectively designated XVIIIb and XVIIIa in order of their construction.

Stratum XVIIIb

Most constructions are assigned to this early phase, but it should be noted they were not necessarily all contemporaneous (Figures 2.4, 2.5). Differences in elevations and styles of some walls suggest the likelihood this is an aggregation of remnants of buildings from different occupational phases.

Walls 1802 and 1809 form a portion of what may be a curvilinear or partially curvilinear building perhaps even apsidal in plan.* Unfortunately, it is too poorly preserved to give an indication of its extent or even its ultimate aspect. If it were indeed apsidal in plan, then it could well be associated with a Late Neolithic (henceforth LN) occupation (see below: Discussion). Its elevations are somewhat lower than those of nearby Wall 1803.

Walls 1808, 1810, and 1812 are part of another construction over which a wall segment (1813) was positioned. These earlier features are possibly a corner of a room that extended to the north and east. Wall 1812 defines a small bin or storage installation attached externally to its southwest corner. Farther to the south, Wall 1801 is a short and straight segment seemingly unaligned with any of the additional structures of this phase. It is assigned to Stratum XVIIIb because it was partially overlain by another wall and because of its relative elevations.

Walls 1803, 1804, and 1807 (Figures 2.7, 2.8) appear to be a portion of a single, large, rectilinear structure with which Wall 1805, because of its alignment, seems to be associated. Wall 1806, a small, narrow segment, *sans* elevations, parallel to Wall 1805, may also be attributed to this structure, although the only evidence for this is its orientation. The relative elevations of these structures suggest they should be placed in the latter phase of this stratum.

Stratum XVIIIa

Wall 1801 (Figure 2.6, background), a somewhat long, straight, and wide segment, is clearly part of a larger structure of which nothing else remained. It preserves the alignment of Wall 1811 of the earlier phase, just below it and to the northwest. Wall 1813, a fragmentary construction of indeterminate shape, is attributed to this same phase by virtue of its relative stratigraphy. Its irregular aspect may be due to

---

* Apsidal (alternately "apsoidal" and *absidiale* {Fr.}) literally means having an apse and is generally understood as indicating the juxtaposition of two right-angle corners opposing a regularly curvilinear (apsidal) end. Much has been made of this supposed house plan, especially for the Early Bronze Age of the southern Levant. However, it would seem that there are few, if indeed any, examples in that period (Braun 1989b; 2001).

Table 2.4 Walls of Stratum XVIIIa

Wall #	SQ	SQ	SQ	SQ	Upper Elevations	Lower Elevations
1801	L 27	L 28	M 27	M 28	80.16	79.52
1813	L 23	M 23	L 24		79.97	79.71

weathering or partial destruction by some later agency.

The several structures of Stratum XVIIIb show little overall coherency, and the only evidence for their mutual association or dissociation is in relative and absolute elevations. Only partially preserved structures are extant and together they exhibit no real sense of cohesion in their alignments that would suggest all were in use simultaneously. Such an interpretation is not inconsistent with the evidence from portable artifacts recovered from associated fills (see Chapter 3).

These buildings are too poorly preserved for us to understand them more than minimally, and any attempt to interpret their significance in terms of architectural traditions is, therefore, highly speculative, especially since curvilinear features are related to two different, chrono-cultural horizons, LN and EB I. Notable in this phase is a curvilinear element, just possibly representing a portion of an apsidal (a curved end on an otherwise rectangular building) structure. Several examples of this type house plan are also known from LN occupations at ʿAin Ghazal (Rollefson, Kafafi, and Simmons 1990: 110-112; Rollefson, Simmons and Kafafi 1992: fig. 7; Rollefson 1998: 45-46) and Byblos (Dunand 1973:24-25). Alternately, this structure could somehow relate to later curvilinear building traditions of the EB I horizon (Braun 1989b; 2001) noted in Stratum XVII and several additional overlying strata, although the differences in relative elevations seem to virtually preclude such a possibility.

The remaining structures are rectilinear and probably belong to the Late Neolithic/Early Chalcolithic (henceforth LN/EC, respectively) horizons. The juxtaposition of Walls 1804 and 1805 suggests a doorway, although these two wall segments are of notably different thicknesses and there is no corroborative evidence for this interpretation. Wall 1803 is a right-angle corner of this structure associated with Locus 1898, and itself is a rather large mass, possibly of mudbrick. It is no ordinary wall and seems likely to have had a specialized function connected with three roughly circular cavities located within it, although precisely what their function may have been is unknown. Possibly they were storage units, pot stands, or receptacles for some other type of artifact.

Stratum XVII

There is a clear dichotomy between structures in the northern and southern precincts of Stratum XVII that probably reflects chrono-cultural differences explained by the existence of a gradient on which the ancient denizens constructed their houses (Figures 2.9, 2.10). The mound appears to have sloped down from north to south and so horizontal excavation apparently unearthed earlier occupations in the north than at the same elevations in the adjacent precinct to the south. There is considerable evidence for this topographical feature in both Stratum XVII and Stratum XVI (see below).

The several fragmentary structures located in the northern portion of the excavated area appear by and large to be rectilinear in plan. They are associated with considerable quantities of pottery assignable to sometime within the LN/EC horizons. By contrast, building remains to the south are definitively curvilinear in aspect and appear to be better associated with pottery reflecting EB I traditions (see below). Another disparity, possibly important but somewhat enigmatic, is found in the type of bricks associated with this level. Differences may reflect chrono-cultural discrepancies that tend to support our interpretation. They are discussed below in detail.

The likely chrono-cultural disparity noted above makes it necessary to divide this stratum into two separate units. However, because the later occupation was not superimposed upon the earlier, and since both stratigraphic entities lie in such close proximity and are actually located at more or less the same absolute elevations, I considered it too confusing to give them different, sequential numbers. Essentially Stratum XVII seems to reflect two different sequences within a very small area. This could be due to the vagaries of preservation or even the existence of open areas during certain time spans. Alternately these differences may suggest the existence of a surface sloping from north to south that could have substantially affected FitzGerald's strati-

Table 2.5 Dimensions of Plano-convex Bricks of Stratum XVII

Length (cm.)	Width (cm.)	Height (cm.)
25	18	6
22	16	8
23	16	5
21	16	8
22	15	5.5
19	16	7
22	15	5
19	15	5
21	18	5
19	14	7

graphic attributions, not only in this Level, but also of overlying structures. Unfortunately, there is not enough diagnostic material with precise associations to structures to allow me to check this hypothesis.

I have elected to preserve the Level number to which they were originally assigned in my own stratigraphic designations. In order to distinguish between them, I have appended a cardinal direction to what I believe to be buildings of different strata in separate precincts so as to differentiate between them and emphasize their disparate chrono-cultural associations. Accordingly, Stratum XVII North belongs to the LN/EC horizons, and Stratum XVII South is attributed to an early phase of EB I. In addition, evidence for architectural phasing within both precincts is noted in Figure 2.10.

Stratum XVII North (Neolithic-Early Chalcolithic)

Only fragments of structures, some quite substantially built, are associated with this stratum. Virtually all are constructed according to rectilinear precepts. Walls 1707 and 1708 form an obtuse angle of a large, apparently multi-chambered building. They seem to share alignment with Wall 1712, but a mutual association is not certain. Wall 1711 is a rectilinear segment of a low stone foundation that also is similarly aligned. These walls could form a coherent plan of a basically rectilinear building, but the disparity in their thicknesses and the materials used in their construction make it somewhat difficult to understand their functions in an integrated structure. Presumably walls of lesser thickness could represent internal dividers, while thicker walls could be either intended for load bearing or external supports meant to withstand the elements and the passage of animals and people. There is some suggestion of the existence of second stories in the Neolithic of the southern Levant (Byrd and Banning 1988: 68) that could account for such proportions.

Two additional, massive wall fragments (1709 and 1710) are noteworthy. They are juxtaposed with an irregular mass of construction or large stone (Figure

Table 2.6 Walls of Stratum XVII North

Wall #	SQ	SQ	SQ	SQ	Upper Elevations	Lower Elevations
1705	J 23					
1707	J 23	K 23			80.39	80.10
1708	J 23					
1709	K 23					
1710	L 23				80.24	
1711	K 22	L 22			80.35	80.24
1712	K 22					
1714	K 23				80.66	
1715	L 22					

2.11) so as to create a bent or slightly curving feature. Totally out of alignment with the remainder of the constructed features in this stratum, they suggest the likelihood of two separate phases of occupation in this precinct.

Additional elements in this precinct are drawn on FitzGerald's plan. Some are indicated as "bins," presumably for storage. They appear to have been cut into the matrix of the site rather than built aboveground. It is not known whether they are associated with any additional, specific features that indicate their supposed storage function.

Notably Wall 1714 forms a tiny, aboveground, elongated cavity, constructed atop the east end of Wall 1707 (Figure 2.11). It is the sole definitive evidence for phasing in this stratum. Other features on the plan appear as slightly irregularly contoured enclosures. Possibly they are indications of pits, but I have been unable to verify this hypothesis due to lack of corroborative evidence, no references to them in the notebooks, and no photographs could be found.

Brick types utilized in this stratum suggest a fundamental association with pre-EB I cultural horizons. FitzGerald rather pointedly noted that in this stratum:

> With one exception they were built of small mud bricks with a rounded upper side, recalling the plano-convex bricks of Babylonia. They vary somewhat in size, the average being about 22 x 15 x 6 cm. In contrast to these were four large flat bricks, laid as part of a curved wall at the extreme south of the area, one of which was 59 cm. in length and 14 cm. thick, its width varying from 42 to 38 cm. (1934:126)

These differences seem to reflect the same chrono-cultural building traditions that are evident in the architectural precepts used for their plans. Plano-convex bricks are a type sometimes associated with Neolithic structures (Kenyon 1960: 65), while the single exception noted by FitzGerald suggests an Early Bronze I dating. The disparity tends to emphasize discrepancies between the buildings in the northern precinct, and at least one curvilinear structure farther to the south. Table XVII North/1 records brick sizes in FitzGerald's field diary.

Most of the structures of Stratum XVII North appear to belong to a settlement that predates the EB I period. In keeping with prevailing architectural traditions, rectilinear precepts seem to have been followed, while the use of plano-convex type bricks (Figure 2.13) are clearly an indication of the early date of at least some of these buildings.

Preservation in this stratum is poor, and the meager remains probably do not adequately reflect the occupations to which they bear witness (Figure 2.12). Some of the rather massive wall segments suggest the settlement in this period may have been of substantial proportions with buildings having more than one story.

Stratum XVII South

The series of curvilinear walls in the southern precinct of Stratum XVII South are somewhat difficult to interpret, partly because they are so poorly preserved and partly because the sequence of construction is unclear. These walls seem to represent the earliest definitive occurrence of curvilinear houses of the Early EB I period at this site (but see above: a curvilinear wall segment in Stratum XVIIIb).

Several curvilinear walls form a construction sequence for which I offer the following, tentative reconstruction. The foundations of Walls 1702 and 1703 are the lowest in this precinct of the excavation (elev. 79.79) and are portions of what appears to have been a curvilinear structure likely to have been the earliest in this precinct. Wall 1703 (Figure 2.14) may be a curvilinear (sausage-shaped?)* addition, constructed after accretion of fill that considerably raised the surrounding surface. That would explain the significantly higher elevation (80.17) of its foundations and those of Wall 1704 (elev. 80.19), a portion of another, probably contemporary curvilinear structure. Unfortunately, however, there are no additional features by which we can confirm this sequence. Wall 1703 is associated with a stone pavement, a feature common in EB I curvilinear houses (Braun 1997: fig. 6.30).

The straight wall segment 1706 does not seem to be aligned with the additional structures and could well represent portions of another building, about which nothing else is known. Farther north is a small, bin-like affair (Wall 1716) that shows no direct relation to the remaining structures in this stratum. It most resembles Wall 1714 and could conceivably be its contemporary.

---

* Numerous "sausage-shaped" houses are known from EB I contexts (Braun 1989b; 2001). The term denotes a plan that has two parallel walls, joined at both ends by a regularly curving segment, effectively creating two opposing apses. Other curvilinear plans associated with this tradition are ellipses, ovals, and circles.

Table 2.7 Walls of Stratum XVII South

Wall #	SQ	SQ	SQ	SQ	Upper Elevations	Lower Elevations
1701	K 27	L 27			80.91	79.79
1702	K 27					
1703	L 27				80.35	80.17
1704	K 26	L 26	L 27		80.34	80.13
1706	L 26				80.39	80.18
1716	L 25					80.63

The curvilinear architecture and association of specific ceramic types from this precinct of the excavation (see Chapter 3) appear to make a good case for an Early EB I dating for these distinctive building remains, and the constructions of Stratum XVII South may easily be interpreted as portions of buildings typical to this cultural horizon. There are, however, some difficulties with this interpretation.

While it is true that the utilization of flat bricks in Wall 1703 argues convincingly for an EB I date for Wall 1704, not all the evidence is corroborative; indeed some of it is confusing and suggests different dates for the additional curvilinear walls. FitzGerald's 1934 discussion of the succeeding Stratum XVI noted: "The excavated surface contained few walls, and those mainly near the Tell edge. With one exception they were built of small mud bricks with a rounded upper side, recalling the plano-convex bricks of Babylonia (126)." Clearly he is referring to Walls 1701, 1702, and 1704 as having been fashioned of plano-convex bricks (c.f. Wall 1703 with its flat-planed bricks). Bricks, visible in Wall 1704 (Figure 2.14: directly below the number 1896), are, as FitzGerald indicates, much narrower than the large flat bricks in Wall 1703 (in the foreground) and appear as well to be rounded on top.

Several explanations for this information suggest themselves to us, none of which is particularly convincing:

1. All these walls are nearly contemporary and date to the EB I period. There is no significance to the differences in types of bricks. This explanation seems unlikely because, so far as I have been able to ascertain, mudbricks in use in EB I are noted for their flat planes, especially on top.

2. All these walls are nearly contemporary and date to sometime within the LN/EC cultural horizons. In this scenario, the curvilinear walls could be understood as portions of circular or possibly apsidal buildings of the earlier periods and the EB I pottery is understood as intrusive. Accordingly, any chronological significance attached to differences between rectilinear and curvilinear architectural traditions and types of bricks within Stratum XVIII must relate to differences within this early horizon.

3. Walls 1701 and 1704 belong to the Late Neolithic–Early Chalcolithic horizons and Wall 1703 belongs to the EB I period. Thus, there is chronological significance to the differences in bricks, despite the shared elevations of the foundations of Walls 1703 and 1704.

4. Curvilinear Wall 1703 dates to the EB I period as do Walls 1701, 1702, and 1704. However, Walls 1701, 1702, and 1704 were fashioned from "recycled" bricks obtained from then extant, earlier structures on the Late Neolithic–Early Chalcolithic horizons.

5. The bricks in narrow Wall 1704 were badly eroded or abraided as the result of the excavation and only appear to have been of the "plano-convex" type in the photograph. This would exempt the bricks in this wall from FitzGerald's observations noted above and suggest that FitzGerald was mistaken and the bricks featured in Figure 2.13 were not derived from these particular buildings.

6. In fact, the apparent disparity in bricks used to construct these curvilinear walls cannot be rationally explained in terms of chrono-cultural disparities and must, for the present, remain a conundrum.

While on the one hand these structural details throw doubt upon the EB I dating of the buildings in Stratum XVII South, on the other hand, there are some compelling reasons for dating them to this period. Notably, the architecture of Stratum XVI, above, includes a complete curvilinear dwelling that may be interpreted as an indication of continuity in architectural traditions. In fact, as the discussion below indicates, the tradition of building curvilinear houses is somewhat long lived and rather tenacious at Beth Shan and other sites. It appears to start in Stratum XVII and continues on into Stratum XIV in which its last vestiges appear.

In addition, the evidence of the pottery from the southern part of the precinct as noted by FitzGerald in the field diary is equally compelling: "Level XVII contains quantities of fragmentary pottery— At S. end of area was a good black burnished fragment, and some ledge handles; at N the ledge handles are extraordinarily few compared to round loop handles" (1933:272). It is clear that FitzGerald's "black burnished" pottery is identical to what we now call 'Gray Burnished Ware' or 'Esdraelon Ware' (Wright 1958), a style of pottery that is one of the hallmarks of Northern EB I (see Chapter 3, Stratum XVII). Ledge handles of the type noted by him and confirmed by us in a review of the ceramic finds, are another of these hallmarks. On the other hand, 'loop handles' from this stratum (as discussed above in Stratum XIX) are associated with earlier, LN/EC cultural horizons.

Stratum XVI

With the exception of two rectilinear wall segments the dominant architectural features of this stratum are curvilinear (Figures 2.15, 2.16). Considering the likelihood of disparate chrono-cultural entities in the preceding Stratum XVII, an analogous situation may also be reflected in the architectural remains of this Level. Additional evidence clarifies the existence a sloping hillside in the Deep Cut.

Stratum XVIb

While the several architectural features in this phase are apparently earlier than the major buildings, they probably represent two chono-cultural episodes, LN/EC and Early EB I. Stratigraphically, Wall 1623 is the earliest element in the building sequence. Its curvilinear aspect suggests continuity with similar structures either in Stratum XVII South (see above) or with the overlying structures that replaced it, and it is probably dated to Early EB I. Several stones beneath the east edge of Wall 1616 may belong to this same phase.

Although the foundations of rectilinear Wall 1601 are at more or less the same elevation (81.07-81.08) as those of the structures to the south, any association between them seems to be spurious. Its rectilinear aspect and that of its precisely parallel wall (1602) to the east contrast with the curvilinear buildings of Stratum XIVa; neither do they share the same alignment. This non-contemporaneousness is explained by additional evidence of a slope up from south to north and west to east in the northern precinct that would account for such a chrono-cultural discrepancy within one level. The foundation of Wall 1602 (elev. 81.20 in the south and 81.46 in the north) compared with that of Wall 1601 reflects the degree of this slope.

Accordingly, I suggest that Walls 1601 and 1602 (Figure 2.17) are likely to be the latest remains of the LN/EC sequence in the Deep Cut and are not properly associated with the buildings just to the south. Since FitzGerald was unaware of the sloping stratigraphy and the diagnostic aspects of the different cultural phases, he automatically (and erroneously) associated all these structures, on the basis of their relative elevations, to the same cultural horizon.

Stratum XVIa

Locus 1885 (Figure 2.18) appears to be the southern end of a sausage-shaped house to which is appended curvilinear Wall 1603 that forms another, adjacent chamber. Wall segments 1604 and 1621 suggest two construction phases for this part of the building. Walls 1606, 1607, 1608, and 1610 effectively subdivide the space between Locus 1885 and another, large and virtually complete sausage-shaped building to the south. Probably they represent a secondary construction phase in this stratum that arose out of a need to utilize space between two independently constructed houses. Such arrangements are common at other sites of the same horizon (Braun 1989b: 27-28; 1997: 24-42, Figure 6.30).

The best-preserved structure in this level is what appears to have been a small, sausage-shaped house with thick walls, presumably of mudbrick (Figure 2.19). Walls 1612 and 1620 partition this curvilinear house into a northern and southern segment. Wall 1611 bifurcates the northern end, a completely curved apse, forming two chambers of unequal size and leaving only a very narrow passage between them. By contrast, the southern end of this building (Loc. 1888) is notable for its one sharply angled corner (in the southwest) opposed by a gently curving wall segment (in the southeast). Presumably this building is a kind of long room defined by what appears to be a threshold of an entrance (between Walls 1614 and 1616) flanked on

Table 2.8 Walls of Stratum XVI

Wall #	SQ	SQ	SQ	SQ	Upper Elevations	Lower Elevations
1601	J 21	J 22	K 21	K 22	81.54/81.42	81.08/81.07
1602	K 21	K 22	K 23		81.84/81.53	81.46/81.20
1603	K 23	L 23	K 24		81.17	80.97
1604	L 23				81.37	
1605	L 23	L 24	M 23		81.44	81.05
1606	M 23	M 24			81.28	80.36
1607	L 24	M 24				
1608	L 24				81.22	
1609	L 24	L 25	M 24	M 25	81.42/81.09	80.79
1610	L 24					
1611	L 24				81.14	
1612	L 25				81.22	
1613	L 26				80.78	
1614	L 26				80.75	
1615	L 26				81.11	
1616	M 25	M 26	L 26		81.24	80.88?/80.94?
1617	K 27	L 27	L 28		80.95	80.29
1618	J 24				81.15?	81.03?
1619	J 24					
1620	L 25					
1621	L 25	L 26				
1622	L 23					
1623	L 24	M 24			80.98	80.87

the west by Wall 1615. Alternately Wall 1615 could be part of another room of which no more is preserved.

This building exhibits a history of construction the precise sequence of which is obscure. Several interpretations are possible, all of which could explain the features encountered by FitzGerald and set down in the plans. The irregular shapes of Walls 1612 and 1620 as well as the inordinate thickness of these constructions suggest they originally functioned as more than internal dividers. However, lack of additional information (especially elevations) prevents me from more than speculating about what these functions might have been.

Wall 1611 is obviously integral to this building, although its precise function is difficult to understand. It effectively divides the small, northern room into two unequal chambers, the more diminutive of which could only have served for storage. This seems a rather unusual utilization of scarce space in such a small house. In addition, it forms a passageway so narrow that it is clearly impractical for access to the eastern room. I speculate that this feature was bench or alternately, it represents a late construction, perhaps fashioned by squatters in a phase when the building ceased to fulfill its original function.

The floor of Locus 1887, paved with potsherds (Figure 2.20), is a feature that is sometimes encountered in sites of the EB I horizon. I recently encountered this phenomenon, the floor of a Late EB I building paved with pebbles and sherds of the Early EB I horizon, at Tel Lod. Two circular features in the adjacent room (Locus 1887) are probably bins noted by FitzGerald (1934:126). They and perhaps a third bin, destroyed by the construction of Wall 1611, apparently belong to an earlier phase of the house.

The angular features of the southwest corner of this house are difficult to explain. In particular, the configuration formed by Walls 1614 and 1615 with 1620 is somewhat out of line with the remainder of the structure's peripheral wall. Together they almost look as if they could have belonged to some preexisting, rectilinear building fragment to which the remainder was attached, although there is no corroborative evidence for this speculation.

Curving Wall 1617 is possibly associated with a stone pavement, although the stones visible in the pho-

Table 2.9 Walls of Stratum XVb

Wall #	SQ	SQ	SQ	Upper Elevations	Lower Elevations
1503	L 26	L 27		81.80	81.43
1510	K 22	K 23	L 22	82.13/82.20	81.89/81.90
1511	L 21	L 22		82.08	
1512	L 23				81.72
1514	J 21	J 21	J 23	81.72	
1515	J 23			82.38	81.63
1516	J 23				
1520	J 23				
1522	M 26			81.43	
1523	L 25	M 25		81.60	
1524	L 25	L 26		81.58	
1525	J 22	J 23		82.43	

tograph (Figure 2.21) do not seem suitable as pavers, while what appears to be a pot is embedded in fill below the tops of the stones. The mudbrick wall appears to have a stone foundation, although it is not drawn on the plans. An alternate explanation is that the stones beneath the wall are part of the same layer unearthed within the confines of this partially preserved structure. Thus, the stones and the pot, which I have been unable to identify within the extant assemblages, might be debris of an earlier deposit, not directly associated with this building.

The curvilinear walls may be interpreted as either the end of a sausage-shaped building or a portion of a circular construction. Unfortunately, nothing more of this building survived; its southern extension apparently eroded away with the side of the mound. There are parallels for both ground plans (Braun 1989b; Braun and Gophna 1995), although the latter is somewhat unusual.

Walls 1618 and 1619 (Figure 2.22) are part of some larger construction that appears to be buried in the balk. It is not certain whether Wall 1618 is part of a building. Wall 1619 is a very narrow affair more in keeping with some type of installation. Their ascription to this late phase is based solely on relative elevations.

The southern precinct shows what appears to be a succession of structures of types common to early phases of EB I. They preserve some basic precepts of curvilinear architecture, although some rectilinear elements are also visible. A pre-EB I date is suspected for the largest of these, located on the slope in the northern precinct.

Noteworthy is EB I utilization of space near the edge of the tell. This rather crowded precinct suggests the likelihood that much of the limited space on the mound was taken up by additional structures. Accordingly, I suspect that large, somewhat open spaces on the plan may not have been devoid of buildings.

Stratum XV

This stratum is made up of aggregations of walls representing two very distinct building phases (Figures 2.23, 2.24). Although FitzGerald apparently plotted them on the same plan because of their physical proximity, the later group of structures (Stratum XVa) shows virtually no continuity with the buildings preceding it. Were it not for the impossibility, given the lack of available data, of separating the finds associated with Level XV, I would have labeled both phases as strata in their own right.

Stratum XVb

This earlier phase is dominated by a series of relatively large rectilinear structures in the northwest precinct of the excavation (Walls 1514, 1515, 1516, 1520 and 1524) that probably extends to the west (Figure 2.25). In addition, there is a part of a room of curvilinear mien (Figures 2.26, 2.27), probably of a sausage-shaped chamber and a fragment of some larger structure in the northeast precinct (Walls 1510 and 1511). Open space between these buildings suggests a path or lane within a somewhat crowded precinct of this settlement. Wall 1512 that appears to have been some type of constructed bin, may be associated with the sausage-shaped structure formed by W1510.

Table 2.10 Walls of Stratum XVa

Wall #	SQ	SQ	SQ	SQ	Upper Elevations	Lower Elevations
1501	L 27	K 27				
1502	K 27	L 27	K 26	L 26	82.23	81.68
1504	K 24	K 25	L 25		82.80	82.20
1505	K 24	L 24	L 25		82.56	81.92
1506	K 23	K 24			82.42	82.03
1507	J 24	K 24				
1508	K 23				82.23	82.03
1509	I 24	J 24	K 24		82 48/82.13	82.19/81.80
1513	J 21	J 22	K 21	K 22	82.64	81.93
1517	K 23				82.68	82.53
1518	L 24	L 25			82.25	82.08
1519	K 23	K 24	L 24		82.88	82.28
1521	L 24					
1526	K 21				82.08	

Further to the south there is evidence of additional structures. Two curvilinear buildings with stone foundations (Walls 1522 and 1523) are only poorly preserved and we can only speculate as to the ultimate plans of these structures. Another wall segment (Wall 1524), also of stones, may somehow be related to them, but it could as well represent yet another construction phase within this stratum. It does not share the orientation of other buildings in Stratum XVb, although its absolute elevation suggests this association. Wall 1503, part of a diminutive, albeit well-built circular building, is considered to be a storage facility because of its size. It is probably associated with the buildings to the north and east.

The curvilinear features of this stratum represent continuity with preceding occupations, while the appearance in this same stratum of a definitively rectilinear structure represents a return to earlier architectural precepts, a process known at additional sites as EB I progresses. A similar phenomenon is paralleled at nearby En Shadud (Braun 1985:12-28) and Megiddo (Engberg and Shipton 1934: fig. 2; Braun 2001) where both rectilinear and curvilinear houses are found in contemporary contexts.

Circular storage buildings should not be associated exclusively with curvilinear architectural traditions. Small circular structures are commonly found in contexts ranging from Neolithic through EB I (Braun 1989b: *passim* and especially n. 25; Braun 1997: 64: 41-41; Levy et al. 1997: fig. 4) and are not specific to curvilinear traditions of house building. This small structure at Beth Shan is notable for its relatively thick wall that is seemingly out of proportion to the size of the space it encloses. I suggest it was intentionally outsized for purposes of insulation so as to maintain a constant temperature within that would be conducive to storage of foodstuffs. I have excavated a similar structure with comparably massive walls in a Late EB I context at Palmahim Quarry.

Stratum XVa

The walls of this phase, albeit fragmentary and of enigmatic function are, nevertheless, well enough preserved to indicate they bear little or no relation to preceding structures of Stratum XVb. Their orientation is quite different, and in some instances they lay directly atop earlier buildings, or, quite obviously, they destroyed the continuity of earlier structures.

One juxtaposition of massive walls 1504, 1505, 1506, 1507, 1509, and 1517 is evidence for some type of structure built along rectilinear lines (Figure 2.28). It includes two walls that form a very broad mass and additional wall segments that bond to give it a rather unusual plan. This feature, probably part of a large edifice, includes an obtuse and an acute angle of what may have been two chambers on opposites sides of a wall of relatively massive proportions. Walls 1501 and 1502, seemingly aligned with this feature, together form another massively thick wall that, if it were complete, would belong to a rectilinear room with the aspect of a parallelogram. Walls 1519 and 1526 have been assigned to this phase because of their relative elevations and orientation.

The most notable feature of this phase is the complete break in continuity that Stratum XVa represents with the structures of Stratum XVb. Clearly the walls of Stratum XVa are part of some larger complex that must have extended to the west and probably to the very edge of the tell on the south, before erosion reduced the area. If the extant features I have assigned to this same building are indeed correctly interpreted, then its relative size and massive proportions suggest some specialized function that, while remaining obscure, is quite different from any of the buildings previously encountered and similarly at variance with those in the EB I levels directly above. Were there more substantial remains then it would suggest significant differences in the social fabric of this occupation. Lack of information prevents me from offering any further interpretation, and so these somewhat outsize mudbrick features remain an anomaly within an otherwise characteristic EB I architectural sequence.

Stratum XIV

FitzGerald's Stratum XIV is a composite plan in which there is evidence of considerable rebuilding (Figures 2.29-2.31). On the basis of extant elevations, I have interpreted it as representing two major phases. Although it is likely that some walls actually continued in use throughout the life span of the stratum, they are not represented on both plans because I lack definitive evidence for this continuity.

Stratum XIVb

The walls of this phase represent a virtually complete rebuilding in this precinct of the site, with only slight evidence for continuity in the orientation of Wall 1417 aligned with earlier Wall 1506. Perhaps remains of the earlier building dictated the orientation of this later structure, although it is difficult to see any connection because of the considerable differences in their relative elevations. The general orientation of buildings and organization of the space in this precinct of the site continues on into Stratum XIII. Here for the first time is the outline of a narrow, crooked lane opening onto a small piazza that bifurcates the excavated area from north to south, effectively dividing the excavation area between three distinctive building units.

A large room built along basically rectilinear precepts, but with externally curving corners (Wall 1429) takes up the northeastern part of this precinct (Figure 2.32 left, middle ground). The corners of this building seem to be the last remnant of the tradition of curvilinear architecture at Beth Shan that began in Stratum XVII. Additional notable features of this building are the sharply angled, internal southwest corner and the rectilinear structure (Walls 1425 and 1426) attached to the remains of its eastern wall.

Also notable in this building are remnants of a stone pavement that is higher (by 16 cm) than the foundations of the southern wall. Floors in EB I houses tend to be level with the bottoms of wall foundations. Thus, this feature indicates a buildup of debris within the room that could suggest a significant passage of time. It may be related to the somewhat massive wall of this house that appears to have been built in two phases, as suggested by the western, stone facade of Wall 1432. FitzGerald noted that Wall 1429 also had stone foundations, but for some reason they were not drawn. The stones may have been completely obscured by the superstructure in a later phase.

Only one short wall fragment (Wall 1460) from this phase was preserved to the west of this building. It is parallel to Wall 1432 and forms a narrow chamber that was apparently built integrally with it. It seems likely that these walls represent a local sub-phase of Stratum XIVb. Although the space to the west of this building is empty on the plan (Figure 2.30), I presume there were other structures here that were obliterated by the superimposed walls of Stratum XIVa.

A large building arranged along rectilinear principles occupies all of the excavated area to the southeast of the curvilinear house (Figure 2.33). This sprawling structure was only partly unearthed; its easternmost portion is buried under the balk and remains to be excavated. Although the west boundary of this wall has a somewhat curved appearance, I do not regard this structure as related to the curvilinear tradition as I do the house to the north. There are numerous examples of curving or "bent" walls at EB sites that in my opinion represent merely opportunistic utilization of available space, especially when it is at a premium or extant structures and the need for passage put limitations on the plans of buildings (Ciasca 1962: fig. I; Braun 1989b: fig. 7).

Rectilinear wall segments (Walls 1410, 1412, and 1413), the western limit of this sprawling, multi-roomed building, apparently reflect its history, one characterized by localized sub-phases of construction. The complex, including a number of rooms of irregular plan with walls of slightly differing widths, seems not to have been planned and executed at one time but apparently grew by accretion.

Table 2.11 Walls of Stratum XIVb

Wall #	SQ	SQ	SQ	SQ	Upper Elevations	Lower Elevations
1401	M 26					
1402	M 25	M 26	L 26	L 27	82.61	82.25
1403	L 24				83.05	82.24
1404	L 25	M 25			82.56	82.39
1405	K 25	L 25			82.79	82.48
1406	K 26	L 26			82.56	82.29
1407	L 26				82.11	
1408	L 26				82.56	
1409	L 26	L 27			82.85	82.59
1410	K 26	K 27			83.36	
1411	K 27	L 27			82.65	
1412	K 25	K 26			83.57	
1413	K 24	L 24	K 25		83.03	82.79
1415	M 24				82.72	
1416	L 24					
1417	K 23	J 23				
1418	K 24					
1420	L 224	M 24				
1421	L 24	M 24				
1422	L 24				82.62	82.24
1423	L 22					
1424	K 23				83.01	
1425	L 22					
1426	L 22					
1429	K 22	L 22	K 23	L 23	83.13/82.90	82.70
1432	K 20	K 21	K 22		83.34	
1439	J 22					
1440	J 22				82.84	
1441	J 22	J 23			83.30	
1444	K 24				82.95	
1445	J 23	J 24			83.27	
1446	J 24	K 24	K 23		83.31	82.85
1447	K 24					
1448	K 24				82.80	
1449	I 23	J 23	J 24			
1450	K 26				82.76	
1459	L 25	L 26			82.89	
1460	K 20				83.77	83.24
1461	L 24	L 25			82.88	82.39
1462	L 23	L 24				

No entranceways are indicated for several rooms (Loci 1869, 1870, and 1871), suggesting that the excavators failed to observe them. Unfortunately there are only a minimum number of elevations indicated for this structure, and we do not know whether the walls were preserved to the same heights along their entire lengths or whether some gaps could be indicative of doorways. These rooms were not subterranean, nor did these walls support an upper story with entrances from above. One interesting feature in this building is short, stubby Wall 1416 in Locus 1896 that appears to have functioned as a pilaster. A similar arrangement is found

Table 2.12 Walls of Stratum XIVa

Wall #	SQ	SQ	SQ	Upper Elevations	Lower Elevations
1410	K 26			83.36	
1412	K 25	K 26		83.57	
1413	K 25	L 24	L 24	83.55	
1414	J 21			83.73	83.37
1419	L 23				
1427	L 24	M 24		83.51	
1428	L 22			83.93	82.96
1430	K 22	K 23		83.49	82.70
1436	J 21				
1437	J 22				
1438	J 22			83.57	
1451	K 20	K 21	K 22	83.74	
1452	K 21			83.24	
1453	L 21			83.50	82.95
1454	L 26			83.11	82.92
1456	L 26				
1457	L 26				
1458	M 26			82.75	

in Locus 1866 (see below), and in both instances they are located in large rooms where they would have considerably reduced the length of span necessary for supporting roof beams of wood.

Walls 1407 and 1408 appear to form an irregularly shaped bin that further divides up a long, narrow room into two chambers. It is an unusual and particularly inelegant arrangement that leaves only a narrow passage between rooms. I was unable to find parallels for this type of arrangement and I am not certain that FitzGerald's plan truly represents the structure as it originally existed. Similar bin-like constructions are found in earlier strata in this precinct. One, formed by Walls 1420-1421, may also have been inside, but it would have been even more impractically situated. I suggest that it was likely to have been external to the building and was constructed after Wall 1462 was destroyed. Together these two features could suggest a later phase of utilization in which some of the structures were so deteriorated that they lost their primary function and eventually served very different purposes.

The western portion of the Deep Cut is taken up by a large, irregularly shaped room (Locus 1866), part of a larger structure obviously built in several stages Figures 2.34 and 2.35). Notable is the segmentation represented by Walls 1439 and 1440, and what may be either an earlier wall or internal bench (Wall 1424). Extant features include a pilaster (Wall 1445) and a hook-shaped segment (Wall 1448), possibly an attempt to create a small compartment within Locus 1867. The entrance to this room may have been just to the south; alternately it could have been farther to the west in the unexcavated portions of this building.

Stratum XIVa

Although recorded elevations suggest a not inconsiderable buildup of fill between this phase and Stratum XIVb, these later constructions show clear continuity with the preceding occupation. Only partial plans of structures were preserved in this phase. They share the orientation of the earlier walls and, in some cases probably utilized portions of them. Walls 1451 (lower elev. 83.38) and 1430 seem to have formed a single feature with one curvilinear end that was only partially preserved. A dotted line on FitzGerald's plan possibly indicates some later construction phase, although I am not certain just what it represents. These walls follow almost precisely the line of Wall 1432 (upper elevation 83.44), while their designated elevations almost coincide.

This feature seems to have been incorporated, probably in its latest utilization, into a compendium of walls that may be loosely categorized as a "building." It consists of Walls 1451, 1430, 1453, and 1452 (the latter associated with a brick floor) and is likely to have also incorporated short Wall 1428. Nothing more of this structure is preserved in the excavated area, but additional portions probably extend into the northern and eastern balks. FitzGerald's plan suggests that this is not the case, but I suspect that it merely reflects the outline of the Deep Cut drawn at a higher elevation. The inward sloping sections explain these discrepancies.

To the west of this structure is a rectilinear building with at least two rooms. Oriented with Wall 1451/1430, it forms a narrow lane similar to that in the underlying (Stratum XIVb) occupation. Wall 1414 was partially constructed atop Wall 1417 and suggests that the rooms directly to the south (Loci 1866 and 1867) may well have continued in use in this phase. The unusual shape of Wall 1438 is difficult to explain. It could be analogous to the pilaster-like jutting wall segments of the preceding phase, or possibly FitzGerald's workmen did not properly define it.

The poorly preserved wall segments in the southeast precinct of the excavation indicate that the earlier structure remained in use with some small changes. Only those walls that could be definitively associated with this phase were placed on the plan of this phase. They suggest that the larger structure was subdivided into several larger rooms. Perhaps Wall 1419 was also incorporated into this building.

The building remains of this stratum suggest a somewhat lengthy occupation with evidence for more than the two major structural phases noted above. Phasing is notable in the obvious numerous additions and changes the several structures underwent during their lifetimes, while continuity is evident throughout the period in the utilization of earlier features and the maintenance of the basic orientation of buildings and the space that separates them. Probably the precinct south of W144 was not empty in Stratum XIVa.

Although three buildings in Stratum XIVb seem juxtaposed in such a way as to suggest their contemporaneousness, the single-roomed house in the northern precinct is different in style from those to its south. Whether these differences actually reflect the same stratigraphic anomalies that apparently indicate chronological disparities observed in earlier strata (see above) is unclear. I suspect that if there is some internal chronology then it is likely to have been preserved in the first of the three buildings constructed. It represents continuity (excepting with Stratum XVa) with earlier curvilinear traditions of house construction and exhibits features that mark it as a type transitional to rectilinear precepts of house building typical for advanced phases of EB I.

It seems likely that this building continued in use and that its existence dictated the orientation of Walls 1462 and 1417. They would have been constructed so as to allow passage between them at the expense of the size of the rooms they define.

The extant plan indicates not only the almost complete return to rectilinear principles for house construction, but also rather crowded conditions on the mound. The Deep Cut is at its periphery, and virtually all the space within it is taken up by buildings. Therefore, we may assume that space was at a premium on this high, steep hill. Such crowding may be indicative of the tenor of the times. Although there are no constructed fortifications at Beth Shan from this period, they have been found at neighboring sites (see Summary), and it is not inconceivable that the mound's steep sides were understood as at least a minimal means of defense that attracted people to the relative safety of the settlement, possibly swelling its population late in EB I.

The internal structure of this precinct of the settlement is noteworthy. The several buildings in both phases seem to be largish, multi-chambered affairs that suggest they served aggregations of peoples greater than the nuclear family. They do not appear to offer access from public spaces, and so I suggest they were somewhat self-contained enclaves probably serving particular social units, perhaps in the nature of extended families.

Stratum XIII

Several phases are noticeable within this stratum, and I have tentatively assigned those structures that appear to have existed contemporaneously to two major and one minor phase on the basis of relative elevations and discernible changes in plan (Figures 2.36, 2.37, 2.38). I am not wholly convinced of the artificial separation as it appears on the two plans because preservation wass uneven and, especially within the upper phases there are considerable signs of structural changes and additions to buildings. In particular, one structure seems almost certain to have survived, with minor changes from Stratum XIIIb into Stratum XIIIa. Since data are scarce, I cannot better understand the sequential nuances they indicate beyond the somewhat simplified stratigraphy suggested here.

Table 2.13 Walls of Stratum XIIIc

Wall #	SQ	SQ	SQ	Upper Elevations	Lower Elevations
1325	K 25	L 25		83.62	
1338	L 25				
1349	M 24				
1365	K 22	L 2 2	J 21		
Postholes	J 20	K 20			

Stratum XIIIc

Three wall segments (Walls 1325, 1338, 1349—no elevations are available for this wall, and it may as well be related to Stratum XIIIb) below a large building in the southwestern precinct appear to belong to the earliest construction phase (Figure 2.37). They share the alignment of the overlying structures. Wall 1350, the foundations of which are notably lower than those of adjacent Wall 1351 (assigned to Stratum XIIIb), may also have originated in this phase. Wall 1365 seems to be a part of a wall that preceded the construction of the mudbrick Walls 1308 and 1377 above it. Perhaps some or all of the postholes in Locus 1849 belong to this phase. I suggest this because the more northerly line, almost adjacent to Wall 1301, is too close for posts to have a likely structural function.

Stratum XIIIb

Two narrow, perpendicular lanes divide the excavated area into three distinct precincts. Remains of a stone wall (Wall 1365) serve as the border for the lane that separates structures in the northern portion of the excavation from additional buildings south of it. Other wall segments bisect the excavation area into eastern and western precincts.

The northern precinct in this phase is dominated by a multi-roomed structure, quite obviously larger than the portions of it exposed within the Deep Cut. Three rooms are visible in its plan (Figures 2.39). Access to this building, part of a complex of chambers, is from a small open area near the juncture of the two lanes, through a doorway, over a well-preserved threshold between Walls 1377 and 1309 (into Locus 1846).

Locus 1846 is a large room of irregular plan. Its southwestern half appears to be more or less rectangular in concept; it has two sharply right-angled corners. However, the northwestern precinct is composed of a series of what appear to be walls (1310, 1311, and 1312) on FitzGerald's plan that truncate the rectangular aspect of this room as well as create a series of offsets or recesses. There is no good corroborative evidence for these lines (only one façade was exposed), and I suspect that FitzGerald's workmen could well have cut into debris or even "created" lines where they might not have existed. These three lines are curiously at odds with the almost regular rectilinear aspect of the remainder of the building and I suspect that these "walls" more properly represent sections at the edge of the excavation than actual structures.

The borders of the Deep Cut on FitzGerald's plans do not always correspond to the strata they are supposed to represent, and it is quite clear that they were measurements taken either at the top of each stratum or perhaps even somewhere above. The cut had sloping sides, and as it became deeper, the area excavated became smaller. That is why walls often do not extend into the balks indicated on the plans. Unfortunately no sections were drawn nor were any pictures of them taken.

Locus 1848, the central room, could be entered from the lane only through Locus 1846. Locus 1846 is a long narrow (ca. 2.5 m wide) chamber that probably was not completely excavated. FitzGerald did not encounter its northern closure wall (1301), although he did ghost it in with a broken line, apparently on the basis of an analogous wall in the adjacent room to the west (Locus 1848). Communication between these chambers was through a doorway with a well-defined threshold, flanked by Walls 1303 and 1304. This latter segment, unaccountably, is curved and joins to a thickened portion of the southern wall, formed by the juncture of two overlapping wall segments (1308 and 1365). These elements suggest some internal construction sequence about which nothing more is known. Bricks from this room are notable for their flat planes (Figure 2.41).

Figure 2.43 indicates that Locus 1848, when excavated, was replete with pottery, including three sizable pithoi (FitzGerald 1935: pl. IV: 25) lined up

Table 2.14 Walls of Strata XIIIb and XIIIa

Wall #	SQ	SQ	SQ		Upper Elevations	Lower Elevations
1301	J 20	K 20	L 20		84.91/	
1302	I 20	J 20				
1303	K 20	K 21			84.89/	
1304	J 21	K 21			84.85/	
1305	I 21	J 21				
1306	K 20	L 20	K 21	L21	84.89/	
1307	K 21	K 22			84.51/	
1308	J 21	K 21	K 22			
1309	L 22					
1310	L 21	L 22			84.90	83.50*
1311	L 21					
1312	L 20	L 21				
1313	I 21	J 21	J 22		85.11	84.03
1314	J 22	K 22	L 22		84.74-84.08	83.68
1315	L 22	L 23	K 23			
1316	J 21	J 22			84.36	83.97
1317	K 21	L 21			84.77	
1320	I 22					
1321	I 22	I 23			84.10	
1322	I 23	J 23			84.08	83.45
1323	I 23				83.73	83.45
1324	I 23	J 23			83.81	
1327	J 23				84.10	83.52
1328	J 23	K 23				
1329	K 23				83.93	
1330	J 23	K 23			84.07	
1332	K 24				83.94	
1333	K 24				83.47	
1334	L 23	M 23			84.03	
1335	L 24					
1336	L 23					
1337	M 24				84.07	83.52
1339	L 23	L 24				
1340	K 24	K 25				
1341	L 24					
1342	L 23				83.52	83.22
1343	L 24					
1344	K 24	L 24				
1345	K 25	L 25			84.05	
1346	L25				83.86	
1348	K 25	L 25			83.91	
1350	L 24	M 24			83.64	82.91
1351	L 24	L 25			83.96	83.51
1352	L 24	L 25			83.64	83.07
1353	M 25					
1359	M 26					
1360	L 21				84.54	
1365	J 21	K 21	K 22	L 22	84.36	84.04
1377	K 22	L 22			84.69	
1379	K 25	K 26			83.62	
1380	I 24	J 24				

*This wall was identified (and numbered 1811) in recent excavations undertaken by A. Mazar in the area immediately to the east (see Figure 1.1). The elevation is derived from a benchmark assigned by Y. Yadin to a mudbrick wall from Stratum VI, re-excavated after more than half a century of having been exposed to the elements. Therefore, there may be some discrepancy between these absolute elevations and the true, preserved height of the wall.

against Wall 1306. Unfortunately, they were not restored and we have only fragments from this stratum (see Chapter 3). Additional vessels, some apparently smaller, appear to have been placed along Walls 1301, 1303, and 1307. FitzGerald (1935: 13) noted the function of this room for storage, especially for grains and legumes (see Appendix 1). This is one of the rare indications that FitzGerald was able to make concerning functions of specific rooms or areas within the Deep Cut.

The almost square westernmost room, Locus 1849, is one of the largest and most complete in this stratum. That it was not an open courtyard seems assured from the presence of a double row of post holes, evidence for the manner in which it was roofed at some point in time. However, it is uncertain whether the internal line of postholes was functional in this phase of the building.

A narrow lane, Loc. 1847 separates this building from the structures to the south. Parallel to Wall 1365 is Wall 1314 that marks the southern border of this east-west thoroughfare (Figure 2.40). It is notable that the upper elevation of Wall 1314 is only 4 cm higher than the lowest elevation of Wall 1365. I attribute these differences in elevations to the existence of a slope here. It reflects an earlier disparity in elevations (noted above) that I suggest accounts for some of the chrono-cultural anomalies in FitzGerald's stratigraphy.

Walls in the western precinct to the south of the lane probably belong to a number of rectilinear chambers created by the juxtaposition of numerous segments. They are obviously part of a complicated construction sequence but, given available data, I am unable to reconstruct it with any degree of confidence. There is no indication as to the possible function of the rooms in this structure, although they seem to form part of a large, composite building. Access to it was probably limited to one doorway opening eastward onto the north-south lane (Figure 2.44).

Of note in this building are FitzGerald's plans that suggest the southern walls were masses of mudbrick (Walls 1328 and 1330) with an open space between. There seems to be no particular structural need for such massive configurations, and their function remains obscure. One wall (1330) or mass, apparently of brick, had a small, round cavity cut into it; another (Wall 1324) may have also been similarly hollowed out and then built over. These cavity-like features could have been utilized for storage, although I wonder that anyone would take the trouble to create such configurations of brick merely to gouge out small cavities. The possibility that these cavities represent later intrusions into mudbrick structures, or even masses of collapsed walls should not be ruled out.

To the east of the north-south lane lies the third precinct. It is dominated by a series of largish, rectilinear rooms at its southernmost extent. Clearly these rooms are only part of a much larger, complex structure that was divided up into smaller apartments. Portions of it remain unexcavated, while additional rooms were probably lost to erosion on the southern slope.

There is no evidence of communication between the rooms in FitzGerald's plan, but at least one doorway can be reconstructed from extant records. A field photograph (Figure 2.45) of the east face of Wall 1338 indicates that the center of the wall had been filled in at some point after its construction. The plan features this doorway, reconstructed from information derived from the photograph of the rear wall (supporting the number) of the large, rectangular room 1856. The sharply defined southern jamb is quite clearly visible, while its northern counterpart seems also to be discernible. Wall 1346, an offset in Walls 1334 and 1345, could be indicative of an earlier construction; alternately it could also have been an external bench facing on the lane.

Stone wall foundations, directly to the north of and adjacent to the mudbrick structure, appear to be later additions to this compound. Together they suggest a coherent plan of small chambers. Wall 1335 may either be a repair of a disintegrated corner (the juncture of Walls 1347 and 1351; Figure 2.45), or alternately, a threshold; a lack of elevations does not permit any more precise interpretation. The close proximity of Walls 1336 and 1334 suggests more than one construction phase, but here again the lack of more precise information does not permit me to draw any conclusions as to their likely sequence.

Stratum XIIIa

Continuity from Stratum XIIIb is evident in the maintenance of the earlier tripartite division into separate precincts within the excavated area (Figure 2.38). Many of the walls in this phase were built directly atop those of the preceding occupation.

The large building in the northern precinct seems to have undergone some minor changes. The construction of a partially sunken, almost circular, stone paved storage facility obviously occurred in this late phase (Figure 2.40). It appears to have been strategically placed against the east face of Wall 1307 so as to leave some space in the southwest corner of the building and

Table 2.15 Walls of Stratum XIIIa only

Wall #	SQ	SQ	SQ	SQ	Upper Elevations	Lower Elevations
1318	J 22				84.95	
1319	J 22					
1326	I 24	J 24			84.50	
1347	K 25	K 26			84.42	
1354	M 26				83.48	83.76
1355	L 24					
1356	M 24					
1357	L 24	M 24			84.40	
1358	L 26					
1361	K 23	K 24				
1362	L 23	L 24				
1363	L 24	L 25			84.70	84.21
1364	L 23	M 23				
1366	K 23				84.78	84.71
1367	K 23				84.93	84.66
1368	L 23				84.85	
1369	L 23				84.85	84.73
1370	L 25					
1371	L 25	L 26				
1372	L 26					
1373	L 25	L 26				
1374	L 25				84.34	
1375	M 25	M 26			84.94	84.21
1376	L 24	M 24	L 25	M 25	84.44 (threshold)	
1378	L 25					

at least a minimal aperture to allow passage into the adjacent room. Wall 1360 effectively bifurcates Room 1846 into two rooms that have no direct communication between them.

Wall 1313 is a long structure that partly delineates the southern edge of the east-west lane in this later phase. While it may have helped to enclose some buildings in a separate precinct to its south, only a few fragmentary buildings could be definitively associated with it. Walls 1318 and 1319 may be a corner of a rectilinear building. Walls 1367, 1366, and 1361 form another right-angle corner that shares a similar orientation. However, they are too poorly preserved for us to declare their mutual association. Still another wall fragment (1326), shares a similar alignment and could also be related to such a structure. It seems likely that this precinct of the excavation was badly denuded or damaged by later buildings.

The southeastern precinct was only somewhat better preserved (Figures 2.46, 2.47). A series of wall segments is visible (Walls 1368, 1362, 1363, 1378, and 1347, from north to south), obviously belonging to different construction phases that maintain a semblance of the narrow north-south lane that began in Stratum XIV. Within this precinct are a large number of wall fragments, most of rectilinear aspect that indicate a similar complicated construction sequence.

Notable in this phase are two walls of vaguely curvilinear aspect. Wall 1364 is ever so slightly curved and may not have been a deliberate attempt at achieving any architectural convention. It incorporates what appears to be a door socket within its outer facing. If in primary position, then it indicates the existence of at least one entrance from the north. Wall segment 1374 seems to be deliberately curved and may be an attempt at achieving a rounded corner. I have suggested an association with Wall 1376, noted by FitzGerald to be a threshold. The juxtaposition with Wall 1363 to form an angular corner is not unparalleled at other sites, but could be indicative of a sequential construction, perhaps with the fortuitous utilization of existing structures.

One notable feature within this complex is a small bin-like structure (Wall 1354) with a stone floor (Figure 2.42). Although its somewhat irregular shape seems to be in keeping with traditions at this site (similar constructions are found in Strata XV and XIV), its incongruous location, taking up almost half the space of the room, suggests to me it was either an above-the-surface structure of a squatter phase, or what seems more likely, it was a silo-like installation dug into fill from a later occupation.

Although many or perhaps all of the walls in this stratum were built anew, there is notable evidence of continuity with structures of the preceding occupation (Stratum XIV). The western wall of the southeastern precinct precisely follows the line of buildings in Strata XIVa and XIVb, and as its predecessors, it is built along rectilinear precepts. So too are the remaining structures in this period and indeed, this is the first occupation associated with the EB I horizon at Beth Shan that has no evidence of curvilinear, domiciliary architectural traditions.

The most remarkable feature in Stratum XIII is the well-preserved structure in the northern precinct that is obviously part of a larger, complex building that appears to have remained buried in the west, north, and east balks. It does not seem to be a typical house, and its rooms are somewhat more commodious than those of complex structures in earlier strata. In that it may be matched by another building complex unearthed in nearby Area M by A. Mazar (1994; personal communication), equated with Stratum XIV. The Area M structure has a series of pillars (albeit large rectangular features) that to some extent parallel the posts that were once set in their holes in Locus 1848.

The narrow lanes and small chamber in the more southerly precincts suggest somewhat crowded conditions, perhaps with living space at a premium as in Stratum XIV. This may be particularly acute in the latest phase in which the large, rectangular Room 1846 was subdivided. That phase and the aboveground storage feature in Room 1857 suggest the likelihood of a squatter phase at the end of the Stratum XIII occupation.

Little else may be said of the fragmentary buildings in the remainder of the excavation precinct. They are a collection of mudbrick walls and stone foundations that give only a vague sense of their original plans. Some of them seem to belong to specialized features, but unfortunately, their functions remain obscure.

Summary

The architectural remains in the Deep Cut appear, insofar as they may be dated by associated material (see Chapter 3), to reflect prevailing traditions in the southern Levant. Rectilinear structures in Stratum XVIII, as well as those in Stratum XVIII (northern precinct), are typical of freestanding domiciles in the LN and EC periods (Braun 1997: 119-122; Getzov 1999: 3, upper left photo). The most northerly walls in Stratum XVI, because they are rectilinear, are also tentatively assigned to these pre-EB I phases of occupation identified by the presence of portable objects of material culture associated to them.

So far as is known at present, the earliest architectural traditions of EB I are curvilinear (Braun 1997: 23-42; 1989b; 2001), and they appear to be reflected in the Deep Cut sequence from Stratum XVII South. This style of architecture is found in the southeasterly series of buildings in Stratum XVI that is apparently typical of early phases in EB I (see discussion of the pottery of this stratum). Noteworthy are the small, virtually complete plan of the sausage-shaped building and the curvilinear walls appended to it on the north. Similar juxtapositions of segments of curvilinear walls have been observed at Yiftah'el and other sites (Braun 1989b; 1997: fig. 5.6, plans 3 and 4).

The Stratum XVI sausage-shaped building exhibits some rectilinear features, a likely indication of its dating to a somewhat advanced (i.e., post-Yiftah'el II) phase of EB I. However, it is uncertain whether they were original aspects of this building or if they represent non-primary phases in which they were introduced. These structures were of non-durable materials and even over a period of several years might well have undergone alterations. Another possible explanation for these seemingly anomalous features is that some may have been inadvertently "created" by FitzGerald's workmen when scraping the unfired mudbrick.

The progression from completely curvilinear precepts of house construction in Early EB I through a gradual return to rectilinear styles with intermediate steps in more advanced phases of this period is now well documented (Braun 1989a: fig. 6; 2001; Kabri 10-9; Kempinski and Niemeier 1992: figs. 3-5), and not unexpectedly the transition is definitively echoed in the remainder of the stratigraphic sequence. The earliest rectilinear structures dated to EB I seem to appear in Stratum XVb, together with at least part of a curvilinear building. Here, as at En Shadud (Braun 1985:67-77), these two traditions of house construction appear coevally.

The anomalous structures of Stratum XVa, all rectilinear, appear to break up what seems otherwise to be a gradual and almost inexorable progression in architectural traditions. However, the buildings of Stratum XIV return to the earlier developmental path, and accordingly that occupation exhibits the last remnant of curvilinear architecture in one house; the remaining buildings are complex aggregations of rooms of rectilinear, albeit somewhat irregular plans. By Stratum XIII all trace of curvilinear architectural traditions seem to have been forgotten. Large complex rectilinear structures fill most of the available space, bringing architectural traditions full cycle.

Too little of the pre-EB I architecture is preserved for any definitive statements to be made concerning the nature of the settlements and the types of houses unearthed in the Deep Cut. Some tentative suggestions for understanding the better-preserved EB I buildings are in order. There is no good evidence for planning during the entire EB I sequence in the Deep Cut. The suggestion is that because this was a high hill with steep sides and limited area, space was always at a premium and people built according to prevailing conditions rather than to their fancy. The results are plans of buildings of irregular shape following general traditions, but with no real sense of any overall organization or planning on a community scale. This is quite typical for villages of these early horizons.

The narrow, crooked lanes and large, composite buildings of the later EB I phases suggest a demographic trend toward greater concentrations of populations from the earlier levels. The single buildings and their additional rooms give way in Stratum XIV to more compact structures that seem to use most of the space available, leaving only narrow passageways between blocks of rooms. Rooms are very small for the most part, and there do not appear to be any internal courtyards, suggesting a very high premium placed upon space. The exception, Locus 1849 in Stratum XIIIa, is a somewhat largish room that may indicate some special function. An adjacent room served as a storage chamber, and there is a suggestion that this portion of the complex may have had a function different from that of other rooms in the surrounding buildings.

This room displays some characteristics of another building unearthed by the Hebrew University of Jerusalem (Mazar 1994) that seems to be contemporary or nearly so. Whether it and the building of which it is a part are indicative of incipient changes in the social fabric of the community in this late period is difficult to know on the basis of the information from the Deep Cut. We must wait for the increment of data on these late phases from the final report on the Hebrew University excavations before proper conclusions may be drawn. Certainly we know that large portions of the mound were occupied with structures in this period, and so it is not untoward to suggest the possibility of a trend toward augmented populations and concomitant social complexity at Beth Shan in these latest phases of EB I. Such a trend seems to be in keeping with developments in the surrounding region and in general in Late EB I.

An interesting sidelight to what appears to be a sizable Late EB I community on the high tell of Beth Shan is the obvious lack of fortifications. Coevally and even prior to this period a number of sites in the region and throughout the southern Levant were fortified, but there is no evidence for any attempt to fortify this hill. It should be noted that other fortified urbanized centers existed in the late phases of EB I at nearby sites such as Tel Shalem (Eisenberg 1997), Tel Beth Yerah (Getzov 1998), Tell es-Sayidiyeh (Tubb, Dorrell, and Cobbing 1996); Tel Megiddo (with monumental buildings and at least a fortified precinct high up on the hill; Finkelstein and Ussishkin 2000), and Tell Abu al-Kharaz (Fischer 2000:202). Additional fortified Late EB I sites farther afield include Jawa (Helms 1991), Tel Aphek (Gal and Kochavi 2000:62-66), Jericho (Holland 1986; Parr 2000), and the Egyptian colony at Tell es-Sakan, just south of Gaza City (de Miroschedji and Sakan 2000). The reason may well be the steep slopes of the hillside the settlement occupied that could have obviated the need for fortifications. However, such natural defenses may not have been a reliable alternative to constructed fortifications. As most of the pottery of Stratum XII suggests—much of it consisting of complete vessels and large fragments of Khirbet Kerak Ware (FitzGerald 1935: pls. 7-10)— the tell seems to have been abandoned after Stratum XIIIa until the Early Bronze III period.

3

Pottery from the Deep Cut at Beth Shan

Discussion of the pottery from the Deep Cut is primarily organized around FitzGerald's original stratigraphy because of limitations of information on the precise provenience of objects. Only in the instance of Stratum XIX (i.e., fill from the pits below Stratum XVIII) was it possible to ascribe material to my emended stratigraphic sequence.

An in-depth study of this pottery suggests that with the possible exception of the Stratum XIX material, none of the stratigraphic collections assigned by FitzGerald to his "levels" is chronologically discrete. Indeed, there is abundant evidence for residual and intrusive material throughout the sequence. This is not unexpected and can be explained by several factors.

Principally, the nature of the deposits is such that most ceramic specimens FitzGerald recovered are quite fragmentary and obviously were not in primary deposition. They were not found on floors or even in destruction debris or in clear contexts known to be close in time to the period in which they were fabricated and utilized. Therefore, it is difficult to understand their associations to find spots (in any case imperfectly known) and then ascribe them to specific features within the stratigraphic sequence. The Deep Cut is a sounding in a long series of occupations that left deposits from successive building and rebuilding events, mostly of modest dwellings with their outbuildings and appurtenances. These structures were primarily fashioned of mudbrick and only occasionally did they boast stone foundations. The remains discovered were often poorly preserved due to natural erosion and human and animal intervention and possibly imperfect excavation techniques. Notably, floors were rarely preserved or perceived.

Thus, most of the artifacts appear to have been in non-primary deposition, a common condition at tells in the region given the vulnerability and/or scarcity of building materials. In particular, the propensity of mudbrick to erode during winter rains is extremely deleterious to preservation of this type of architecture.

The continued use of this part of the mound with all its incumbent re-utilization and alteration of materials and structures, especially the leveling and digging of pits, obviously wreaked havoc with the original sequence of deposits as they were laid down. The Deep Cut removed an archaeological deposit replete with "post-depositional" disturbances, only some of which may be understood.

The manner in which the excavation was undertaken can also explain the mixed chrono-cultural nature of the ceramic assemblages of the several levels (see below: The Data and their Limitations). FitzGerald's (1933:278 reverse side) journal includes a list of "Rooms of Levels Below Level XIV" that cryptically notes: "The levels being shallow, the 'Rooms' usually go down into the level below." Thus, we know that very often the workmen dug below levels of foundations in operations "within" rooms; nor is it sure just when and how they may have collected pottery or where they stopped their probes. According to the notes in the journal, this was done only twice weekly. The journal does not tell us whether all the pottery was saved and stored or whether collection was desultory. We also have no way of knowing whether any selection process may have been employed that might have differentiated between diagnostic and more nondescript body sherds. In addition, some walls were obviously trenched around their perimeters (Figure 2.27). Judging by the few elevations taken for wall foundations, it appears that little interest was taken in minute detailing of fills and their associations to structures.

Most of FitzGerald's stratigraphic assemblages are clearly of mixed chrono-cultural origins. That he was not aware of such a situation is eminently understandable because he had no frame of reference, no previously excavated, stratigraphic ceramic sequence beyond his own observations at this site, with which to compare artifacts. In truth, more than six decades later, even with our knowledge of a large body of evidence on the archaeological record, we still have problems with the chrono-cultural identification of some pottery types. It is sometimes impossible, especially from fragments to distinguish between objects associated with the LN/EC horizons and those of Early EB I.

This particular problem and its relationship to the pottery of the Deep Cut is discussed below at some length (see below, *Excursus*: Is The "Middle Chalcolithic of Beth Shean" Really A Cultural Horizon?) because of the important implications it has for the study of pottery of late prehistoric periods. In most cases the associations I have made are based on interpretations that correlate chrono-cultural information intrinsic to the objects and the structures to which they are at least tentatively attributed. I need not remind the reader of the subjectivity of this approach and its obvious limitations. Accordingly, I note that in some instances, chrono-cultural identifications are difficult and I freely admit the possibility of some error in my judgment.

FitzGerald associated all the ceramics from the Deep Cut with the different levels he perceived, and he published those he considered important within that stratigraphic framework. It appears that he automatically related material from findspots within "rooms" to those same structures, based on relative elevations. Occasionally, ceramic deposits are noted as "upper" or "lower" within rooms, but it is not clear just what he meant by this. Sometimes this latter designation seems to refer to deposits below foundations, and in those instances FitzGerald appears to have automatically assigned such material to a preceding level. However, nowhere is there specific written evidence of this. In other cases there is also a possibility of more than one phase associated with a room above levels of foundations, particularly when the latter were of mudbrick and where accumulation of deposits was considerable.

FitzGerald was not oblivious to the problem of assigning material to correct levels, and he worked out a sequence for the structures, apparently while still in the field with the excavation fresh in his mind. His preliminary report to the director (FitzGerald 1933b, 1933c) was sent from the Beth Shan camp sometime before December 31, 1933, and his final stratigraphic designations (FitzGerald 1934; 1935) are identical to those in his later reports.

As noted above, the lack of chrono-cultural homogeneity in the ceramic assemblages assigned to the different levels presents problems for dating buildings. Unfortunately the data FitzGerald left do not allow for any major revision in dating structures by associated finds because his notation system lacks a degree of precision that would allow for relationships between artifacts and structures to be verified. Thus, we may only make educated guesses as to how correct FitzGerald's stratigraphic associations are. I have attempted, where possible, to do this in the following discussion.

Following earlier examples of the Beth Shan Field Directors who encountered substantial architecture, FitzGerald designated his excavation units as "rooms" (nd; 1933. These rooms are what today we generally regard as loci. Such usage is at least minimally informative and appropriate enough when actual walls or other architectural features were present to define areas and volumes of excavation (provided elevations were noted). However, the system of notation he employed is far less precise and of considerably less utility, especially for the earlier levels of the Deep Cut where well-defined architectural features are lacking. It is even more problematic when there is little precision in the three-dimensional definition of rooms and virtually no precision for the ultimate provenience of artifacts.

Precise locations and absolute elevations for the ceramic finds were noted in only a handful of instances. Unfortunately, the findspots for most of the objects cannot be pinpointed. In virtually every instance finds are ultimately provenienced only to rooms and most of these rooms were rather sizable affairs or were actually large open spaces between structures.

Precise elevations, the crucial third dimension for understanding stratigraphic relationships, are also unavailable. Some walls were preserved to a substantial height (sometimes more than 1.0 m), and artifacts attributed to a room could come from anywhere within fill encompassed by it. Nor can we know of the likelihood of disturbances to the archaeological record that could account for intrusions that displaced or deposited material from different chrono-cultural horizons. Nowhere is there any indication of soil layers or color differences within Levels XVIII–XIII that could inform us of such activity. Most tellingly, there is no indication of pits or robber trenches or similar intrusive features, except in the very lowest level, and as any excavator knows, the likelihood of their absence in such a site is virtually nil.

Accordingly, material FitzGerald assigned to his rooms may have ultimately derived from the rooms themselves or from earlier or later deposits. I cannot evaluate FitzGerald's observations better than to suggest chrono-cultural identifications of the ceramics based on their diagnostic attributes. Since there is no possibility to improve upon the stratigraphic ascription of the ceramic assemblages, the discussion below follows FitzGerald's sequence.

The Sample

Pottery available for study is an unquantified sample retained from the total assemblage recovered. Evidence that this material was sorted and some of it discarded is found in FitzGerald's (ND) notes. It is quite clear that this took place before pottery was shipped to its present locations, probably before a division with the Department of Antiquities took place late in December of 1933 (FitzGerald 1933b). As noted in Chapter 1, numerous sherds, some diagnostic (i.e., rims and bases), were recorded, even drawn and then ultimately discarded. What, if any, attempt was made to restore pottery is unclear.

In one instance in Stratum XIII, three pithoi found smashed, their bases still *in situ*, were clearly identified and even photographed (Figure 2.43). Although the vessels were apparently complete, or nearly so, we have only large fragments of these partially restored vessels. No body sherds from them are found in either stored collection; presumably, the remaining pieces were discarded. As far as I have been able to ascertain, pieces of many other vessels deemed of little or no importance were also discarded, probably at the excavation camp. There is even circumstantial evidence to confirm discarding in the field likely to have derived from FitzGerald's 1933 season (see Chapter 1). The Deep Cut appears to be the only probable source of EB I pottery; earlier work on the tell was in much later levels that would not have produced the quantities encountered in that dump.

Extant in the present assemblages are only reasonably well-preserved diagnostic fragments (e.g., rims, handles, spouts, bases, and specially decorated pieces). Anyone familiar with the quantities of pottery generally encountered in tells of the northern valleys of the southern Levant (of which Beth Shan is quite typical), knows that the material retained by FitzGerald must be only a small and highly selective sample of a vastly greater assemblage recovered. In addition, there is no evidence for sieving of materials, and we may assume that sherd recovery was dependent upon the skill and motivation of the workers, dispositions and inclinations for which we have no information.

Pottery Typology

Pottery from the Deep Cut derives mostly from the LN through EB I periods and includes recognizable types, the products of accepted conventions, mental templates abroad at different times that dictated permutations of morphology, fabric, and decoration. Some of these are rather long-lived traditions, and identifying them allows for only broad chrono-cultural attributions; others are more specific and consequently can be dated more precisely by parallels.

Further limitations on our ability to recognize specific types derive from the fragmentary nature of the material available for study, and so, quite often, the reader will note that suggested chrono-cultural attributions are less than specific. It is particularly reflected in the use of the broad-term LN/EC, indicating that no further precision can possibly be derived from available information.

By contrast, some pottery of the EB I horizon from Beth Shan tends to have diagnostic features that often allow more specific comparisons. Some of that material fits into a ceramic typology specifically designed for a Northern variation of Early Bronze I, originally developed for the excavation report of 'En Shadud and afterwards extended to the study of ceramics from Yiftah'el II (Braun 1985: 29-66; 1997: 56-89). However, Beth Shan has additional types that indicate it belongs to a somewhat different, localized region, while it also apparently exhibits a greater chronological range, extending into the latest phases of the period. Indeed, the Deep Cut appears to have one of the better EB I sequences found to date in the region.

The Illustrations

One set of line drawings (Figures 3.1 to 3.22) illustrates a selection of the most diagnostic ceramic artifacts from the Deep Cut that are prominent in the following discussion. They include objects from the two collections, the overwhelming bulk of which belongs to the University Museum. The remainder is part of the IAA collection in Jerusalem.

A second set of illustrations is a reproduction of FitzGerald's (1935) original plates I–VI from *The Museum Journal* in which there is some overlap with the figures. I feel that this replication is justifiable, primarily because the plates have been cited innumerable times in the literature and their reappearance here will be indispensable to scholars. Another incentive for their inclusion lies in the current unavailability of some objects to be drawn anew because they could not be located. Thus, the addition of FitzGerald's plates allows representation of the most compete assemblage possible for the different levels, albeit with some duplication. When the original drawings represent types that are not included in the new figures, the discussion cites the plates.

Technical Conventions

Since it was impossible to change the drawings to conform to conventions that are more usual, I have organized the publication to compensate for it. In excavation reports from the southern Levant, red and related earth colors and their variations are generally indicated on line drawings as shaded areas. However, with the exception of those objects from the IAA collections and several with selective rendering of particular styles of painting or burnishing from the Museum collection, evidence of this convention is mostly absent in the accompanying illustrations. The reader must rely on descriptions accompanying the figures to know whether a particular vessel was otherwise treated in red.

The Pottery Assemblage by Stratum

The Pottery of Stratum XIX

Material available for study from this stratum includes examples of morphological, technical, and decorative features typical of the LN/EC horizons (Figure 3.28). Following are brief discussions on the most diagnostic of these artifacts illustrated in the accompanying figures. A summary discussion deals with their significance for understanding what appear to be the earliest human deposits on the tell. All of the pottery from this stratum was fashioned by hand, as is usual for early periods in the southern Levant. There is no evidence for the use of a wheel, although at least one vessel seems to have been fashioned on a tournette that was probably rotated slowly.

Bowls

One fragment of a simple, shallow, rounded bowl (Figure 3.1:1) is notable for its rather coarse fabric and somewhat unusual decoration. Of light color, it is painted inside and out with thick, uneven, radial lines of red paint. In addition, there are smudges and irregularly shaped drops of the same paint in intervening spaces. Simple bowls of similar mien have a long history; they are found in LN/EC contexts at Teleilat Ghassul (Garfinkel 1992: fig. 96:2-12; Lovell 1999: fig. 239). Yannai et al. (in press) have found numerous examples of similar shallow bowls decorated with semicircles of red paint on the rims in Stratum V at 'Ein Assawir, an occupation they date to EC. This same, simple form is also well attested in EB I contexts, but the coarse fabric and decoration of this specimen as well as its findspot, proclaim it as belonging to the LN/EC horizon. Bowls with similar, red-striped decoration are found in the basal (LN) levels of Abu Hamid, another Jordan Valley site (Dollfus and Kafafi 1993: fig. 9-17).

The mid-portion of a Pedestaled bowl (Figure 3.1:2) is a fragment of a large vessel of uncertain overall morphology. Such bowls have a long history of development beginning in the Aceramic Neolithic Period, when they were fashioned of lime plaster (known as either "white ware" or by the French term "vaisselles blanches"; de Contenson 1979) or stone. Eventually, in later periods, the type developed in several ways including one noted for its fenestrated bases. Bowls of this general morphological type are associated with LN/EC sites such as Munhatta, the Rabah Stage (Garfinkel 1992: figs. 102; 103: 1-11) and Ein Assawir (Yannai et al., in press).

Holemouths

Holemouths are one of the simplest shapes and appear in the earliest pottery repertoires of the southern Levant (e.g., in the Sha'ar Hagolan phase of LN Pottery ; cf. Garfinkel 1992: fig. 42) and in most other regions of the Near East. Generally they have either simple tapered or rounded rims attached to vertical or nearly vertical walls that form deep wells ending in rounded or flattened bases. When fragmentary they are often hard or impossible to distinguish from fragments of bowls that share similar characteristics. Some examples, apparently with specialized functions, are notable for loop handles attached vertically to their walls. One simple example with slightly tapering rim (Figure

3.1:7) is so fragmentary that the attitude of the wall is uncertain. It may be a portion of a deep vessel with a nearly upright wall that would give the vessel a rather wide aperture.

Small Holemouth Vessel with Handle

A single fragment of a small, deep vessel with simple, tapered rim and flat loop handle is the most complete fragment of any vessel recovered from the pits of Stratum XIX (Figure 3.1:3). Little more may be noted of its rather inelegant shape, but some general morphological parallels from the Jordan Valley sites of Jericho (Droop 1935: pl. XLV:1; Kenyon and Holland 1983: fig. 37:15) and Ghrubba (Mellaart 1956: figs. 4: 28, 5: 100) suggest a general date within the LN/EC horizon. The very coarse fabric and lack of finish of this example, in concert with its crudely applied red decoration, mark it as clearly belonging to an early ceramic horizon.

Jars

Only a few diminutive sherds can be definitively assigned to this generic type. It is an upper portion of a small storage vessel, a rimless neck and segment of shoulder (Figure 3.1:4). Despite the fragmentary state, its notable features hint at the overall morphology and decoration of the vessel. The diagnostic feature, typical of LN/EC, is its horizontal ropelike band around the neck, produced by depression of a blunt, flattened instrument applied obliquely at regular, narrow intervals. Similar decorations are found on vessels from nearby Tel Tsaf in the Jordan Valley, dated to EC (Gophna and Sadeh 1988: fig. 11: 3) and farther afield in the Néolithique Récent of Byblos (Dunand 1973 fig. 91:2707).

Additional examples of a decorative, ropelike effect in this assemblage are in the form of raised bands, slashed diagonally. This type of decoration first appears in the Neolithic, continues throughout the Chalcolithic, and is also quite common in Early EB I (see below). Sometimes it is difficult or even impossible to distinguish between the productions of these periods (representing several millennia of human activity, especially on otherwise non-diagnostic fragments. However, those in this group unmistakably derive from earlier horizons as indicated by their findspots and the exceedingly coarse fabrics from which they were fashioned. There is no apparent evidence of intrusive material from the EB I occupation in the pits of Stratum XIX, although such material seems to be found in Stratum XVIII.

One sherd, probably the neck of a small jar (Figure 3.1:5), is paralleled at Byblos in the Néolithique Moyen and Néolithique Récent (Dunand 1973: pl. LXX: 28068, fig. 19: 27027) levels. A second fragment (Figure 3.1:6), with its less well-demarcated segments of rope, seems more similar to decoration on a bowl from Byblos dated to the Neolithique Récent there (Dunand 1973: pl. LXXV: ll/6, LX).

Tubular and Loop or Strap Handles

The most numerous sherds retained by FitzGerald from the pits are handles (Figures 3.1:14-16). They are invariably of types described as loop or sometimes strap, and by Garfinkel (1992: 54) as tubular, although these distinctions are somewhat arbitrary (dependent upon what degree of depth in a loop and what degree of flatness is required to fulfill definitions of these types). For purposes of this discussion, tubular handles are recognized for their extreme width proportionate to the relatively small size of the aperture of the tube-like feature they form. Notably there is a great degree of variety in size and finish in the looping and tubular appendages found in these pits at Beth Shan.

Following chrono-stratigraphic information from Munhatta (Garfinkel 1992: 54, 79, 293 and passim; but apparently *contra* Garfinkel 1999: fig. 111, who assigns similar handles from Stratum XVIII to his "Middle Chalcolithic"), it would appear that the crudest and widest (the most obviously tubular) examples tend to belong to a pre-Rabah, Neolithic phase known from the basal levels at Tell Abu Hamid (Lovell 2001:162). Although ceramic evidence for that particular horizon is nowhere represented at Beth Shan, it may be that this type of handle reflects an analogous chronological sequence, i.e., that these handles date to a pre-Rabah phase of LN. Several examples from Beth Shan typify this group.

The loop handles from these pits tend to be somewhat more carefully fashioned than tubular handles, although whether this observation is related to function and/or chronological differences is unclear from available data. Lacking additional information on the morphology of the vessels to which these handles were appended, one cannot date them more specifically by analogy beyond noting that they belong to a lengthy LN/EC tradition. Examples of them are paralleled at a number of nearby sites in the Jordan Valley and Lower Galilee, including the basal level at Tell Abu Hamid (Lovell, Kafafi, and Dollfus 1997: fig. 4:6), Munhatta (Sha'ar Hagolan and Rabah stages respectively; Garfinkel 1992: 55, 79), Tell es Shuna I (de

Contenson 1960: fig. 7), Jericho (Ben Dor 1936: pl. XXX: 1-3, 7; pl. XXXII: 27) and LN Yiftah'el (Braun 1997: fig. 15.5:5).

A Handle-like, Fragmentary Object

A solid ceramic, handle-like object, for which I know of no parallels, is included in the material from Pit 19-3 (33-11-71) (Figure 3.1:12a-c). It is of light buff fabric mottled with light pink, has a gray core, traces of red slip and brown painted lines forming what may be chevrons in opposing positions. The longest segment of this object is a thick, flat strip with rounded edges, bonded at right angles to an almost cylindrical post-like segment. This solid cylinder, partially broken off at the opposite end, has a small stub that goes off on a tangent. It, in turn, is also broken where it was formerly attached to yet another segment or, alternately this second break could merely have been some stylistic adjunct, a small, non-functional fragment that broke off. This latter possibility seems somewhat remote, considering that structurally such an appendage would have been of limited vulnerability in a pattern of breakage. It would have required a hard, well-placed blow to fracture in that way. This object does not seem to be have belonged to a simple, utilitarian pot, but rather may have had a specialized function that remains obscure.

Assorted Bases

Several types of bases are found in Stratum XIX (Figure 3.1:8-11, 13). By shape and fabric, they fall clearly within the chrono-cultural parameters of the remainder of the assemblage. They include stumplike bases (Figure 3.1:13), a type paralleled in Neolithic contexts (Kenyon and Holland 1983: fig. 124: 2; Garfinkel 1992: fig. 130:2), and simple, flat bases, some notable for the coarseness of their fabrics. Such types are the most common for vessels of the Neolithic period.

Another type of base (Figure 3.23) is most often associated with Chalcolithic pottery traditions and seems to be a technological innovation of potters of that period. It is characterized by what may be termed a narrow, almost vestigial ring, formed apparently when a circular base of clay was attached to a work surface (probably a tournette) by pressing hard around its circumference. It is not certain, but in some instances the surface may have had a slightly raised circular hump, designed to keep it more stable, on which the pot was fashioned. When the vessel was removed from the surface a low ring remained. It was probably smoothed over by a simple tamping down when the vessel was almost dry. This type of base is generally associated with Chalcolithic assemblages (Commenge-Pellerin 1990: pl. II: 1, pl. III: 1, 3) and may be considered as one of the hallmarks of the period (Roux and Courty 1997), although more recently it has been noted in very early southern EB I contexts (Braun 2000; Braun and Gophna 2004:206).

Pottery retrieved by FitzGerald and available for study from the pits of Stratum XIX makes up a collection that includes numerous large fragments of a variety of vessels but no complete, nor even nearly complete objects. Accordingly, I assume the material derived from these cavities was not in primary deposition and that these pits are repositories of discarded objects, although to what extent their placement there may have resulted from deliberate human intervention remains obscure.

Dating of these objects, primarily based on parallels, is fraught with difficulties since there is not a great deal of standardization in the pottery of these early periods and the parallels are mostly generic. They suggest that the relative date of the LN pottery is later than the Yarmukian period and perhaps later than Jericho IX, based on the following observations. They appear to hold true not only for Stratum XIX, but also for all the LN/EC pottery from the Deep Cut:

1. There is no evidence for hallmarks of the Yarmukian horizon, i.e., pots painted with yellow and red incised herringbone decoration (Stekelis 1972), or for the nude, steatopygious female figurines with coffeebean eyes (Stekelis 1952; Perrot 1972: 412-416) that are additional hallmarks of that chrono-cultural entity.

2. Large, coarse vessels of the early phases of LN (Garfinkel 1992: figs. 64-70; Braun 1997: fig. 15.1-15.3 passim) with grass-wiped exteriors, vegetal tempers, and knob ledge handles are also absent in this assemblage.

3. None of the sherds I examined could be classified as "white ware," a type of object similar to pottery but made of lime preparation, associated with Early and LN (Braun 1997:123), but which does not seem to survive into the Rabah or Post Sha'ar Hagolan Phase.

It seems quite clear that the entire assemblage of this stratum available for study is not homogeneous. Isolated assemblages from the several pits include objects that cannot be more specifically related to two sequentially contiguous cultural horizons, LN and EC, while one object could even possibly be dated later. Thus, on the basis of available information it is impossible to determine definitively how long a utilization of the site these materials represent. Suffice it to note that there is evidence for utilization of the site either continually or intermittently within the LN/EC horizon.

Although the very presence of these incomplete artifacts indicates considerable activity on the site in whatever period or periods they represent, nevertheless, their relationship to the pits from which they were retrieved is unclear. It seems likely, given the nature of these cavities, that the material in them was in non-primary deposition, which says only that they were placed within, sometime after the pits were created, and before the succeeding occupation sealed them. Presumably some of the material was deposited during the occupation of Stratum XVIII, while some of it appears to have originated later.

One last observation suggests the ceramic deposits of Stratum XIX do not document mere casual visits, but rather derive from real occupation of this high hill overlooking the surrounding plain. No other explanation would account for the considerable quantities of pottery found within the pits. Additional excavation of this stratum would presumably produce more of the same material and possibly evidence of a sedentary occupation.

The Pottery of Stratum XVIII

The pottery repertoire of Stratum XVIII is represented by a relatively large number of sherds displaying a limited range of shapes and vessel types likely to be derived, *grosso modo*, from two chrono-cultural horizons (Figure 3.29). While some of the types are difficult to associate solely with one or the other horizon, others are hallmarks that inform us of their specific origins. Most of the vessels in this assemblage were hand made. The few exceptions, fashioned or altered on some sort of rotating mechanism, are noted below.

Bowl Types

The wide assortment of bowl types suggests differing functions for the end product as well as varied technological approaches to ceramic production. The types suggested below are broad categories of vessels with very generalized similarities.

Pedestaled Bowls

The midsection of a small, pedestaled bowl of coarse fabric is the sole portion of this vessel to survive (Figure 3.2:1). It is not known whether it may have originally been fenestrated nor what the shape of the bowl might have been. However, the fabric is of a type often associated with LN/EC pottery, while the morphology certainly does not preclude such a date (Garfinkel 1992: fig. 103). A second example (Figure 3.2:3) with a high "trumpet-like" base and larger bowl with a flat bottom seems also to belong to the same horizon. Several fragments of additional, pedestaled vessels are derived from Strata XIX and XVII (Figures 3.1:2, 3.5:5-6).

Bowls

One large, deep bowl with tapering rim is notable for a horizontal band of rope decoration below its rim. It is closely paralleled at nearby Tel Tsaf (Gophna and Sadeh 1988-89: fig. 10:9) where it is apparently derived from an EC occupation of Stratum I. A base, probably of a bowl (Figure 3.24), is notable for the imprint of a telltale string-cut, swirling pattern made when it was detached from a rotating surface. This method of production, unknown in the Neolithic period, is commonly encountered in Chalcolithic contexts from early phases (C. Commenge 2001: personal communication).

Holemouths with Handles

One example (Figure 3.2:4) does not strictly belong to this category of vessels. Unusually, it has a ledged or guttered and slightly splayed rim. Its vertical handle, widely splayed at its points of attachment, is a characteristic common to Neolithic handles. The more rounded features of a diminutive specimen (Figure 3.2:5) could suggest a somewhat later date. A third, rather large vessel is notable for its somewhat flat handle and three widely spaced horizontal bands of red paint below the rim, features that suggest a Neolithic date for this fragment.

Holemouth Types without Handles

There is a great deal of variation in size, fabric, and decoration within this generic type that suggests different chrono-cultural origins for this group. Several examples (Figure 3.2:7-8, 10, 11, 13) display typical tapering rims atop nearly vertical walls that indicate a tendency toward depth in morphology. The coarse fabric of one vessel (Figure 3.2:10), decorated with a vertical stripe of red paint, may indicate a Neolithic rather than a later origin. Other examples have thicker walls and rounded or almost flattened rims (Figure 3.2:9, 12, 14), features that tend to become more common in the Chalcolithic and later periods, but that are also known as early as the Sha'ar Hagolan Neolithic phase (Garfinkel 1992: fig. 64:2-4, 65:6-9). Additional vessels in this group tend to be of better-levigated fabrics, more carefully shaped, and have a finer finish, characteristics, that suggest they date to the Chalcolithic period (cf. Sadeh and Gophna 1991:143).

The larger examples (Figures 3.2:8-14, 3.3:1-4) are rather deep vessels that tend to have wide apertures and tapered rims, morphological characteristics common from the earliest Neolithic occupations until the advent of EB I (LN though Chalcolithic) when the overall morphology of holemouth vessels changes. Two small fragments of holemouths can be dated with confidence to the LN/EC horizon based on morphology and painted, horizontal-striped decoration (Figure 3.2:8, 14). A broad, almost horizontal band on one example is a type of decoration commonly encountered (see above: bowls) in that horizon. A series of lines created by allowing paint to drip vertically (Figure 3.2:12) may be a regional characteristic of the Jordan Valley where it has a long history extending from LN times into EB I (Parr 1956: figs. 13-14; Kenyon and Holland 1983: fig. 2: 1, fig. 14: 7-8, fig. 17:13; Gustavson-Gaube 1985: fig. 9; Lovell, Kafafi and Dollfus 1997: fig. 4:1; Garfinkel 1999: figs. 109:1, 113:1).

One fragmentary vessel has thin lines horizontally incised into its inner and outer surfaces by some sharp tool, probably as the vessel revolved on a tournette. A similar feature has been found in the Middle Levels at Abu Hamid (Lovell, Kafafi, and Dollfus 1997: fig. 5) and on Chalcolithic bowls at Nahal Qanah (Gopher and Tsuk 1996: fig. 4.2: 10-12).

Jars

Closed vessels are represented by a variety of fragments. They can be roughly identified as belonging to two major categories—jars with very short necks or splayed rims and others with longish necks and splayed rims.

Jars with Short, Wide Necks and Splayed Rims

This type is another very broadly defined morphological category (Figure 3.3:5-12). It too made its appearance in the earliest LN assemblages (Garfinkel 1992: fig. 70:6-8; Lovell 1999: figs. 4.40, 4.41) and remained popular until the onset of EB I. Variations on this theme are found in all sizes, from virtual cups to pithoi. These variations actually form a continuum with other morphological types defined as holemouths (cf. Lovell 1999: fig. 4.38: 1-6), the major difference being the splaying of the rim. One example was painted red (Figure 3.3:11). Another was similarly painted and adorned with a horizontal band of incisions near the juncture of the rim and shoulder (Figure 3.3:12) and should probably be associated with the LN/EC horizon. Incised decoration is not common, but examples of similar treatment are known in types that appear to belong to this horizon (cf. Figure 3.5:13; Leonard 1992: pls. 1:2, 2:2; Gophna and Tsuk 1996: fig. 4.6:14).

Jars with Longish Necks and Splayed Rims

This type is identifiable only from several neck and rim fragments; nothing else is known of its morphology. One example, notable for its crescent-shaped incisions (Figure 3.3:12), is paralleled in the LC of Teleilat Ghassul (Lovell 1999: fig. 4.39:3), where it may be understood as the precursor or prototype of the three remaining jars in this group (Figure 3.3:13-15). Garfinkel (1999: fig. 110:1, photo 93) has ascribed this type (including these specific vessels) to a "Middle Chalcolithic"; however, my own research leaves me reasonably confident that it is one of several intrusive fragments of vessels from the Early EB I strata (XVII-XVI) above (see *Excursus* below). I suggest that the type's superficial resemblance, especially in the details of ropelike decoration, to earlier LN/EC examples (Garfinkel 1992: figs. 106-7; 1999: photo 61) led Garfinkel to erroneously date these vessels to such an early horizon. I interpret these same vessels as variants of Type 52 in my Yiftah'el-'En Shadud typology (Figure 3.7:2; cf. Braun; 1997:77-81). Additional examples of this type are found in Strata XVII and XVI in the Deep Cut, where I do not believe they are intrusive.

Miscellaneous Vessels

A deep, small egg-shaped vessel with rounded base (Figure 3.4:14) has a hand-made wall of uneven thickness and is poorly finished. I have been unable to find any convincing parallels to it. Another vessel fragment in Stratum XVII (Figure 3.9:4), also egg-shaped, is somewhat similar but more skillfully fashioned. The overall morphology of these vessels remains obscure.

Handles

Several handles are illustrated from the assemblage of this stratum. One is a large straplike affair with two sets of incised parallel lines on its upper edges that form an incomplete chevron pattern (Figure 3.4:1). Similar incised decoration is found at Munhatta where Garfinkel (1992: figs. 135, 137) attributes it to the Rabah Stage. Droop (1935: pl. XLI: 13) identified a handle from Jericho similarly adorned as Chalcolithic, which, since Kenyon's (1979: 51-52) excavations at the site, would place it within the LN/EC horizon, rather than in later Chalcolithic contexts. The loop or strap handles from this stratum are notable for the broad area of attachment to the vessel, a characteristic of LN/EC handles. These objects are very similar to handles from Stratum XIX and appear to derive from the same chrono-cultural horizon (see above).

Decorated Sherds

Several fragments of vessels of indeterminate shape are illustrated so as to represent forms of decoration found on the pottery of Stratum XVIII. A portion of what appears to be the neck of a jar is also assigned to the LN/EC horizon (Figure 3.4:10). Its rope decoration is a slashed, narrow, raised band, a style similar to that found in both LC (Leonard 1992: pl. 3:23) and Early EB I contexts.

A closed shape has a small ledge handle or flattened knob (Figure 3.4:7) that is paralleled on vessels of the LN/EC horizon (Garfinkel 1992: fig. 108). Several body sherds have ropelike decoration formed by thin bands of clay with small rounded (finger?) indentations at more or less regular intervals (Figures 3.4:9, 11, 12). Although this type of decoration is known in EB I, I find it more common in the LN/EC horizon (Leonard 1992: pl. 1:3; Lovell 1999: figs. 4.15:5, 4.16:5, 4.24:4).

Two large body sherds of similar fabric and decoration, probably of the same jar, appear to belong to the same vessel, although they do not join (Figure 3.4:13a, 13b; Pl. III:17 18). The thin brown lines drawn to produce a chevron effect and an additional element (analogous to a metope in architecture, another vessel, illustrated in l. III:18, may give a suggestion as to the kind of pattern of which this represents only a part) were drawn by a steady, if not particularly skillful hand. This type of decoration is not uncommon in pottery of the LN/EC (Mellaart 1956: fig. 5) horizon.

A ledge handle with indented profile (Figure 3.4:8) seems to me quite typical of EB I types (cf. Figures 3.9:11, 13, 14; 3.12:2, 3, 4). It differs from earlier LN/EC examples that appear to be stubbier and protrude less from walls of vessels (Garfinkel 1992: fig. 106; see *Excursus* below).

Assorted Bases

Flat bases are ubiquitous in the Deep Cut and were pretty much the rule for jars and bowls of all the periods from Neolithic through EB I, with the exception of specialized types (i.e., fenestrated pedestaled vessels) (Figure 3.4:15-20). Despite their apparent sameness, sometimes specific features allow us to understand technology used for their manufacture that elucidates chrono-cultural origins of these objects.

Two additional flat bases (Figure 3.4:15, 17) can be more closely dated. They have telltale vestigial rings (see above; Figure 3.23) that are one of the hallmarks of Chalcolithic ceramic traditions. Recent research shows them to have appeared in the Middle Chalcolithic at Teleilat Ghassul in the southern Jordan Valley (Lovell 1999: figs. 4.29: 1-5, 4.30: 3-4). Although variations of this type of base have also been associated with an Initial EB I in the south (Braun 2000:125), where they are distinguished from local LC types by their fabrics and careless finishes, there is no evidence yet to place them within EB I contexts in the region of Beth Shan, or anywhere else outside the southern region. Indeed, this technological aspect is conspicuously absent at Yiftah'el II, one of the earliest identifiable EB I sites, where there is no Chalcolithic admixture in the assemblage. Thus, at Beth Shan these bases are definitively associated with the Chalcolithic horizon.

Summary

Pottery attributed to Beth Shan XVIII is apparently derived from fills that at least in part may be associated with stubs of walls and poorly preserved constructions. However, since no object is complete, or even nearly so, their relationships to find spots may be virtually spurious in terms of dating structures. These fragments also reflect their overall morphology only poorly, and thus comparative study of them is of limited value. Therefore, our understanding of this material is rather restricted. With few exceptions, we can only attribute it to the LN/EC horizon; no greater precision is possible. Exceptions are several jar fragments with clear Chalcolithic features and a ledge handle datable by good parallels to Early EB I. Thus, the Stratum XVIII assemblage is best understood as a chrono-culturally mixed bag and should not be used as the basis for a chronologically homogeneous typology (see *Excursus* below).

Excursus: Is the "Middle Chalcolithic of Beth Shean" really a Cultural Horizon?

In *Neolithic and Chalcolithic Pottery of the Southern Levant* (1999), Y. Garfinkel deals in considerable detail with the periodization of the Chalcolithic culture. Central to his thesis is a tripartite division of Chalcolithic into early, middle, and late phases. The phases are identified with a number of sites and different "wares" that, in Garfinkel's opinion, are homogeneous and representative of these phases.

Of particular interest to this discussion is Garfinkel's use of a term he has coined, "Middle Chalcolithic." He virtually defines this chrono-cultural phase by two aggregations or "assemblages" of ceramics, "Beth Shean Ware" (henceforth BSW) for the northern regions and "Qatifian Ware" for southern sites.

BSW is named after the site and refers to the FitzGerald's Level XVIII ceramic material that Garfinkel accepts as a homogeneous representation of a "Middle Chalcolithic" cultural phase. Because Beth Shan is central to Garfinkel's thesis, and his interpretations are so at variance with the observations in the present report, it is necessary to review the methodology of his work and to comment upon his observations in considerable detail.

Garfinkel's "Middle Chalcolithic"

Garfinkel's "Middle Chalcolithic" chrono-cultural phase is primarily based on the concept of "BSW" copiously illustrated in more than 200 line drawings and a number of black and white and colored photos. However, nowhere in his work does he expressly define the parameters of this "ware," nor even deal with the stratigraphic or sequential position of such an entity with such a sequence that would justify its name.

So far as I have been able to make out, BSW and "Middle Chalcolithic" pottery in general are never precisely characterized by what they are; rather they are "defined" by default by what they are not. Garfinkel's own words express the poverty of this non-definition: "The pottery does not fall into either the typological framework of the EC (as defined in the previous chapter) or that of the LC (to be defined in the next chapter)" (1999:153). Utilizing these "non-criteria" Garfinkel then proceeds to empirically define BSW by selecting pottery examples from 23 separate archaeological deposits that he claims are "Middle Chalcolithic." The resultant aggregation of ceramics is apparently his definition of BSW.

De facto, Garfinkel's (1999: figs. 94-115) BSW is an extraordinarily eclectic collection of morphological types that range from minuscule bowls to sizable vessels identified as pithoi. Handles include loop and tubular types, small lugs, and smooth and "thumb indented" lug types (everywhere else identified as "ledge" handles; e.g., Amiran 1969:35-40).

BSW is decorated in numerous ways, or not at all. Types of decoration include plastic ropelike applications, incisions, and application of red paint as a slip, in a "dribble" technique and in "finely executed designs," usually in a net pattern. Fabric classifications are apparently not considered in this definition, although they would be the essence or at least one of the major elements of what I use to determine a ceramic "ware."

The term "ware" is usually reserved for specific fabrics and/or morphological types of generally more limited distinguishing features such as Gray Burnished Ware (Braun 1997:60) that indicates bowls of a very distinctive aspect or even "Abydos Ware," an eclectic but rather limited collection of jugs and storage jars with distinctive morphological and decorative features (Amiran 1969:59-65).

In my opinion the term BSW is not truly a "ware" in any sense generally accepted for ceramic studies dealing with late prehistoric societies of the southern Levant. Rather, Garfinkel employs it as a generic term to indicate (in this instance) northern "Middle Chalcolithic" pottery, perhaps a legitimate enough use were it provably a homogeneous chronological collection representative of a single, chrono-cultural horizon. Such an assumption, however, is highly problematic for a number of reasons.

As Garfinkel notes: "Because this phase has not yet been clearly defined in the archaeology of the southern Levant, the survey of sites is more comprehensive than that presented for other periods" (1999:153). By this proposal he suggests that quantitative data, presumably in lieu of qualitative data, will produce a more reliable or at least a less problematic BSW construct. While his inclusions are an impressive array of drawings and photographs of ceramic vessels and sherds from numerous sites in the northern region, their sum does not necessarily constitute a definitive assemblage of northern, "Middle Chalcolithic" pottery; nor does it seem to me is it likely ever to be proven so! The reasons for this evaluation are outlined below.

A Detailed Critique of Garfinkel's "Middle Chalcolithic" Construct

The primary unsound aspect of his BSW construct is his utilization of Beth Shan as the "type site." His uncritical dependence upon FitzGerald's stratigraphy and stratigraphic associations of artifacts is, first of all, of rather equivocal validity (see Chapter 2 and above and below in Chapter 3). Well before the present work was conceived, different scholars were aware of the problematic chrono-cultural identification of the material of Level XVIII in FitzGerald's work. Perrot (1972:416) classified the material as "Ouadi Rabah," while Moore (1973:59, 65) indicated its non-homogeneous nature by classifying it as both LN(2) (Moore 1973) and EC. Mazar (1993:215) recognized Neolithic and Chalcolithic elements in it. More recently, in his critique of Garfinkel's (1999) work, Banning noted the mixed nature of "Middle Chalcolithic" material in the following statement:

> Admittedly the published evidence for this period is far from ideal, but such errors, combined with the use of badly mixed material from such sites as Beth Shan, create a confusing mixture of earlier and later material. Although there must be a period or periods to fill the time between Wadi Rabah and the Ghassulian, and some of the assemblages indeed belong here, the grouping of material in this chapter is unconvincing. (Banning 2001:80)

I fully concur with Banning's assessment. Notably, Garfinkel totally ignores the material from the pits below Level XVIII (Stratum XIX). They are apparently filled with LN/EC handles that appear to be of the same type as a number from Stratum XVIII, yet he considers neither the likelihood nor even the possibility that residual material from the period represented in the pits could be found in debris of Stratum XVIII. In addition, his assumption that Stratum XVIII is chronologically homogeneous is rather extraordinary considering there are no complete or even nearly complete vessels associated with these deposits. As noted above, there is no material *in situ* from floors or living surfaces; all the artifacts from these levels derive from fills that are not definitively related to each other and thus are likely to have been deposited there at different times and under differing circumstances. Indeed, as noted above, the evidence seems to point to precisely such a pattern of deposition.

However, merely questioning the Middle Chalcolithic designation of the Beth Shan assemblage is to deal only with the specific ceramic types found there. There is an even more fundamental flaw in Garfinkel's basic methodology in the definition by default of his "Middle Chalcolithic" construct. It assumes rigid parameters for an "Early Chalcolithic" and a "Late Chalcolithic" that may be used (by extrapolation through absence of ceramic types) to determine a "Middle Chalcolithic." From my experience (Braun 2001) such sharp definitions between chrono-cultural phases in ceramics fail to stand the test of reality.

Traditions of ceramic production, especially as expressed in methods of manufacture, morphology, and types of decoration, were passed on from one period to the next. Sharp, clean breaks or well-defined parameters such as Garfinkel postulates were quite rare, if they existed at all. Indeed, most chrono-cultural horizons are artificial, heuristic constructs, attempts at periodization imposed by scholars onto the archaeological record. Very often they tend to blind us to what might be defined as zones of transition between them, and the use of ceramic evidence to identify and define them is fraught with difficulties. O. Bar-Yosef has best expressed the problematic nature of the kind of data available in his treatment of the Pottery Neolithic period. I suggest that his cautionary note applies equally to material from Beth Shan and additional sites that Garfinkel attributes to "Middle Chalcolithic":

> A final difficulty lies in the determination of relative age on the basis of changes in shape and decoration of pottery vessels. In later periods, characterized by a combined chronological base (based on inscriptions, comparisons with Egypt, and accumulation of identical or similar typological sequences), pottery can usually be used as a good criterion for dating a given stratum. However, an attempt to apply such a criterion to the Pottery Neolithic, without independent control over the results may lead to many errors. (Bar-Yosef 1992:33)

As Garfinkel noted in the opening statement of his Chapter 5: "The Middle Chalcolithic has not previously been clearly defined" (1999:153). I suggest that not only has he failed to ameliorate this situation, but that there is an excellent reason for such a state of affairs and that his contribution may have inserted serious errors into the literature. That is because quite simply there are not enough data of unequivocal veracity to allow us to define such an entity as "Middle Chalcolithic" with any degree of confidence, certainly not in the broad sense he suggests. Lovell (1999: figs. 4.19-4.29) indicates a "Middle Chalcolithic" pottery assemblage from the Chalcolithic site of Teleilat Ghassul, the name of which is virtually synonymous with Chalcolithic ("Ghassulian"). The pottery attributed to this phase has a rather limited repertoire of shapes. However, cornets—a type absent in Garfinkel's (1999: fig. 133: 1-14) "Middle Chalcolithic" but associated with his "Late Chalcolithic" so-called Ghassulian Ware, are included by Lovell. The primary reasons for this lack of definition are the lack of even a single, good published sequence (with well-defined stratigraphic units definitively associated with significant, well-preserved, and properly associated ceramic corpora) from which one may build a LN to Chalcolithic sequence and the regionally idiosyncratic nature of ceramics of these periods. This is obvious in the different chrono-cultural attributions of the same pottery assemblages by different scholars noted above.

Garfinkel's suggestions for corroborative evidence for Middle Chalcolithic in the archaeological record suffer from the same types of problems. Aside from pottery, he suggests additional diagnostic features called by him "striking attributes": circular silos lined with flat stones, basalt chalices, and infant jar burials. However, none of these "striking attributes" is solely or even definitively associated with sites he assigns to his "Middle Chalcolithic" construct.

Circular silos and other outbuildings are common features in Late Neolithic through MB contexts (Braun 1989b; Milevski 1992; Bienert and Viewger 1999: fig. 12) and do not seem to be ascribable to one particular phase of the Chalcolithic period as Garfinkel would have us believe. In particular the type of structure he refers to appears at a number of sites of the LN/EC and EB horizons—in a Chalcolithic occupation at Tel Teo (Eisenberg 1989: fig. 2A), in phases of the Enéolithique Récent occupation of Byblos (Dunand 1973), at the Late EB I village of Horvat 'Illin Tahtit (Braun and Milevski 1993:10), and in the EB II town of Arad (Amiran 1978: pl. 155:1-3).

In particular, it should be noted that despite Garfinkel's attempt to assign Tel Teo VII–VI to his "Middle Chalcolithic," his chrono-cultural ascription is far from assured. In his preliminary report the excavator Eisenberg (1989) was uncertain where to place these strata within the Chalcolithic sequence. He suggested at the time that the evidence was equivocal and pointed to both a relatively early and a relatively late placement within the Chalcolithic sequence. However, a more recent evaluation (Eisenberg, Gopher and Greenberg 2001:204-207) suggests at least some contemporaneity with Ghassul IV, generally understood to be "Late Chalcolithic." This date is emphasized by the presence of a churn in the Tel Teo Chalcolithic assemblage (fig. 6:5-8). The churn is a vessel type conspicuously absent from Garfinkel's "Middle Chalcolithic" but notably prominent in his "Late Chalcolithic." However, Lovell (1999: fig. 4.23) includes one fragmentary example in her "Middle Chalcolithic" at Tuleilat Ghassul.

Basalt "chalices" (pedestaled bowls) are, so far as I have been able to ascertain, often found in Neolithic contexts. Several were encountered at Yiftah'el in Pre-Pottery Neolithic or LN contexts. Most of their parallels suggest a pre-Chalcolithic date (Braun 1997:129-130). Since Garfinkel would attribute them to "Middle Chalcolithic," I can only wonder whether he would do the same for the Late Neolithic pottery of Yiftah'el with which these vessels are stratigraphically associated. This pottery includes examples painted in broad bands in the style known as Jericho IX, a phase Garfinkel associates with LN. Thus, it would seem that the LN ascription of at least some of these basalt vessels is assured.

Infant jar burials are also not solely a "Middle Chalcolithic" phenomenon, although certain vessels may well have features that allow them to be so dated. At least one such burial is undeniably dated to LN, despite Garfinkel's attempts at ascribing it to his "Middle Chalcolithic" (Banning 2001:80). Others are found in LN contexts at Tel Teo where there are also two of undeniably EB I *bona fides* (Eisenberg 1989: fig. 8; Eisenberg, Gopher, and Greenberg 2001:39, 97). Both the position of one of these vessels and its morphology (it has striking parallels to several vessels from Yiftah'el II; cf. Braun 1997: fig. 9.10:6), leave no doubt as to its EB I chrono-cultural ascription. Thus, this type of burial is not specifically related to one particular chrono-cultural horizon. Indeed, all the "striking attributes" Garfinkel suggests are exclusively characteristic of "Middle Chalcolithic" are distributed over far-flung chrono-cultural horizons, and their employment in defining his construct is an additional reason to regard it with suspicion. If we cannot prove all the sites that Garfinkel claims to be Middle Chalcolithic to be contemporary on the basis of architectural and mortuary traditions, and there is no other corroborative evidence for this claim, then it is no longer valid to view pottery from them as a single assemblage representative of "Middle Chalcolithic."

Some Pot Types From the Deep Cut— "Middle Chalcolithic" or EB I?

Garfinkel's (1999: color plate III:5, photo 93, figs. 108:7, 109:7, 110:1-2, 112:8-11) inclusion of a large number of jar rims and ledge handles from the earliest level in the Deep Cut leaves me in the uncomfortable position of having to defend my alternate interpretation of them as deriving from an EB I occupation. While I cannot "prove" their assignment to a later chrono-cultural horizon, I believe that I can make a good case for it.

I am also convinced that when Garfinkel composed his work he was unaware of Early EB I pottery traditions and so was unable to spot these items as intrusive. In addition, he did not have the advantage given me to study FitzGerald's documentation of the Deep Cut extensively and so he was unacquainted with the impressive sequence of EB I occupation that appears as early as Stratum XVII. Neither could he have understood the reasons for the chrono-cultural admixtures of ceramics in the early levels without an intimate knowledge of the architecture and associated materials from FitzGerald's levels and the manner in which the Deep Cut was excavated. It should also be noted that there is an unexplained affinity and similarity between ceramic styles of the LN/EC and Early EB I horizons that can and does create some confusion in identification of pottery from these two cultural horizons (Gustavson-Gaube 1986; who noted what she termed "Late Chalcolithic/PNB-related" pottery at Tell es-Shuna North). Two jar fragments from Stratum XIX and one from Stratum XVIII with somewhat similar plastic rope decoration around their necks (Figs. 3.1:4, 6 and 3.4:10; Garfinkel 1999: fig. 109:7 and probably photo 83: bottom center) are good examples of LN/EC pottery types that have affinities with EB I types. Their features are paralleled in a Neolithic vessel from Jericho (Garfinkel 1999: fig. 59:1).

Several fragments of large jars and holemouths with applied "rope decoration" near the juncture of neck and rim were recovered in Strata XVIII through XVI. I identify them with EB I types; Garfinkel assigns them to his "Middle Chalcolithic." My point of departure in identifying the EB I pottery from the Deep Cut comes from an intimate acquaintance with the Early EB I site of Yiftah'el II (e.g. Figure 3.7), with its relatively sizable and quite homogeneous (i.e., devoid of Chalcolithic material) assemblage. The pottery was derived from a large-scale exposure of dwellings in which much of the material was found *in situ* on floors. Thus, the chrono-cultural ascription of the EB I pottery from Yiftah'el is as reasonably secure as any archaeological deposit may be, and the assemblage is one eminently useful for comparing with material from Beth Shan. Both sites are northern, located within interconnecting valleys, and are known to have contemporary or nearly contemporary occupations. Following is a discussion of the vessel types in question.

Large Jar and Pithoi Rims

Several fragments of large jars with applied "rope decoration" near juncture of neck and rim were recovered in Strata XVIII through XVI (Figures 3.3:13-15, 3.6:1-7, 3.10:10-11) in the Deep Cut. I had already identified them as early EB I types on the basis of parallels with Type 52 vessels from Yiftah'el (Figure 3.7:2) when Garfinkel's book appeared. I noted somewhat with surprise that Garfinkel (1999: fig. 110:1, 2) assigned two examples of this type to his "Middle Chalcolithic" and that both are from Beth Shan, Level XVIII; he appears to have ignored the later stratigraphic provenience of additional examples of this type published by FitzGerald. A third vessel fragment with similar rim profile that Garfinkel (1999: fig. 110:3) associates with this group lacks the distinctive rope decoration and probably does derive from an earlier horizon.

Garfinkel's work prompted me to conduct an especially assiduous search for parallels to support my own view, or in the event that were wrong, to change my dating for this type. To date I have been unable to find very similar vessels with necks and splayed rims in good Chalcolithic contexts at other sites. However, I have encountered them at Yiftah'el II (Figure 3.7) and in a survey assemblage I once viewed from a site in the Beth Shan Valley that includes Gray Burnished Ware, a hallmark of Early EB I. I have also found similar types at Jebel Sartaba (Area XIV; McNicoll et al. 1992: pl 17:1,2) in what the excavators describe as a Chalcolithic "Post-Ghassulian" phase that could be a very late Chalcolithic or Early EB I phase, a phase so elusive that I have elsewhere labeled it somewhat whimsically "the lost horizon" (Braun 1996:104-105). In any event, such dating precludes a "Middle Chalcolithic" ascription.

Garfinkel's ascription is somewhat understandable because these jars actually do have affinities with Chalcolithic types (Garfinkel 1999: fig. 105:3,9: Lovell 1999: figs. 4.15:, 4.16:5, 4.24:4). Some related types, perhaps even prototypes, come from the "Late Chalcolithic" occupation of Teleilat Ghassul (Lovell 1999: fig. 4.39:3) and the LC site of Tall Fendi (Blackham, Fisher, and Lasby 1998: fig. 6:7). These vessels have the distinctive short necks and tapered rim of the Beth Shan examples, but the "rope" decoration formed by crescent-shaped indentations is quite different and seems to be popular in the Chalcolithic of the Jordan Valley (Blackham, Fisher, and Lasby 1998: fig. 67-9; Banning, Blackham, and Lasby 1998: figs. 7:5-6, 8:18).

Garfinkel (1999: fig. 105:1-2) has, I believe, also erred by including two holemouths with rather small apertures from Tell el Mefjar in his "Middle Chalcolithic" construct. These last are best paralleled at Yiftah'el II (Braun 1997: fig. 9.11:9) and are likely to be EB I in date. The site has both Chalcolithic and Early EB I material (Leonard 1992:18).

It is impossible to tell whether the findspots of these relatively large fragments at Beth Shan reflect their ultimate chrono-cultural origins, but it is notable that sizable fragments of them appear in contexts as late as Stratum XVI, while they are unknown in the pits of Stratum XIX. Although it is possible that these selfsame fragments derived from Stratum XVIII could be "residual" in Strata XVII–XVI (deriving from a LN/EC occupation), I suggest they are more likely to derive from the earliest EB I occupations. Thus, I would argue that they are intrusive in Stratum XVIII and more or less at home in Strata XVII–XVI. They are not, however, the sole examples of intrusive EB I artifacts in Stratum XVIII.

Ledge Handles

Garfinkel (1999: fig. 112:11) has assigned one ledge handle (unaccountably termed by him "lug handle") from Stratum XVIII to "Middle Chalcolithic" along with three additional examples from other sites (1999: fig. 112:8-11). The Beth Shan handle is taken from FitzGerald's excavation (Garfinkel 1999: fig. 112-11; possibly fig. 3.4:12) and is quite similar to another from Tell es-Saydiyeh et-Tahta, a site with a sizeable EB I occupation (Tubb, Dorrell, and Cobbing 1997), also identified by Garfinkel (1999: fig. 112:9) as "Middle Chalcolithic" in origin. These examples appear to me to be typically EB I in their morphology (cf. Amiran 1969:35-40; Braun 1997: figs. 9.21:1, 4, 9.22:1, 3, 9.27:5-8) and not earlier; they are thinner and more delicate than LN/EC types (Garfinkel 1999 fig. 112:8,9; Braun 1997: fig. 15.5:7-8).

Not unexpectedly numerous examples of the same type of indented ledge handles were found in the later deposits of the Deep Cut (Figures 3.9:11, 13, 14; 3.12:2, 3, 5; 3.15:5, 7; 3.16:7; 3.17:10, 11) and other sites (Braun 1985: fig. 25:1-7) where they are certainly derived from EB I occupations. Considering the parallels cited above, I suggest the ledge handle from Stratum XVIII identified by Garfinkel is also intrusive and likely to have derived from one of the later levels, Stratum XVII–XV.

Another example of Garfinkel's (1999: fig. 112:9) ascription of a typical EB I type to "Middle Chalcolithic" is a smooth-edged handle. Its quite delicate profile indicates it to be of a type common at sites in the Jordan Valley and farther east in advanced phases of EB I. Handles of similar mien, painted in a "drip" style similar to Garfinkel's example, have been found at Jebel Abu el-Thawwab (Kafafi 2001) in clear EB I contexts.

Summary

The pottery of Stratum XVIII is apparently a mixture of Neolithic, Chalcolithic and EB I types, all fragmentary and in non-primary deposition. Their presence suggests that there were significant intrusions into this stratum that seriously compromised its chrono-cultural integrity. Thus, one can only question the validity of Garfinkel's attempt to use it as the type-site for his "Middle Chalcolithic" construct. While I do not deny the possibility that there may be a "Middle Chalcolithic" occupation within the occupational sequence of the Deep Cut, it is clear that FitzGerald's excavations did not produce a ceramic assemblage by which it may be defined.

The Pottery of Stratum XVII

The pottery of this stratum shows a clear chrono-cultural bifurcation that apparently reflects an analogous dichotomy of architectural evidence (see Chapter 2) (Figures 3.30-3.31). Included in this assemblage are types that are attributed to the LN/EC horizon as well as others that derive from the northern variation of Early EB I. Accordingly, the discussion below deals with the material as two separate assemblages.

Part A—The Early (LN/EC) Pottery of Stratum XVII

Only a limited number of pot types is represented in this assemblage, but rather fortunately the examples include good diagnostic fragments that allow us to closely identify them with the cultural horizons from which they derive.

Bowls

Three types of bowls are represented in this stratum.

Deep Bowls with Tapered Rims and Narrow Bases: Two example of this ubiquitous bowl type (Figure 3.5:2; Pl. III:13) are represented in the illustrations. The deep form of this bowl is virtually unknown in EB I contexts and is at least an indication of its early date.

Pedestaled Bowls: Only a portion of the upper bowl and the beginning of the pedestal (Figure 3.5:5) are still extant in one specimen. The pedestal is pierced by a small, circular hole. Similar objects are found in LN/EC contexts (Garfinkel 1992: fig. 104), but they are also known from Beth Shan where without doubt they were found *in situ* in Late EB I strata (Pl. IV:23, 24).* The depth of this deposit and a lack of additional Late EB I material in this stratum incline me to date this fragment to the earlier horizon.

Another example (Figure 3.5:6) has a "trumpet-like base" (cf. Figure 3.2:1) that is apparently not pierced. Nothing of its bowl remains and so the complete morphology of the vessel is obscure. Probable parallels to these vessel fragments appear to date them to the LN/EC horizon (Garfinkel 1992: fig. 104; Amiran 1969: pl. 2: 12-15).

Fenestrated Pedestaled Bowl (Figure 3.5:8): Only a small fragment of a buff-colored base of this bowl type is extant, but its distinctive shape, with rounded fenestration, clearly indicates the type of vessel it represents. The morphological type is well known in basalt examples from Chalcolithic contexts (Gopher and Tsuk 1996: fig. 4.2:3-9) and is apparently translated into the medium of clay in the same period. It is one of the few ceramic types that continue into EB I in its northern variation, although they are not well known in the north in the Chalcolithic period. This buff-colored sherd—unpainted, unburnished, and crudely finished—is difficult to date. Its fabric is remarkably similar to that of an Early EB I vessel from Yiftah'el (Braun 1997: fig. 9.4:1), although the Beth Shan example does not appear to have been painted red. Thus, it may represent additional information on utilization of the site in the Chalcolithic period; alternately, it could derive from the Early EB I occupation.

Deep Bowl with Tapered Rim (Figure 3.5:7, Pl. II:11-12): This type is ubiquitous in the LN/EC horizon. Some remains of paint are still visible on its surface. One example, unusually, has two vertical strap handles, placed side by side.

Egg-shaped Cup-Bowl (Figure 3.9:4): This vessel is nicely fashioned with even walls and a smoothed finish painted a deep red. It bears a superficial resemblance to another vessel from Stratum XVIII (Figure 3.4:14); both are similar in morphology to rhyta and may have functioned similarly. This example is clearly an open type vessel as discernible from its painted interior. The closest parallels I could find are several vessels from Ghassul (Koeppel 1940: pl. 77:6; pl. 78:2) with bodies of similar size and shape. However, one of these last is a closed type, while both differ from the Beth Shan example in the addition of a pair of opposing, loop handles (see below).

Jars

Several distinctive jar types are included in this assemblage. They may be specifically attributed to the LN/EC cultural horizon.

Bow-Necked Jar (Figure 3.9:2): The very distinct upper portion of a jar is of a type definitively associated with the Neolithic period, although its wide, curved, bulging neck, set atop a large body, is unusually long. Most bow necks (Amiran 1969: pl. 1:9; Garfinkel 1992: fig. 123) tend to be relatively shorter. Another related type, also segmented, has a long neck with tapering straight walls (Kenyon and Holland 1983: fig. 113: 2, 20: Braun 1997: fig. 15.3: 6, 11, 16, fig. 15.5: 1-3, 6).

Small Jar with Strap Handles (Figure 3.9:1): A portion of a small, almost barrel-shaped jar with flat base and two opposing, vertical strap handles (placed more or less midway on its sides) is one of the few, sizable fragments preserved from the early strata in the Deep Cut. Unfortunately the uppermost portions were not recovered, so its complete morphology remains obscure. Extant portions of the vessel, fashioned of unpainted, somewhat coarse fabric, are consistent with fabric types and morphological features of the LN/EC horizon. Generic parallels suggest this early dating is correct (Ben-Dor 1936: pl. XXIX: 11; Koeppel 1940: pl. 78: especially 9 and 10-12; Mellaart 1956: fig. 6:122).

Small Jar with Everted Rim (Figure 3.5:11): A large fragment of the upper wall and rim of a small jar is notable for the decoration it bears. It is painted red with an attempt to leave a reserved area the shape of

---

*Several complete vessels, one quite similar to another excavated by FitzGerald, were found more recently in a Late EB I destruction that should be more or less contemporary with FitzGerald's Levels XIV–XIII, making the total number of this type an impressive assemblage. I am grateful to Prof. Amihai Mazar, of the Hebrew University, who directed my attention to this group of vessels.

thin crescents arranged horizontally to form a pattern in the buff-to-pink fabric around the wall of the vessel. A band of short, thin, shallow, horizontal incisions arranged at regular intervals accents the lower part of its broad, splayed rim. A similar type of reserved technique, using the unpainted color of the fabric on a rim of this type, was found at `Ein el Jarba (Kaplan 1969: fig. 4:14). In addition, numerous examples of this type of rim (some painted red) are attributed to the Rabah Stage at Munhatta (Garfinkel 1992: fig. 124), suggesting a date in the LN/EC horizon for this jar. The incised decoration could also indicate a Chalcolithic origin for this vessel (Mallon, Koeppel, and Neuville 1934: fig. 52:2; Dollfus and Kafafi 1986: fig. 8:9, fig. 10:7; Epstein 1998: pl. XVI:4, 11, 13; Gophna and Sadeh 1988-89: fig. 2).

Holemouths

There is a deal of diversity in this group, although all the vessels share characteristics of early types, a deep profile and tapered rim. The upper portions of two diminutive vessels have small loop handles and simple, tapered rims (Figure 3.5:10). Additional examples (Figure 3.5:12-15) are unadorned and typical of the early horizon. Another fragment has "rope decoration" near its rim. Although it is reminiscent of EB I, Type 52 vessels at Yiftah'el II, I tend to date it to the earlier horizon on the basis of its overall, deep morphology (cf. Lovell 1999: fig. 4.16:5) that is unattested in EB I assemblages.

Bases: Two bases in this assemblage can be dated to the Chalcolithic horizon because of morphological characteristics. The larger (Figure 3.9:6), perhaps belonging to a jar, has the distinctive vestigial ring at the circumference of its underside, an indication of rotary motion technology used to fashion the vessel (see above: Stratum XVIII: Bases). A second, part of a diminutive vessel (Figure 3.9:3), probably of a goblet, has a distinctive, raised foot that is well attested to in Chalcolithic contexts (Mallon 1932: pl. LXVIII: 2, 5; Mallon, Koeppel, and Neuville 1934: fig. 36:12; Lovell 1999: fig. 4.18:3).

Handles

Early type handles recovered in this stratum vary considerably in size and style and indicate the likelihood that additional ceramic types, not represented in the illustrations were present at the site. Unfortunately, such appurtenances can be associated with several morphological types such as jars, kraters, and bowls (Droop 1935: pl. XLI–XLII; Garfinkel 1992: fig. 1-11); which precise types of vessels these fragments represent remains obscure.

Strap and Loop Handles (Figure 3.9:5-9, 12): Several straplike handles were made by fashioning a coil, shaping it, and then attaching it to the body of the vessel (Figure 3.9:7-9, 12), a technique encountered throughout the LN/EC horizon. Other handles in this stratum may perhaps be dated with some greater precision because of specific diagnostic features.

Two examples are straplike but were made by circular piercing of ledgelike appendages. One, quite unusually, is horizontal (Figure 3.9:5), the other vertical (Figure 3.9:10) and nearly triangular in section, is much more typical of handles of the Chalcolithic period. These two features are arguably two of its hallmarks (Mallon, Koeppel, and Neuville 1934: figs. 36:1, 5; 37; Dayan 1969: fig. 8: 1-3), although they may actually make their appearance at the very end of Late Neolithic. The type seems to develop along a trajectory, with the earliest examples tending to be small and somewhat carelessly fashioned (Garfinkel 1992: 78; Lovell 1999: fig. 4.9: 1, 3-4). By Late Chalcolithic, these handles are generally produced with greater care, and conventions for their manufacture are apparently more rigidly adhered to. Triangular sections seem to become the rule for medium-to-larger examples, while less attention is paid to smaller appendages fashioned by pinching. Chalcolithic potters virtually eschewed the strap handle in favor of a circular hole in these vertical types.

Summary

This small assemblage of pottery is additional evidence for occupation of the site within the LN/EC horizon. With only a single definitive exception, all the fragments of these early pottery vessels derive from contexts in the northern precinct of this stratum, precisely where rectilinear structures are located, thus suggesting a more than casual if not absolutely proven association. They appear to confirm the pre-EB I dating for the buildings there.

Part B: The Later Pottery of Stratum XVII

This group of artifacts includes a number of features that are hallmarks of an early (Yiftah'el II) phase of EB I. For the most part, the pottery is distinct from Chalcolithic types, although several objects could be alternately interpreted as representing a very late variation of Chalcolithic, possibly even an elusive interface between these sequential horizons. This may be somewhat wishful thinking because to date, archaeologists have failed to isolate such a phase for Northern EB I. Recent work in the southern reaches of the southern Levant, however, has helped to identify some of its features in the south (Braun 2000). The type numbers referred to below are direct references to the Yiftah'el II -'En Shadud ceramic typology (Braun 1997).

Type 11 Gray Burnished Bowls with Projecting Sinuous Line

Included in this assemblage are three small, but nonetheless diagnostic fragments of bowls of a class of fabric and morphological types that has come to be known as "Esdraelon Ware" (Wright 1937; 1958; 1971; Braun 1985:65-66;) or "Gray Burnished Ware" (Henceforth GBW) (Figure 3.5:1, 4). One rim and portion of a wall is not only gray and burnished, but also has the characteristic carination that helps to identify early bowl types of this group (Braun 1985:65-66).

Type 6 Large Bowl with Everted Rim

This is a well-known type that is found in the 'En Shadud phase of EB I, a time span somewhat later than Yiftah'el II. Numerous variations of this type are known at that site and 'Afula, but do not seem to be common at Beth Shan (Braun 1985: fig. 16), suggesting a rather parochial, regional pattern of distribution with the Jezreel Valley as its center and Beth Shan likely to be located at its periphery.

Type 8 Small Hemispherical Bowls

Although not technically hemispherical, this type of bowl is noted for its simple, gently contoured shape (Figure 3.5:3). The morphology is known in LN/EC contexts (e.g., Figure 3.1:1), but is virtually absent in the Late Chalcolithic of the southern Levant. It reappears in EB I and becomes a standard for the EB Age. The fabric of this example and the somewhat high walls are more typical of EB I bowls and, accordingly, I have assigned this one to the later chrono-cultural horizon.

Type 52 Jar/Pithos

This is an excellent example of the jar type that Garfinkel (see above, Stratum XVIII; *Excursus*; cf. Figure 3.8:2) assigned to LN/EC, but which I interpret as EB I. The presence of a parallel in Stratum XVI (see below) seems to corroborate my dating.

A Base

One flat base of a large vessel and a low portion of its wall bearing the typical diagonally impressed rope decoration of Early EB I could belong to a Type 52 pithos (Braun 1997: fig. 9.17:6,8) (Figure 3.6:8).

Ledge Handles

Three of the five ledge handles (Figure 3.9:11, 13, 14) illustrated are of fabrics and have scalloped or impressed contours typical of Early EB I. Two additional ledge handles (Figure 3.9:10, 15) fashioned of hard-fired fabrics, are thin and long and narrow, features more typical of Late EB I deposits.

Summary—The Later Pottery of Stratum XVII

This small inventory of artifacts attributed to Stratum XVII suggests they are derived from Early and Late EB I contexts. Notably they come from the southern precinct of the Deep Cut and some of them seem likely to have been associated with the curvilinear buildings of this stratum, although none is large enough nor well enough preserved to be in definitive association to them. Accordingly, I suggest an EB I date for the buildings in the southern precinct of the Deep Cut.

The Pottery of Stratum XVI

The rather small assemblage from this level includes a number of sherds that belong to pre-EB I horizons (Figures 3.32-3.33). It is uncertain whether they are residual objects or associated with some of the structures ascribed to this stratum.

Part A: The Early Pottery of Stratum XVI

This small group of vessels includes LN/EC types and several bowls that display well-developed, definitively Chalcolithic traditions.

Bowls

A large, deep example with tapered rim, carinated profile, and narrow base is covered with a heavy, red slip that still bears traces of polishing and a slightly raised, crescentic, decorative element at the line of carination (Figure 3.10:7). This LN/EC type that includes red-painted and burnished examples, is paralleled at Munhatta (Garfinkel 1992: figs. 88:1, 2; 97:22). Another deep bowl (Pl. III:11), with narrow, flat base and folded rim, is of a type unknown in EB I and should probably also be assigned to the LN/EC horizon.

One example of a small, deep bowl with curving sides has a base of a type with a typically rough surface and vestigial ring that marks it as Chalcolithic. It also bears marks of the wheel by which it was made, a technological improvement that Chalcolithic potters made upon their Neolithic predecessors (Commenge-Pellerin 1990:10-15; C. Commenge personal communication: 2001). This technology was widely employed for making bowls found at nearby Abu Hamid (Roux and Courty 1997) in the Jordan Valley. This particular specimen of well-levigated clay, greatly resembles (in color, fabric and form) bowls from the Northern Negev (Gilead and Goren 1995:143-149, 206-207); its fabric is dissimilar to that of most other vessels in the Beth Shan Deep Cut assemblages.

The base of another bowl of similar mien (Figure 3.12:4; 3.24) bears string-cut marks, although only on a small portion of its surface, made by detaching the base while the vessel was revolving. This technological feature found in early pottery is generally associated with the Chalcolithic period and, so far as I have been able to ascertain, unknown in Neolithic contexts. The remainder of the base has a rough, stippled surface and a large depression, also typical of Chalcolithic technology (see above). Thus, it appears that this bowl was twice removed from work surfaces, in two different ways, both typical of Chalcolithic potting techniques. These techniques of fabrication are completely unknown in the earliest EB I assemblages of the northern region.

A Storage Jar

The upper portion of a storage jar with tapered rim is of a type that has its origins in the LN/EC horizon (Garfinkel 1992: fig. 122, especially 3 and 6) (Figure 3.10:9). Although the distinctive crescent type of decoration with which it is adorned is also found within that period (Garfinkel 1992: fig. 139: 1-8) and continues on through the Late Chalcolithic period (Mallon, Koeppel, and Neuville 1934: fig. 62: 1-3; McNicoll et al. 1992: pl. 18:1) into EB I (Helms 1992: fig. 171: 10), the jar's overall morphology suggests a relatively early date for its manufacture.

Holemouths

The morphology of several deep holemouths with tapered or flattened rims suggests an attribution to the LN/EC horizon (Garfinkel 1992: figs. 113-115) (Figure 3.11:1-3, 10).

Handles: Two handles represent pre-EB I cultural horizons. A wide, flat loop handle (Figure 3.12:7) of somewhat coarse fabric can be dated on typological grounds to LN/EC. It is of an earlier type than a thin, pierced loop handle (Figure 3.12:6) that bears distinctive features associated with developed Chalcolithic ceramic traditions. One ledge type handle (Figure 3.12:5) may belong to an early pre-EB I horizon; its morphology seems to fit better that of handles from such an early period, although it does not entirely preclude it from a place in the EB I assemblage of this stratum. In truth, it is sometimes difficult or impossible to distinguish between the ledge-like handles of LN/EC and crudest examples of Early EB I.

Miscellaneous Body Sherds with Rope Decoration (Figure 3.12:8, 9): The type of rope decoration on these sherds, a flat band with small oval indentations (Blackham, Fisher, and Lasby 1998: figs. 12:1, 13:6, 15:5, 8, 9, 24), and the relatively coarse fabric of these objects, suggest to me they should be dated to the LN/EC horizon.

Summary

Little may be said of the significance of this small assemblage of LN/EC and Chalcolithic pottery. Most of the fragments could well be residual and thus have no bearing on the dating of the structures of this stratum. The small bowls, however, fashioned according to purely Chalcolithic techniques, do confirm human activity at the site sometime within this period.

The EB I Pottery of Stratum XVI

The limited repertoire of EB I shapes from Stratum XVI includes bowls, all of related types, several holemouths, a small jar and a pithos. They are relatively small fragments and their association to the structures of this stratum is uncertain, although their easily recognizable chrono-cultural *bona fides* are secure.

Type 11 Bowls

Gray Burnished Ware Bowls with Projecting Sinuous Line (Figure 3.10:1, 3, 4-6, Pl. III:1-5): Fragments of these bowls are distinguished by the presence of typical projections and a distinctive, dark lustrous finish.

A Spouted Type 7 Bowl

Only the rim and a small portion of this vessel is extant (Figure 3.10:8). The type is attested to at 'En Shadud (Braun 1985: figs. 17, 26:3, 4), in a somewhat advanced, but still relatively early EB I context.

Type 52 Pithoi

These are additional variations on this type and the appearance in the debris of this level of sizable fragments of them suggests they may well have originated in the EB I occupation. There is considerable variation in the morphology of this group, especially in the manner in which the neck and rim were fashioned. The vessel in Figure 3.10:10 is closer in style to one from Meser (Dothan 1959: fig. 8: 13), but its buff fabric is highly reminiscent of pithoi of this type from Yiftah'el II.

Type 56 Holemouths with Rope Decoration

As at Yiftah'el II (Braun 1997:62), there is a great deal of variety and little sense of standardization in this group of vessels (Figure 3.11:4). However, unlike those from that site, one of these vessels (Figure 3.11:4) shows evidence of fireclouding and appears to have been a cooking pot. It has a narrow band of rope decoration placed externally just below the simple tapered rim.

Additional Holemouths

This group of rims without the characteristic rope decoration of the Yiftah'el II phase of EB I suggests they derive from a later occupation, perhaps one more or less contemporary with 'En Shadud, where the decorative feature was completely absent (Figure 3.11:5-9). These vessels also have general affinities with holemouths from the later occupation (see below).

Ledge Handles

Two ledge handles (Figures 3.12:2, 3) are characteristic of Early EB I (Braun 1997: fig. 9.27: 6-10) types. A third (Figure 3.12:5; see above) may be dated to this period only equivocally; its thickness and coarse scalloping could indicate an earlier, LN/EC origin.

Another ledge handle (Figure 3.12:1) is finely fashioned of well-levigated clay, fired to a hard fabric and red slipped. These features and its smooth profile suggest a later date (Braun 1996: V.C.2.g). Such handles are especially popular at Jordan Valley sites (Betts 1992: figs. 237-238) in Late EB I-EB II.

"Umm Hammad Ware"

This name denotes a very special style of pottery first identified by de Miroschedji (1971:37-38) who called it "ceramique Proto-urbain D" according to Kenyon's (1960) chrono-cultural division of EB I. "Proto-urbain" is the French equivalent of Kenyon's (1979) chrono-cultural "Proto-Urban" horizon that is more or less equivalent to the early and somewhat developed phases of EB I noted in this work. Since Proto-Urban supposes a chrono-cultural construct that incorporates three different ceramic groups (Proto-Urban a, b, and c, respectively) supposedly representing separate ethnic populations and chronological associations that do not seem valid to me, I prefer the type-site name for this pottery that associates it with the Jordan Valley site where it was recovered in great quantities (Figure 3.12:2, 10; Pl. III:3). It appears to be a relatively Late EB I phenomenon (Helms 1992:29,42-43,101-113), although characteristics of the ware (the copious use of rope decoration and large, thick, flat rims on pithoi and jars) suggest affinities with much earlier, Chalcolithic types. From the samples seen, most are truly deserving of the characterization as ware; their fabrics tends to be of a dark red-brown to gray, quite hard, and modeled with finely detailed plastic features. This ware appears to have been mostly associated with its namesake site; evidence for it is rather desultory at other locations. Several pieces of this ware are found in the Deep Cut in Stratum XVI and below. One large body sherd (Figure 3.12:10) is noted in addition to a ledge handle (Figure 3.12:2) and a pithos rim fragment (Pl. I:3).

Miscellaneous

An otherwise nondescript body sherd of a relatively well-levigated fabric but somewhat coarsely fashioned surface is notable for three parallel incisions made prior to firing (Figure 3.12:11; Pl. III:8). It appears to have been somewhat more complete when recovered, as FitzGerald's drawing indicates. Unfortunately, it is not known what the complete graffiti looked like. Extant marks are of a size that suggests they are more than just a simple potter's mark. The date of this fragment is uncertain but anytime within the range of LN/EC through EB I would not be inconsistent with its physical characteristics.

Summary: The EB I Pottery of Stratum XVI

The EB I pottery of this level suggests a mixing of early and late EB I elements. In general most items seems consistent with the evidence of the curvilinear architecture. However, since the ceramics are quite fragmentary and do not seem to have been in primary deposition, we cannot be entirely assured they accurately reflect the date of these structures and associated fills.

The Pottery of Stratum XV

Although the material from this stratum is also rather fragmentary and probably was not recovered *in situ*, nevertheless, virtually all of it can be dated with confidence to EB I (Figures 3.33-3.34). Accordingly, it is possible to date the structures of this occupation to the same period with a somewhat greater degree of confidence than was possible for Stratum XVI.

Bowls

Several types of bowls are associated with this stratum.

Type 8 Small Hemispherical Bowls

Several of these diminutive bowls, a hallmark of the EB period, were recovered. Examples are either undecorated or slipped in red (not illustrated).

Type 7 Large Bowl with Inverted Rim and Overhanging Lip

This is a simple shape common at 'En Shadud (Braun 1985: fig. 17) (Figure 3.13:5). The fabric of this vessel is consistent with a somewhat advanced EB I date.

Type 10 Small Bowl with Conoid Projections

This bowl type is definitively associated with advanced phases of EB I (Braun 1985: fig. 1:11) (Figure 3.13:2), though significantly absent at Early EB I sites of the Yiftahel II phase. One example is red slipped and polished (lightly burnished). Others with the same morphology range from GBW examples to black and red and may be burnished or unburnished (Gal and Covello-Paran 1996:29; Yannai and Grosinger 2000: fig. 9.6:7; Goren and Zuckermann 2000:165-166).

Type 11 Gray Burnished Ware Bowl with Projecting Sinuous Line

Only one definitive example of this type, a fragment of a protrusion, was recovered in this stratum (Figure 3.13:4).

Type 12 Gray Burnished Ware Bowls

Three additional fragments of bowls were recovered from this stratum and could be of Type 11 (Figure 3.13:7, Pl. V:27), although they do not have the distinctive protruding line that definitively assigns them to that group and, automatically to Early EB I. Thus, they may also be of a related type (Type 12) without the projecting line that apparently has a later chronological range (Braun 1985: 65-66; Braun 1997: 106; Gal and Covello-Paran 1996:29-30; Goren and Zuckermann 2000).

Type 13 Small Bowls with Everted Rims

The single fragment (Figure 3.13:1, 3) in this stratum is of a type that appears indicative of regional production in the Northern Valleys of Israel (Braun 1985:129).

Type 21 Fenestrated Pedestaled Bowl

The morphology of this type is an example of continuity in ceramic traditions from the Chalcolithic period, but this mid-segment of a bowl (Figure 3.13:6) is a particularly fine example of GBW that dates it to EB I.

Although not a commonly encountered variant of the flat-based type, similar examples are known from a number of sites (Braun 1997: fig. 9.4:2 and parallels).

Jars

Several types of jars were recovered in this stratum. All are paralleled at Northern EB I sites.

Type 15 Amphoriskos

A small fraction of this type, the unmistakable juncture of neck and body of one vessel, allows its generic identification, although the precise shape of its body is obscure (Small Jar with Two Handles; Figure 3.14:2). Its splayed rim and short handle suggest it belongs to types associated with developed EB I (Braun 1997: fig. 20:1-2).

Type 17 Jars with Necks

Several vessels belong to a category that shows a great deal of variation. One (Figure 3.14:6) is decorated in the "grain wash" or "band slip" style of painting (Amiran 1969:41). A second, with a somewhat similar but less thickened rim, unadorned, is of a type that is popular in the Late EB I of Beth Shan (Figures 3.18:7, 3.22:3, 5-6; A. Mazar personal communication 2001; Mazar, Ziv-Esudri and Cohen Weinberger 2000) and other sites and continues on into EB II (de Vaux 1948: fig. 6:1-2).

Another jar, unadorned and fashioned of coarse fabric, is fire clouded and appears to have been a cooking pot (Figure 3.14:10). It may be a precursor or prototype of a northern type of cooking pot that appears in either Late EB I or EB II (Braun 1996b: fig. 10:5). The jar with a row of oblique, incised marks banding its neck (Figure 3.14:9) is somewhat unusual; its rim is similar to those of large bowls with everted rims (Type 6).

Type 19 Holemouths

Four spouted rims of holemouths exhibit a morphology shared with other examples, but they were made of better levigated clay and slipped (Figure 3.15:1-4, Pl. IV:7). Obviously they have a specialized function related to liquids. One example of this type was fire-clouded and may have been a cooking pot. One has a band of oblique, incised decorations. One deep holemouth fragment (Pl. IV:7) appears to be of a very distinctive type found only occasionally at sites in the Jordan Valley (see below). Another, with ridged rim (Pl. IV:6) was not available for study, but its morphology suggests it may be related to an 'En Shadud type (Braun 1985: fig. 21:10-22).

Juglets

These fragments are eminently recognizable as belonging to a highly varied class of vessels that is virtually ubiquitous in Late EB I assemblages (Amiran 1969: pl. 9: 22-24; Dothan 1970: fig. 1) (Figure 3.14:1, 3). Although not preserved in these examples, a common feature in EB I juglets is a high loop handle, a type of strap that rises over the top of the vessel to attach at the rim.

Ledge Handles

An assortment of these handles includes numerous variations that reflect differences in the kinds of vessels to which they belonged and possibly different chronological and geographical origins (Figure 3.15:5-6). Two examples (Figure 3.15:5, 7), both of relatively coarse fabric with indented exteriors, appear to reflect Early EB I styles (Braun 1997: fig. 9.27: 6-8) and may be earlier than the remaining examples. The smooth-edged variety is a latecomer in the EB I sequence (see above) and is particularly popular at Jordan Valley sites (Betts 1992: figs. 237-239).

Two Small Spouts

These small, but distinctive fragments belong to "teapots," a type (Amiran 1969: pl. 9:11-13) so named because of its resemblance to modern vessels (Figure 3.15:8, 10). The EB I examples are painted red and are found in advanced ('En Shadud phase) and Late EB I contexts.

A Strap Handle

This strap handle has the look and feel of a LN/EC appendage and is understood to be residual (Figure 3.15:11).

Grain-wash

A body sherd of a large jar painted in a dark gray variation of grain-wash decoration (Figure 3.15:11): The dark color of this painted specimen is less well documented in the literature, but is actually commonly encountered.

A Unique Multiple-legged Bowl-Plate

A large fragment of a flat-bottomed, shallow vessel with several (3?) thick, rounded legs (Figure 3.13:8) was, until very recently, without a published parallel. Its coarse fabric and red painting do not preclude it from originating in pre-EB I levels, but it could also be dated to EB I, or perhaps even later. A somewhat similar looking object (Getzov, Paz, and Gophna 2001: fig. 9:3) comes from a southern EB III context. Level XII in the Deep Cut (FitzGerald 1935: pl. VII) contains much EB III pottery, and if we assume this vessel is intrusive from a later occupation, then such a late date for this object cannot be excluded.

Summary

Clearly a chronological progression is reflected in the Stratum XV ceramic assemblage. Gone are virtually all early LN/EC and later Chalcolithic elements found in Stratum XVI, while most of the EB I objects are paralleled in advanced phases of the period. These changes in ceramic styles more or less parallel developments in architecture. Clearly, this stratum belongs to an advanced, but not the latest phase of EB I.

The Pottery of Stratum XIV

The Ceramic assemblage of Stratum XIV includes several EB I types that were not previously encountered in earlier levels (Figures 3.35-3.36). In addition, there are a number of obviously intrusive artifacts that date to the EB III period, and even one sherd that derives from a second millennium BC occupation. This indicates the likelihood of later penetration of this level, although on what scale cannot be estimated. Somewhat paradoxically, the assemblage includes a larger admixture of earlier types than is found in Stratum XV.

Late EB I Pottery

Several types are included in this assemblage. These advanced EB I types are generally fashioned of hard fired fabrics.

Bowls

There are only a few fragments of bowls in this assemblage and only two types are represented. The absence of Type 11 bowls and GBW is undeniably a function of chronological progression.

Type 8: Small Hemispherical Bowls (Figure 3.16:11, 3): Two illustrated examples of this ubiquitous type show considerable variation in morphology. Some examples have soot-blackened rims indicating their utilization as lamps.

Large Bowls with Inverted Rims (Figure 3.16:4, 6, Pl. V:24): The morphology of these vessels presages the appearance of platters in EB II. They are a Late EB I type bowl that continues on into EB II (Amiran 1969: pls. 9:7, 15:4-6; Braun 1996: fig. 11:1). A general lack of specifically EB II pottery types in the Deep Cut suggests that these particular examples are likely to derive from EB I deposits.

A Deep Bowl: The steep, almost vertical sides and tapered rim of this bowl proclaim it as belonging to the LN/EC horizon. It is assumed residual in this stratum.

An EB II–III Platter: The sizable fragment of a platter painted red and pattern burnished is clearly later than EB I. Its rim, slightly indented on the outside, suggests it should be dated to either late in EB II or EB III (Esse 1991:45, 76-83; cf. Braun 1996b:17; Bourke 2000: fig. 13.6:1-3, 8) and that it is intrusive from a later occupation.

A Deep Bowl with ledge Handle (Figure 3.16:7): This bowl is of especially well-levigated, hard-fired fabric and seems to be related to some of the better holemouths, both in overall features and in morphology. Its sharp lines, finely fashioned, wavy handles, and relatively thin walls reflect the skill of the potter who made it. Parallels come from Late EB I contexts at Megiddo (Engberg and Shipton 1934: Figure 3:7), Umm Hammad (Betts 1992: fig. 268:1) and Tel Shalem (Eisenberg 1996: fig. 13:10).

Diminutive Amphoriskoi

This type of vessel, with narrow neck and two small lugs placed on the shoulder, is very typical of Late EB I and EB II in both settlement and mortuary contexts (de Vaux and Steve 1949: fig. 8:27) (Figure 3.16:8, Pl. V:10). One example is notable for a potter's mark on the underside of the base.

Larger Amphoriskoi (two-handled jars)

One vessel with a biconical body is somewhat unusual (Figure 3.16:9). A somewhat similar body shape in a jug comes from what may be a contemporaneous assemblage (Parr 1956:148). Two additional examples (Figure 3.16:19, 11) are variations on the theme of small, two-handled jars, commonly encountered in Late EB I and EB II contexts.

"Teapots"

One fragment of a particularly rounded example (a "teapot"; Pl. V:11) is notable for its spout and two small lugs on its shoulders. Another is represented only by its spout (Pl. V:3). A fragment of what appears to be a very long spout (Pl. V:4) is atypical.

Juglets

Two examples have the distinctive, high loop handles associated with the EB I-II horizon (cf. Fischer 2000: fig. 12.2:10) (Pl. V:12-13).

Holemouths, Type 19

Most of these vessels seem at home in Late EB I (Figure 3.17:5, 9). The different rims and kinds of decoration may indicate diverse functions. The use of incised decoration near the rim is well attested in the Jordan Valley (Betts 1992: fig. 263:3-8). Two examples (Figure 3.17:1, 30) are painted in grain-wash style and are of well-levigated and hard-fired fabric. One ridged example (Figure 3.17:2) is closely paralleled at 'En Shadud (Braun 1985: fig. 22:1-7). Another (Figure 3.17:5), with particularly narrow aperture and long, thickened rim accented by a thin, horizontal band of rope decoration, is a highly stylized type that appears to be of limited production and distribution within the Jordan Valley (Betts 1992: fig. 169:7).

At least one of these vessels (Pl. V:2) was of a spouted sub-type commonly encountered (Fischer 2000: fig. 12.4:9). It is notable for rope decoration near the rim, a style that suggests it derives from an Early EB I occupation. Potters' marks, incised before firing, such as one near the rim of one vessel (Figure 3.17:9), are commonly encountered in EB I contexts (Fischer 2000: fig. 12.4:6) and may be a sort of coded message possibly understood by people outside the Beth Shan community.

Necked Jars, Type 17

FitzGerald (Pl. V:23) published a small jar that when created apparently boasted ledge handles, but which were no longer extant when he found it. It appears to have been either painted or burnished in a net pattern. This type of decoration is common in Late EB I contexts in the north and continues on into EB II.

Rail Rim Pithos, Type 26

Only one fragment of this type is known to me from the Deep Cut (Pl. IV:17). However, the type is popular at other EB I settlements in the region including 'En Shadud (Braun 1985: fig. 23) and in a later EB I occupation at Tel Kittan (Eisenberg personal communication).

Jar Fragments and Handles

A variety of small jars is represented by body sherds with delicate handles, lug, ear, and strap types (Figure 3.18:10-11, 14-15). These vessels are made of hard fired fabrics, some of which were painted in variations on the grain-wash style.

A Spouted Vessel

A wide spout with small hole is probably from a somewhat squat, rounded jar (Amiran 1969: pl. 9:28) (Figure 3.19:1).

Lug-Handled Pithoi

There is some variation in this group that may well be a sub-type of pithos with a specialized function necessitating suspension from relatively small lugs on the shoulder. I was unable to find good parallels for these handled examples at other sites—another example of this type was recovered in Stratum XIII (Figure 3.22:4)—but somewhat similar appendages, high loops placed on the shoulders of storage jars from Late EB I of the south, seem to have had an analogous function. Fragments of rims of similar style are known from nearby Pella (Bourke 2000: fig. 13.1:1,2), but it is not certain that those vessels also had lugs on their shoulders. Several pithos rim fragments published by FitzGerald (Pl. IV: 18-19) may be variations of these types.

Ledge Handles

Several diminutive, and a number of large examples are of the smooth-edged variety and are at home both in the Jordan Valley and in Late EB I (Figure 3.17:7, 8, 10-13, Pl. V:I:11, 12). The smaller examples are notable for incised marks. Other ledge handles have wavy edges and are also typical of EB I.

A Strap Handle with Anthropomorphic Hand

This appears to be a high loop handle, probably of a small jug (Figure 3.19:2a-c). It is notable for its flatness and sub-rectangular section. The hand, in relief, comes up over the top of the highest part of the loop. I know of only one somewhat similar object from this period, a smaller but also notably flat handle adorned with a highly stylized, probably anthropomorphic face (Braun 1985: fig. 24:4). The generic similarity of this object to high loop handles, in particular to the handle from 'En Shadud, as well as its fabric and color, suggest a tentative dating of this object to EB I.

A Vessel with Egyptian Affinities?

A vessel, purportedly a "pithos" (so identified by a handwritten note on the photo album from the 1933 season) from Room 1866, is noteworthy (Figure 3.27). The badly fragmented vessel was photographed but appears neither to have been drawn nor otherwise documented, and no record of it is found in the assemblages available for study. Unfortunately, there is no specific indication of its size in the photograph, but its overall shape is suggestive of the morphology of Egyptian vessels and local, south Levantine variations that are sometimes called "Egyptianized" (Andelkovic 1995: figs. 16:10, 17:3, 21:4, 7, 9). Nothing is known of this vessels' disposition.

The Early Pottery of Stratum XIV

Several finds from this stratum appear to derive from earlier occupations. A number of holemouths are of types not common in Late EB I. One (Figure 3.16:6) seems to be more of an Early EB I type as may be discerned in the rope decoration near its flattened rim. The flattened rim of another (Figure 3.16:7) suggests an even earlier date for this type, perhaps one in the LN/EC horizon. A jar fragment with folded rim (Figure 3.18:8) and four strap handles (Figure 3.18:12, 13, 16, 17) are of fabrics and styles that suggest they derive from LN/EC contexts.

Summary

The EB I pottery of this stratum dates to very late in the period, with most of the styles presaging developments in EB II. This dating is matched by the change in architecture that sees a return to rectilinear precepts that become the rule in the following period.

While the bulk of pottery retained from this stratum points to a date late in EB I, there is a disturbingly significant quantity of earlier material somewhat difficult to explain. Some, or even all of it, may be regarded as residual; other explanations may better account for its association with fills of this stratum. I suspect it could be the result of a later disturbance that penetrated to earlier levels and re-deposited artifacts in Strata XIV and XIII (see below). Such activity would account for not a little of the mixed nature of the different assemblages throughout the Deep Cut. Unfortunately, there is no other indication of this in the record left by FitzGerald.

The Pottery of Stratum XIII

This assemblage is characterized by what appears to be the latest EB I material found at the site (Figures 3.35-3.36). However, there is also a considerable quantity of much earlier LN/EC material as well as an admixture of EB II-III ceramics, obviously intrusive from later occupations (see FitzGerald 1935: pl. VII).

Late EB I Pottery

There appears to be very little difference between the Late EB I pottery of this stratum and that of Stratum XIV.

Carinated Bowls

These bowls are a type that appears in Late EB I contexts and transcends the period into EB II (Figure 3.20:1-6, 8; Pl. V:15-18, 22). Beck (1985) noted the dating and distribution of this kind of bowl. It is included here with some notably larger specimens as well as examples with small, ledge handles. The type is morphologically related to the platter of the EB II-III horizon that it presages (Braun 1996b: figs. 9, 10:1, 2; Fischer 2000: fig. 12.5).

Shallow, Rounded Bowls

Functionally this type seems to be similar to the carinated bowl with its shallow well and its large rim (Figure 3.20:8-9). This group differs in its curving profile; one example (Figure 3.20:8) has an unusually exaggerated, incurving rim.

Large Bowl with Inverted Rim and Overhanging Lip, Type 7

One small fragment is very similar to the examples from 'En Shadud. Another (Pl. VI:1) is notable for its loop handle, a type that appears also in Stratum XIV (Pl. VI:2) (Figure 3.20:7). Similar handled types are known from a Late EB I occupation at nearby Tel Shalem in the Jordan Valley (Eisenberg 1997:13, 17).

Large Deep Bowl

FitzGerald (Pl. V:19) published a fragment of a large bowl with flat base, apparently with a red band on its rim. This may be similar to bowls that Engberg and Shipton called "holemouth bowls" (Engberg and Shipton 1934: chart no. 14), although the drawing is not clear enough to determine this absolutely.

Holemouths

These are of the same types as found in Stratum XIV (Figure 3.20:10-11). One is spouted and best described as a "vat" (Figure 3.20:10); the other (Figure 3.20.11), is decorated in one variation of the grain-wash style of painting. Other, plain holemouths (Figure 3.22:7-8) are typical generic types at home in Late EB I or the EB II-III horizons (Bourke 2000: figs. 13.2.-13.4).

Diminutive Amphoriskoi

These vessels are ubiquitous at sites of EB I and EB II. Two examples (Figure 3.21:1, 3), although somewhat poorly preserved, are of a type usually painted red and highly burnished. Others may be painted in a net pattern or remain unpainted (Pl. V: 5-7). The finest examples were apparently highly prized and commonly traded, either for their contents and/or for their intrinsic value. Included in this group is a double vessel (Pl. V: 6), a somewhat rare but not unknown type (Amiran 1969: pl. 11:12) in this period.

Jug

This small jug is of a type common in Late EB I and EB II contexts (Parr 1956: fig. 15:145, 147) (Figure 3.21:3).

Pedestaled Bowls

This large, finely fashioned, high trumpet base appears to belong to a specialized vessel, one of a large group of unusual shapes generally assumed to be ritual objects, recovered from Beth Shan (Figure 3.21:6, Pl. IV:23-24). In Late EB I contexts nearby on the high tell, A. Mazar (personal communication 2001) excavated several additional variations on this theme, one of which is quite similar to this example. FitzGerald (1935: pl. IX:26) published another from Stratum XII that I believe may also belong to this group. All examples I know of are virtually unique in form, but share major features, a shallow bowl set atop a very high base.

Spout

This type of spout is typical of small jars known as "teapots" (Figure 3.21:8).

Tube Handle

This minuscule tube handle is of a rare type that may be part of a vessel of Egyptian origin or inspiration (Figure 3.21:9). It is reminiscent of handles found on Late Proto-Dynastic and Early Dynastic stone vessels. The dark buff color of the well-levigated fabric is unusual in the assemblage and could have been imported to the site. The look of it is comparable to others made of loessy clay from the Negev or even Nile silt. This may be a second of two EB I vessels with Egyptian affinities found at the site (see above), both from FitzGerald's excavations, though A. Mazar (personal communication 2001) has noted that the renewed excavations have not encountered any EB I Egyptian imports or imitations. This type of handle, however, is also occasionally encountered on local vessels (Braun 1985: fig. 24:12), so its exotic origin or inspiration is uncertain.

Ledge Handles

Both smooth edged and indented edged types are found in this assemblage (Figure 3.21:10-14, Pl. VI:7-9). One example (Figure 3.21:14) is of special note; it belongs to a jar of "Umm Hammad Ware" (see above), some few examples of which have been found at the site.

Jars

As in Stratum XIV, several types of jars were recovered in this stratum, all paralleled at Northern EB I sites.

Type 17 Jars with Necks: One example has a widely splayed neck (Figure 3.22:1) and may be of a post EB I date (see vessels of the Intermediate Bronze period; Gal and Covello-Paran 1996: fig. 11:11). Another, with straight neck, painted in red seems well placed in a Late EB I assemblage on the basis of its simple rim, fabric, and decoration. Several pithoi with large, rounded rims (Figure 3.22:3, 5-6) are of a type also found in Stratum XIV and are apparently well known at the site (see above) and at Tell Abu al-Kharaz (Fischer 2000: fig. 12.4:1-6). Notable is the decorated rim, both incised and painted in a kind of drip style (whether intentionally or not is not clear; Figure 3.22:3). A sole example with small lugs on its shoulders (Figure 3.22:4) and rounded rim is paralleled in Stratum XIV (Pl. IV:13, 14).

Flat Bases

These flat bases of closed vessels are typical of pottery of the Neolithic through Intermediate Bronze horizons. The fabric of the smaller (Figure 3.21:5) suggests it may belong to a pre-EB I vessel, while the larger (Figure 3.21:6) cannot be dated with any degree of confidence.

A Bowl-like Object

FitzGerald published a unique bowl with flat base and large knob placed centrally on the interior, in juxtaposition with a curving wall of a bowl with thickened, rim (Figure 3.21:4, Pl. V:14). I am not wholly convinced they belong to the same vessel. Accordingly, the base fragment is illustrated alone in this volume. In any event, this object appears for the present to be unique and of a specialized and obscure function. Since it is a rather large fragment it is not unlikely that its findspot reflects its ultimate chrono-cultural origins in Late EB I, although it could have been introduced there by some disturbance (see below).

Earlier Pottery

Included in the assemblage of this stratum are several LN/EC sherds similar to those encountered in Strata XIX–XVII (Figure 3.21:15-18, Pl. VI:5, 6). Their size and the relative quantity of retained examples suggest to me they were more likely to have been deposited in the debris of this level as the result of some major intrusion resulting from a post-depositional disturbance of the lower levels of the stratigraphic sequence at the site. Most of the illustrated examples are handles (Figures 3.2:14, 3.4:2-4), but one small base (Figure 3.21:5) may belong to this group, as well (Figure 3.1:8, 11, 13) as a body sherd with rope decoration, highly reminiscent of a bowl of Stratum XVIII (Figure 3.2:2).

Summary

Not unexpectedly the bulk of pottery retained from this stratum is dated to late in EB I. Parallels suggest that some types have limited geographical distribution at sites in the northern and Central Jordan Valley. However, the platter-like bowls enjoy wider distribution at both northern and southern sites and continue into EB II. If indeed they belong to the EB I horizon in Stratum XIII, then they reflect the move to mass production of specialized types of pottery noted by Beck (1985) as early as EB I. Such an interpretation seems likely given the lack of metallic ware in this assemblage, a kind of pottery generally associated with EB II-III (Greenberg and Porat 1996). Alternately, those bowls could derive from a later EB II occupation for which there is only scarce evidence.

4

Small Finds: Metal, Stone, and Flint Objects

The small finds available for study are those objects retained by FitzGerald and shipped to the Museum directly after the division of spoils with the Department of Antiquities of the Mandate Government of Palestine. It is unknown where additional finds may be, although from the card index in the Museum's Archives it is clear that at least some ceramic and flint artifacts were "discarded" by FitzGerald. Notes to that effect were appended to some drawings of objects on index cards, although there are no details as to when, how, and where they were disposed of. Only ceramics could be located in the IAA database for the early levels of the Deep Cut, and so the discussion below deals only with a limited and presumably highly selective group of objects. I suspect that some of the objects recovered may be in the IAA's storerooms but because they could not be identified, as in the case of one copper axe head that looks as if it might be one of the Beth Shan examples, their provenience remains obscure. Included in the discussion are several metal implements, numerous flint tools, and a variety of ground stone and flaked stone objects.

Metal Objects

Three substantial metal objects were recovered from the Deep Cut as well as a small number of small awl-like and needlelike points. The best preserved—including one axe head, one adze head, a knife blade, and one needle—were discovered in Stratum XVI. Unfortunately, the present whereabouts of the two large artifacts are unknown. One axehead, looking to be of pure copper, is in the Museum. I suspect that at least one of these axe heads may be in the Israel Antiquities Authority's collection, but is listed as of unidentified provenience because no markings were found on it when it was to be entered into a new, computerized database. Consequently I must limit my remarks to observations based solely on viewing one object and photographs and published line drawings (Figure 4.1; Pl. III:21-25). Presumably all of the metal objects from the Deep Cut are of copper or natural bronze alloys; tin bronzes do not make their appearance in the southern Levant until the end of the 3rd millennium BC.

An Adze and an Axe Head

One flaring adze head and a similar type axe head are of a generic type that first makes its appearance in the Chalcolithic period and remains popular well into the EB Age. The more delicate adze head (Figure 4.1:3, Pl. III:21) is distinguished by its thin section. The axe head (Figure 4.1:2, Pl. III:23) also has a flaring blade, but is notably massive, with a thick, heavy butt that bespeaks its different function.

The relative thinness and widely flaring blade of the adze are most reminiscent of the morphology of two objects from the Chalcolithic hoard from Nahal Mishmar (Bar-Adon 1980:113, nos. 168-169), although the Beth Shan specimen is not nearly so long.

Elsewhere the possibility has been suggested (Shalev and Braun 1997:94) that Chalcolithic axe and adze heads tend to be somewhat thinner and longer than EB I types. However, there are still not enough reliable data to fully support this observation, and it should be acknowledged that such typological differences might as well be ascribed to function (i.e., the difference between axe heads and adzes) as to chrono-cultural variation.

The axe head is very similar in morphology to two pure copper examples from Yiftah'el II (Shalev and Braun 1997:93-94, fig. 11.3), both dated to Early EB I. Other similar objects are less well provenienced chronologically, and it is uncertain to what (if any) extent the simple, functional morphology of these tools is indicative of their chrono-cultural origins.

Thus, lacking additional information on the precise provenience of these artifacts from Stratum XVI, we may merely note that these two objects of different, and possibly chronologically diverse morphologies, may have originated in Stratum XVI where they were found. However, one or the other, or perhaps both these items could also derive from earlier or later occupations. They appear to originate in either a Chalcolithic or Early Bronze I occupation.

A Knife Blade

A short, somewhat rounded blade of a knife is of a general morphological type that cannot be dated with any accuracy (Figure 4.1:1). The type is as equally at home in Early EB I (Macdonald 1932: pl. XXVIII:1) as in the Intermediate Bronze period (Meyerhof 1989: pl. 30:3:109). Presumably its findspot reflects it chrono-cultural origin during Early EB I.

Metal Needles

Two metal needles are attributed to Stratum XVI (Pl. III:22,24). One, so far as I have been able to ascertain, has a unique, double eye. Another is notable for its eye being placed at some distance from the end of the needle. A very similar, complete (albeit bent and twisted) copper needle was found between paving stones in a floor of a curvilinear house of Yiftah'el II (Shalev and Braun 1997: fig. 11.1).

Awl

What appears to be an awl of rounded section is one of several found in fills in the Deep Cut (Figure 4.1:4).

Ground Stone Objects from the Deep Cut and Elsewhere on the Tell

FitzGerald recovered a number of groundstone objects in the Deep Cut. They include several large fragments of stone bowls, pestles, a celt, and a variety of pierced, disk-like objects, maceheads, and miscellanea. FitzGerald also saved flint tools his workmen were able to recognize, and they are represented below in a series of photographs of them he apparently commissioned while still in the field.

Early Bronze I Basalt Bowls

Several bowls fashioned of black basalt volcanic rock are of morphologies that clearly associate them with the EB I horizon. A number was found in the Deep Cut and several others were recovered from different contexts on the tell. The best preserved of them are discussed below according to a typology that characterizes most of the basalt bowls of EB I (Braun 1990).

A Type I, EB I Basalt Bowl

A large fragment of basalt bowl including most of its well and base was recovered in Room 1897, indicated by FitzGerald to derive from Level XVII (FitzGerald 1933a:277-278) (Figure 4.2:2). Presumably, it was retrieved somewhat early in the excavation of this room; the field diary (FitzGerald 1933a: 274-276) indicates virgin soil was reached in this room below Stratum XIX. The relatively large size of this fragment, its thick base, and thin, almost vertical and slightly splayed walls are characteristics consistent with EB I Type I vessels that appear as early as the Yiftah'el II phase (Braun 1990). The major significance of this artifact lies in its provenience in such a deep deposit where it corroborates the likelihood of at least part of Stratum XVII dating to EB I.

A Stone Bowl Base

Another sizable, distinctively EB I artifact was also found in Stratum XVII (Figure 4.2:3A-D). It is a complete, thick base of a typical EB I stone bowl (probably Type I in Braun 1990), with only a small portion of its wall still extant. Remarkably, this fragment was re-used as a shallow mortar or perhaps door socket, or possibly for both functions. Centrally-gouged out shallow impressions in both its underside and the flat, inner surface of what had originally been the well of the bowl indicate two attempts at its re-utilization. There is no evidence of smoothing or polishing of these depressions that would result from prolonged rotary motion, so the vessel fragment's use as base of a potter's wheel or as a mechanism for prolonged rotary motion seems to be precluded.

A Complete Type I Bowl from Stratum IX

Additional basalt bowls of Type I derive from non-EB I proveniences on the high tell at Beth Shan (Figure 4.2:1). One complete example was recovered from the "Thotmes Temple" and is an obvious "heirloom" put to use in a cultic context. It is one of two such examples from Beth Shan; a second is of another bowl type (III) and was found in the Stratum V temple (see below). We may only speculate as to how these vessels made their way into two such disparate contexts, the late 2nd and not so early 1st millennia (Strata IX and V respectively). The best case scenario that may be suggested is that these durable bowls of unusual mien were somehow recovered nearby, in post EB I times, and were considered rare and precious enough to be dedicated for use in temple rituals. It is intriguing to think that both bowls may have been even recovered simultaneously and that one might have been passed along from one generation to find its way into the temple of Stratum V.

Type III Basalt Bowl

So far as I have been able to ascertain, another EB I type of bowl with rectangular base, cylindrical (outside and inside) and four strap handles rising up vertically from the corners of the base to join the top of the rim of the well, is unique to the southern Levant and this cultural horizon (Figure 4.3). Some years ago I published a rare, and what I then believed to be degenerate variant of this type from Stratum XIII (Braun 1990:93-93; Braun 1996: fig. 14). It differed from all other examples (Figure 4:4) I had encountered by the aspect of its handles. Outwardly they were roughed out as the strap handles of other vessels, but unusually they were left attached to the vessel's well along their full length, rather than only at the rim and base.

The Museum's collection contains another complete, albeit much larger example of what I then regarded to be a sub-type. It was recovered from the "South Temple" of Stratum V (Figure 4.4, 4.5:1A-C). Examination of both these unusual vessels indicates that, in contrast to other bowls of this type, both are unusually roughly finished on their external surfaces, including their handles, while the surfaces of their wells are quite significantly smoother. Therefore, I suggest that these features are best explained as evidence of unfinished objects, the unfinished production of a workshop located onsite or nearby.

To fashion even a simple Type I bowl of hard, dense basalt is a highly labor-intensive process; to produce one with walls of even thickness and a smooth surface requires great expertise. Most Type III bowls are of high quality. If we bear in mind that such a great deal of labor was required to fashion them, then we can only wonder why, after so much time and effort was expended to rough out two such objects as the bowls under discussion, they would have been left with such roughly finished exteriors. In my opinion, the answer to this question is that these two vessels remain unfinished, and their creators, assumed to have been skilled craft persons, were neither careless of their products nor too lazy to finish them properly. The following arguments are offered in support of this hypothesis.

The artisan or artisans who made the Beth Shan bowls chose hard vesicular basalt that cannot be successfully chipped (as flint or even limestone)—the availability of much softer limestone as well as a single example of a limestone bowl of this type (Braun 1990: fig. 3:3) indicates that a much softer medium was also an option—but must be roughed out by a laborious process of pounding, crushing and grinding. Only after initial shaping of the basic form desired could the artisan then smooth and polish the piece in order to achieve a truly finished product. All other bowls of this type I examined appear to exhibit considerable skill in their manufacture. They are noteworthy for their symmetry, the even thickness of their walls, and the smooth finish of their external surfaces.

Strap handles are portions of a vessel most vulnerable to breakage, and it seems to me that prior to their detachment they would have served as useful grips during various stages of work, perhaps right up to the finishing touches on the handles themselves. Accordingly I contend that only after the basic form of the vessel was completed and its surfaces smoothed would the artisan have detached them from the body of the well.

There are large basalt flows atop the limestone bedrock in the region of Beth Shan and the entire site is strewn with (and constructed of) virtually every type of black and brown variety of the former as well as cream and rose-colored variations of the latter stone type. Quarrying for desired material is not even necessary, although it too is a local option. Unfortunately, however, we have no way of knowing whether FitzGerald encountered debitage from such a workshop in the Deep Cut and whether there might have actually been a workshop nearby.

Stone Maceheads

Several fragments of stone maceheads were recovered in the Deep Cut. Such objects are known from as early as the Chalcolithic period (Bar-Adon 1980:117-131; Bourke 2001: fig. 4.19) and continue on into use in the EB Age). There is no way of telling whether the stratigraphic ascriptions of these not too large objects reflect their chrono-cultural provenience. All the different morphological types found appear to have a widespread chronological distribution. Several piriform examples (Pl. VI:19, 26, 27) derive from Strata XIV and XIII and are paralleled in Chalcolithic contexts in the Judaean Desert (Bar-Adon 1980:121) as well as in EB I contexts at Horvat 'Illin Tahtit and Palmahim Quarry. Others are either barrelshaped (Figure 4.8:1, Pl. 3:26) or spherical (Figure 4.8:3, Pl. III:27), types that may also reflect Chalcolithic or EB I origins (cf. Bar-Adon 1980:119:307, 423; Bourke 2001 fig. 4.19:6; Amiran 1978: pl. 76:1). Another more flattened type (Figure 4.8:2) is also paralleled in these periods (cf. Bourke 2001: fig. 4.19:2; Amiran 1978: pl. 76:4-10). However, its morphology and somewhat lesser mass could also suggest a function as flywheel for some type of rotary motion device.

Celts

This type of tool is associated with the LN/EC horizon and does not make a transition into the EB Age. Thus, these objects are derived from the earlier, pre-EB I occupations.

A Polished Stone Celt

This small stone object was polished to a very smooth finish on all but its wide base (Figure 4.8:4). Polished stones of roughly this shape are common at sites of the LN/EC horizon (Wheeler 1983).

A Basalt Celt

This heavy, blunt object was somewhat crudely fashioned (Figure 4.8:5).

A Limestone Celt

This somewhat crudely shaped stone was polished (Figure 4.8:9).

A Stone Phallic-like Object

A slightly elongated, hard gray limestone cylindrical object, marked by a line ringing its tapering end, appears to be a phallic representation (Figure 4.8:7). It was roughly pecked out of what appears to be hard limestone.

Pottery Tokens

Two diminutive, crudely fashioned objects are tentatively defined as tokens, although they could be gaming pieces (Figure 4.8:7, 8).

A Pierced Pebble

Considerable effort was expended in drilling through this naturally smooth, elongated, flat pebble. Its function remains obscure (Figure 4.8:10).

Pierced Discs

FitzGerald recovered a variety of small pierced discs of stone and pottery (Figure 4.9). They are small objects and their find spots do not necessarily reflect their chrono-cultural origins. Such objects are commonly found in the several cultural horizons represented in the Deep Cut (Amiran 1978: pl. 76; Wheeler 1982). Several of the objects are probably spindle whorls. One (Figure 4.8:1) incompletely pierced disc is apparently unfinished.

Flint Tools

As was the custom in the early part of the 20th century, relatively little attention was paid to the collection of flint artifacts, and so there are neither debitage nor cores in FitzGerald's collection. Thus, we have no information as to whether flint might have been knapped at the site and there is no possibility to quantify the material recovered in the excavation. The extant assemblage appears to roughly reflect the chrono-cultural sequence of the site as understood from the pottery.

A series of illustrations commissioned by FitzGerald in the field indicate something of the range of types assigned by him to the different levels (Figures 4.10-4.19). Presumably they are representative of the entire collection from the Deep Cut, although there is no way to validate this observation. The lowest levels include several kinds of arrowheads, bifacials (some polished), denticulates, scrapers, and blades, all types well identified with the LN/EC horizons. The selected assemblages of the later levels, beginning with Stratum XVII, have an increasing number of Canaanean blades, and by Stratum XV these artifacts, a hallmark of the EB Age, dominate the objects chosen by FitzGerald to represent the successive occupations.

Summary

Notably all metal objects from the Deep Cut were recovered from Stratum XVI, but whether this indicates a period of intense use of metal is uncertain. Presumably the objects were found separately, since FitzGerald would have noted the unearthing of them in a cache.

The stone object assemblages, both ground stone and chipped stone, are typical of the periods represented in the ceramic assemblages, LN, Chalcolithic, and EB I. Unfortunately, the highly selective nature of the collection throws only a modicum of light on activities carried out at the site. The Type III basalt bowls are notable for the suggestion they make of craft specialization in EB I at Beth Shan. They suggest the production of sufficient surpluses in the economy of the settlement or some nearby occupation that would free artisans to go about the laborious business of creating these bowls that would then have been exchanged for other products. Material from Beth Shan may have been traded as far north as Me'ona (Braun 1996b) and as far south as Arad (Amiran 1978: pl. 78:8), the most distant sites where such vessels have been found to date. Such products could have put Beth Shan or a nearby local production center at the center of a small trade network.

The pierced discs in this collection are likely to be an indirect indication of weaving activity at the site. Several or perhaps all of them probably functioned as spindle whorls for making thread. This is very much an amateur, home-based industry and should not be considered commensurate with the level of labor-intensive basalt bowl production that required considerable expertise. It should also be noted most of the holes in the whorls were probably drilled with the aid of flint tools and in this connection it is suggested that some of the larger examples of these pierced discs, or possibly even the flattish "macehead" (Figure 4.8:2), could have served as flywheels for use with drills. Although we have little direct evidence for actual rotary motion machines in late prehistoric periods, their end products are eminently visible in the Chalcolithic and EB I basalt bowl industries (Braun 1990; van den Brink, Rowan, and Braun 1999).

5

Fitzgerald's Deep Cut: A Summary Statement

The Deep Cut is a window onto the earliest utilization of the high tell of Beth Shan. It documents human activity on this hill overlooking the banks of a perennial stream during the time span beginning late in the Neolithic period and concluding late in EB I. While the evidence buried in the early deposits of the tell is far from clear on many points concerning the nature of the episodes of human activity there, it does indicate a sequence of material culture remains laid down by successive human endeavors in several chrono-cultural periods. As presently understood, FitzGerald's work leaves us with a story of intermittent events, some likely to be temporary in nature and of very limited duration, others representing long-term, sedentary activity. Table 5.1 outlines the record of human utilization of the site within the Deep Cut as I understand it. Following is a short interpretive summary of the archaeological record.

Stratum XIX

Portions of the mound were utilized during LN and EC times. During this timespan pits were formed, either naturally or as the result of human activity, or possibly through both agencies. Eventually, and possibly through both natural and human actions, they became receptacles for discarded pottery fragments and other artifacts. While there is no direct evidence within the Deep Cut for sedentary occupation of the mound concurrent with this process, it seems likely that the ceramic and other objects in this stratum actually do derive from such an occupation on other, unexcavated portions of the mound.

Had the Deep Cut been expansively published earlier, then FitzGerald's plans and photos may well have considerably altered interpretations of the archaeological record for south Levantine late prehistory. For example, I believe the idea of pit dwellings, at least those supposedly identified with the amorphous cavities of this stratum, would not have made much headway had their true nature been accurately described, and Beth Shan (below Level XVIII) would not figure prominently in every list that purports to document such types of supposed dwellings.

Stratum XVIII

Although there is little in the way of architecture in this stratum, the evidence of a few wall segments and a sizable quantity of artifacts indicates there was a sedentary occupation in this stratum. Unfortunately too little is known of it for us to comprehend its essence. Notably, the ceramic material from this stratum represents a mixed bag of LN/EC types with an admixture of Early EB I types indicating intermittent utilization of the mound within the time-span covered by LN through Chalcolithic chrono-cultural horizons. The presence of EB I materials in this level is understood as evidence that these early deposits were disturbed by later intrusions. It is also particularly unfortunate that the ceramic assemblage from this site has been used as an example of a "Middle Chalcolithic" phase, considering the rather obvious chrono-cultural heterogeneity exhibited by the assemblage derived from Level XVIII.

Table 5.1 Sequence of Chrono-cultural Periods in the Deep Cut (Dates based on Braun (2001b)).

Level	Stratum	Description	Chrono-cultural Horizon	Approx. Date BC
Below XVIII	XIX	Pits and cavities, some natural and others man-made or altered, material cultural debris indicating utilization of site, possibly, but not necessarily from sedentary occupation, derived either from nearby or from overlying, probably mixed chrono-cultural deposits.	LN to EC	6th-5th millennia
XVIII	XVIII	Occupational debris, scant evidence of permanent structures; probably mixed chrono-cultural deposits.	LN to EC	6th-5th millennia
XVII	XVII north	Sedentary occupation; probably mixed chrono-cultural deposits.	LN to EC	6th-5th millennia
XVII	XVII south	Sedentary occupation	Early EB I	3500-3400
XVI	XVI	Sedentary occupation; probably mixed chrono-cultural deposits.	Early EB I	3400-3300
XV	XV	Sedentary occupation; probably mixed chrono-cultural deposits.	Developed EB I	3300-3200
XIV	XIV	Sedentary occupation; probably mixed chrono-cultural deposits.	Late EB I	3200-3000
XIII	XIII	Sedentary occupation; probably mixed chrono-cultural deposits.	Late EB I	3200-3000

Stratum XVII

The likely chrono-cultural bifurcation of this stratum suggests the remains of a sedentary, pre-EB I occupation were unearthed in the northern precinct of the Deep Cut, while the ruins of much later, Early EB I houses occupied the southern portion at approximately the same elevations. In that sense, FitzGerald's utilization of the term "level" takes on a literal meaning, although it is doubtful whether he intended it in that particular context. Apparently, the hill sloped in this precinct, and rather than carry out massive earthmoving operations, people built their houses accordingly. FitzGerald excavating on level surfaces, unwittingly encountering a duality of chrono-cultural horizons reflected both in architectural and in ceramic traditions within one "stratum."

He was unable to understand the eclectic nature of the ceramic assemblage because at that time there was no sequence by which he could have known of the chronological disparity of the pottery he recovered. Even today, we still encounter problems identifying pottery derived from LN/EC and Early EB I traditions because of the many similarities between them. With benefit of hindsight we now know there is no substantial evidence for LC artifacts in the Deep Cut, and it seems likely there was a gap in occupation of the tell, although a few ceramic objects suggest limited activity within that period. Settlement seems to have been resumed sometime early in the EB I period.

Stratum XVI

Stratum XVI suggests continuity in Early EB I with the later occupation of the preceding stratum. Had a plan for the Stratum XVI curvilinear house (dated early in EB I by typical pottery) been available to scholars directly after FitzGerald's excavation, then it might well have acted as a counterweight to interpretations derived from a Megiddo Stage IV house (Engberg and Shipton 1934:fig. 2) of supposedly "apsidal" mien. The Medgiddo building that has so inordinately influenced interpretations of the archaeological record of EB I, was actually formed by the juxtaposition of two construction phases, one curvilinear, the other rectilinear with only a single, constructed, right-angled corner (Braun 1990). Rather unfortunately, the plan of the house at Megiddo, rather than the Beth Shan XVI domicile, was (and occasionally continues to be) touted as evidence for an architectural tradition, despite its essentially unique character. The curvilinear house of Beth Shan XVI remains little known, although it is a quite typical example of an Early EB I curvilinear house. Only recently, with additional discoveries, has this Early EB I house type come to be well documented (Braun 1990; 2001). Thus, despite evidence for a curvilinear tradition of house construction unearthed in Stratum XVI at Beth Shan as early as 1933, the type was largely ignored, or worse, misinterpreted as apsidal.

Stratum XV

While the ceramics of Stratum XVb appear to reflect continuity with an EB I sequence, the architectural features unearthed in Stratum XVa seem to be very much at variance with prevailing traditions and represent a break in continuity for which I can find no good explanation. The precise function of the especially thick walls and unusual plans of the buildings, apparently without parallel, must remain a conundrum for the present.

Stratum XIV

Structures of Stratum XIV show more continuity with Stratum XVI than with the preceding occupation and fit well into the pattern of settlements known from this time span and region. They exhibit some evidence of curvilinear traditions but by and large follow rectilinear precepts. Thus, this stratum demonstrates a somewhat gradual or partial return to earlier styles of house building also documented at other sites (Braun 2001).

A notable feature in this stratum is the suggestion of a crowded precinct in which space was at a premium, perhaps a reflection of the political and social tenor of the times. The large, composite buildings encountered in this stratum are typical of the period and probably suggest that social units greater than a nuclear family were domiciled within them. This may possibly be interpreted as a change in social patterns from Early EB I, in which smaller houses (generally understood to have domiciled nuclear families or other social units of limited size as at the site of Yiftah'el II) seem to have been the rule. Evidence from the Hebrew University's excavations of the adjacent precinct at Beth Shan indicates the mound within this time span was occupied over most of its surface and that one or more of the structures may even have been of a public nature (Mazar 1994). Whether such an interpretation is fully justified is still unclear, but undoubtedly there is evidence for trends toward a more complex, hierarchical type of social organization in the later EB I phases of the site. The buildings are large, complex affairs with numerous rooms that suggest relatively large concentrations of populations. Some of the larger buildings or rooms apparently reflect this new social reality.

The pottery of this period indicates a trend towards more standardized forms, also of generally higher quality. They suggest origins of pots at production centers, perhaps produced by specialized classes of artisans, but whether Beth Shan may have played a role in what appears to be a system of production and trade, is unknown for the present. What may be stated on the basis of the limited evidence of the Deep Cut is, that on the whole, Beth Shan seems to be pretty much within the mainstream of Northern EB I traditions. Minimally, it was by this time a recipient of prevailing ideas and paraphernalia of the Late EB I cultural horizon. Certainly, its strategic location at the intersection of two major valley systems accounts for these developments. This is more evident in the adjacent precinct excavated by Mazar, equated with Stratum XIV, but hints of it are found also in the Deep Cut.

Stratum XIII

This stratum represents a clear continuation of the preceding occupation, and is noteworthy for a complete return to rectilinear architectural styles. The Deep Cut situated at the edge of the tell seems to have at least two types of buildings, one typical of large, multi-roomed domiciles, the other possibly of a more public nature. It was in part used for the storage of grain (Appendix 1). The full significance of this structure and those of the preceding stratum must await publication of the Hebrew University's report for it to be properly understood within the greater context of the site. Suffice it to note that the buildings in the Deep Cut are part of an obviously crowded and complex agglomeration of buildings that indicate a degree of social complexity concomitant with that of towns. This Late EB I occupation on the high tell was apparently a flourishing community at a time when other nearby sites appear to have grown into major settlements, some of them boasting fortifications such as Tel Beth Yerah (Getzov 1998; Getzov, Paz, and Gophna 2001:22) and Tel Shalem (Eisenberg 1997). Perhaps this occupation on the high tell was protected by the steep slopes of the hill; alternately it may have occupied a political niche offering it protection that would obviate a need for fortifications. A nearby site at Tell Istaba (east of the monastery excavated by FitzGerald 1939a), is notable for large quantities of Late EB I pottery eroding out of the earlier levels. It suggests another, similarly unfortified, contemporary settlement in the vicinity that would possibly have made a pair or perhaps even belong to a cluster of settlements of some political prominence.

Notably, although most of the pottery of this stratum clearly represents a Late EB I occupation as known from other sites, a relatively large quantity of LN/EC types collected by FitzGerald remains as a curious, exotic element within the assemblage. It is best explained as intrusive or residual and should be understood as evidence of the problematic nature of the archaeological record of the Deep Cut that has produced chrono-cultural admixtures of ceramics and other artifacts within assemblages assigned to one or another level.

Some Observations on Beth Shan XII

Although Level XII is beyond the scope of this work, a few observations on the nature of the settlement above Stratum XIII are in order. The earliest identifiable pottery of that period which I was able to discern appears to belong to the EB III horizon. That includes well-known types such as platters and bowls with pattern burnishing (FitzGerald 1935: pl. VIII:20, 23, 25) and quantities of "Beth Yerah Ware (FitzGerald 1935: pl. VII). So far as is understood, there is no appreciable evidence for an EB II occupation in the Deep Cut and such appears to be the case for the adjacent precinct (Mazar, Ziv-Esudri and Cohen-Weinberger 2000:259). Thus, the occupation in the Deep Cut may be said to end concurrently with EB I, and as far as may be discerned in FitzGerald's notes, the site appears to have been peacefully abandoned or, at best, only sparsely settled within the EB II horizon.

A Personal, Summary Statement

Although I fully appreciate the opportunity entrusted to me by the University of Pennsylvania to bring a report of FitzGerald's work into print, I cannot but feel that in one sense it is unfortunate it took more than seven decades for such a project to come to fruition. There is a lesson of timeliness that may be learned from this inordinate delay, one that indicates just how much a full report of FitzGerald's pioneering efforts was missed in the early years of archaeological investigation in the southern Levant. The sounding that we know as the Deep Cut brought to light very early on some important and fascinating pieces in the puzzle of the early ceramic cultures of the southern Levant. FitzGerald obviously realized the possibilities for understanding them that could arise from his work, and laudably he rushed two preliminary accounts into print. Unfortunately, his other duties (including several excavation reports on later occupations of the site) left him unable to complete a final, detailed publication. Indeed, he appears not to have worked at all on this material, and as a result, he has retained only a minor place in the pantheon of early 20th century excavators who probed the late prehistory of the southern Levant. Had it been more detailed, his Deep Cut contribution would have greatly enriched our knowledge of early pottery horizons and earned him a more prominent position among scholars working on these periods. Nevertheless, to my mind he remains an under-appreciated scholar.

More than seven decades after the excavation of the Deep Cut the reader might question the wisdom of preparing and publishing a detailed account of so limited a sounding, especially when in the interval between the excavation and the present, considerable knowledge has accrued on the periods FitzGerald's work revealed. I suggest that however tardy the report, it is a necessary contribution to the literature on a number of levels.

All excavation is destruction and it is incumbent upon a director to leave a detailed and scientific account of his observations, and to make it available to the public at large. On the most primary level, this report fulfills FitzGerald's obligation, but it goes even beyond that for it remains, until the present, the sole source of information on the earliest strata of the mound. The Hebrew University's excavations stopped in Late EB I occupations that are tentatively correlated to Stratum XIV and have not been probed below.

On another level, it is hoped that somehow this report will manage to dispel some of the unclear aspects of the evidence from the early levels that has fueled so much discussion in the past. I have attempted to present an accurate record of just what was (and was not) found within the Deep Cut, and in doing so I hope to alter researchers' perceptions of what can and cannot, and what ought and ought not, be discerned from available data.

One of the objectives of my exercise was to present as full a complement of FitzGerald's data from the excavation of the Deep Cut as was possible, given the available records. The harvest, while perhaps not the most bountiful, was richer than one might have suspected from the early publications. Perhaps the most valuable contribution in the present volume is the presentation of the architectural plans for the first time in a publication. They offer us a rather astounding glimpse at some of the chrono-cultural developments that we have come to know from other sites excavated many years after FitzGerald's work.

I have endeavored, with benefit of hindsight, to analyze this information in light of the relevant data on findspots of artifacts and use it to interpret the stratigraphic sequence in the Deep Cut. My hope is that the researcher will find in the pages of this report enough raw data and that my interpretation will assist in better understanding of the numerous finds published so many years ago. Readers must judge to what extent I have given them their archaeological context and the degree to which I have elucidated their likely relationships (or lack of them) to structures and fills that made up those early deposits on the mound.

FitzGerald's Deep Cut, documented by him in a manner acceptable in the time when he worked, gives us a picture of a series of late prehistoric events that reflects the chronological progression of cultures within the northern region of the southern Levant. While far from a perfect view, it does offer us at least a glimpse, occasionally with startling clarity, into the earliest human endeavors on one of the major sites of the southern Levant. By shedding light on the earliest of levels there it helps to complete a vertical, albeit minimal, record of the excavated portions of the tell.

Appendix 1
New Data on Some Cultivated Plants and Weeds of the Early Bronze Age in Palestine

Naomi Feinbrun*
(Hebrew University)

In December 1933 some samples of seeds were brought to me for determination by Mr. G. M. FitzGerald, who had found them in excavations in Beth Shan. Substantial quantities of seeds had been found in room No. 1848 of the XIII level in large stone jars. [N.B. This discription is in error. These vessels are ceramic pithoi (Eliot Braun).] FitzGerald (1934) estimates the age of the XIII level of Beth Shan as of more than 2000 B.C., i.e., Early Bronze Age. According to a later evaluation by Albright (1935) the level in question was dated as of the period of 3000-2500 B.C., synchronic with the I-II Dynasty of Egypt (Early Bronze I).

The four samples brought to me and designated as 1848 A, B, C, D, contained carbonized but perfectly preserved seeds. Sample A contained a considerable quantity of barley mixed with a few wheat grains and a few small grass grains; Sample B contained lentils; Sample C common beans; Sample D lentils mixed with common beans. We will discuss the lentils and the beans as having particular interest.

Lentils

Data on prehistoric lentils (Buschan 1895; Barulina 1930:1937) may be summed up as follows: Neolithic findings in the southern part of Middle Europe and in Asia Minor (ancient Troy); Bronze Age findings in the same part of Middle Europe, Crete and Egypt (Fra-Abu-Negga); Iron Age—in Southern and Middle Europe (Figure A1.1).

Literature thus mentions lentils in prehistoric times in only three countries east of Greece (Crete, Troy and Egypt). The Beth Shan discovery of Bronze Age lentils are to date the easternmost finding of this vegetable and apparently the richest in quantity.

According to the taxonomic subdivision of *Lens esculenta* by Barulina (1930, 1937) the Beth Shan lentils belong to ssp. *microsperma* (Baumg.) Bar. – average of 50 measured was 3.4 mm, varying between 2.75 and 4mm. More precise determination being impossible from seeds alone, it can be assumed, on the basis of indirect proofs that they belong to the proles of *asiaticae* of the ssp. *microsperma*. Palestine being situated in the center of the area of distribution and presenting 21 of its 31 existing varieties of proles *asiaticae* (Zaitschek 1938). Determination of the varieties based on the color of seeds was, naturally, impossible.

A Weed of Ancient Lentils

Among the seeds of sample B we found a few carbonized seeds which we could identify as of Galium

---

* This article first appeared in *The Palestine Journal of Botany, Jerusalem Series* 1(2) (1938). It is reproduced here through the courtesy of Prof. Uriel Safriel, the late Prof. Feinbrun's nephew and scientific executor. Minor changes have been made in punctuation and spelling to an otherwise intact text.

tricorne L. This species is a common weed of present day lentils. This find is testimony to the age of this anthropophyte.

Common Beans (*Vicia Faba* L.)

Prehistorical findings from the east Mediterranean are very rare. Muratova (1931; 1937) reports two findings of the Neolithic (Troy and Egypt) and one of the Bronze Age (Crete). No findings are reported east of the above countries.

The seeds from Beth Shan are very small, averaging 5.5-5.75 mm in length, with a maximum of 6.75 mm; their thickness index (thickness to length is 0.7-0.8)(Figure A1.2). The seeds are, however, destitute of peel and radicula, so they may have been somewhat larger. According to Muratova, such small-seeded beans can be classed either in ssp. *paucijuga* (All.) Murat. confined to India or into ssp. *eu-faba* Murat. var. *minor* Beck with much wider and more westerly distribution. A more exact determination is impossible on the basis of seeds alone, but geographic evidence speaks more for its belonging to the second group. At any rate, they belong to the smallest-known forms of common beans. All these small-seeded forms display the same bolster-shaped seeds as the Beth Shan common beans. The Palestine common beans of today are quite different. Muratova reports for this country only the forms *divulgata* and *macrosperma* of the var. *major* (large-sized beans, 1.88-3.05 cm in length) and f. *mediterranea* of the var. *equina* (medium-sized beans, 1.25-1.65 cm in length). Geographically nearest are the forms of var. *minor*—f. *syriaca*, endemic for Syria and f. *aegyptica*, endemic for Egypt but they too have much longer (1.10—1.20 cm) and somewhat compressed (index of thickness 0.54-0.62) seeds. The small-seeded common beans seem to be no longer in cultivation in Palestine.

Buschan has already shown that prehistoric beans were small, although big ones were also found. The second fact noticed was that East Mediterranean and Middle European findings comprise smaller and rounder sees than West-Mediterranean. As to the origin of cultivated beans, Muratova concludes: (1) that the small-seeded bolster-shaped beans are more primitive; (2) that the development tended toward enlargement and flattening of seeds and diminution in diversity of forms; (3) that the center of diversity of common beans lies in the mountainous parts of Irano-Turanian Asia. Our findings seem to confirm this view. It is worth noticing that Beth Shan lies in the Irano-Turanian phytogeographical territory of Palestine (cf. Eig *Palestine Journal of Botany, Jerusalem Series* 1 (1938):4-12).

References

Albright, W. F.
1935 Presidential Address: Palestine in the Earliest Historical Period. *The Journal of the Palestine Oriental Society* 15: 193-234.

Barulina, H. J.
1930 Lentils of the USSSR and of Other Countries. Supplement of the 40th *Bulletin of Applied Botany, Genetics and Plant Breeding*: 1-319.
1937 Leningrad (Tourn.) Adans. In *Flora of Cultivated Plants* 4:127 ff.

Buschan, G.
1895 *Vorgeschichtliche Botanik der Culturund Nutzpflanzen der alten Welt auf Grund praehistorischer Funde*. Breslau.

FitzGerald, G. M.
1934 Excavations at Beth-Shan in 1933. *Palestine Exploration Fund Quarterly Statement* 66: 123-34.

Muratova, V. S.
1931 Common Beans (*Vicia Faba* L.) Supplement 50th Bulletin of Applied Botany Genetics and Plant Breeding: 1-298.
1937 *Vicia* L. in *Flora of Cultivated Plants* 4: 75. Moscow-Leningrad.

Zaitschek, D. V.
1938 Studies in Palestinian Lentils II. *Palestine Journal of Botany: Jerusalem Series* 1:55-64.

Appendix 2
Room List

Following is a list of principal rooms or loci assigned by FitzGerald to the excavation within the Deep Cut, according to his stratigraphic ascriptions. In order to give easy reference to locations I have superimposed a new 5.0 m x 5.0 m grid based on two extant coordinates from FitzGerald's plan. In addition, I have added my notes on the "rooms" or, as I term them, "loci." A room is equivalent to a locus. The designation was made by FitzGerald in line with earlier excavations and was maintained throughout the excavation of the Deep Cut.

Table A2.1 Rooms of Level XVIII

Room	SQ	SQ	SQ	SQ	Observations
1897	J 22	J 23			Open space at W edge of excavation, to west of pit of –XVIII.
1898	J 22	J 23	K 22	K 23	Possible fill of rectilinear structures; presumably above pit of –XVIII.
1899	L 22				Open area to S of pit and mudbrick bin and remnants of structures.
1900	L 25				Possibly refers to extant structures, amorphous masses of wall debris or mudbrick.

Table A2.2 Rooms of Level XVII

Room	SQ	SQ	SQ	SQ	Observations
1891	J 21	J 22			Open space W of W1708.
1892	K 21	K 22	L 21	L 22	Open space E of W 1708; several pits, bins, and walls are evidence of poorly preserved structure and activity in this precinct of the excavation.
1893	K 22	L 22	K 23	L 23	Open area S of wall fragments and bins to E edge of excavation; bounded by grain bins.
1894	J 23				Open space S of W 1707 to edge of excavation; several pits, bins, and walls are evidence of poorly preserved structure and activity in this precinct of the excavation.
1895	L 24	M 24			Open space S of several grain bins bordering 1893 to E edge of excavation.
1896	K 25	L 25	K 26	L 26	Open Area with several curvilinear walls and other wall fragments and bins; several phases represented here.

Table A2.3 Rooms of Level XVI

Room	SQ	SQ	SQ	SQ	Observations
1881	J 21				Possibly a part of a room of which only 1 wall is extant in the NW part of the sounding.
1882	K 21	K 22			A partial room with only 2 partial parallel walls extant.
1883	L 21	L 22	K 21	K 22	An open space (?) E of 1882 to edge of excavation.
1884	K 23				An open space with some wall fragments W of a curvilinear structure.
1885	L 22	L 23			Part of an apsidal end of a curvilinear structure; this has a brick floor.
1886	L 23	M 23			Space between 1885 and 1887/8; walls here connect these two curvilinear buildings.
1887	L 24				The N end of a completely preserved plan of a curvilinear house; it is divided into two chambers; there seem to be pits in this end; the shape of the divider wall suggests the excavators missed some bricks and that there were several phases.
1888	L 25				The S end of a curvilinear house; the unusual shape of the chamber suggests problems in defining the brick structure; stones below may be either an earlier structure of the same type or belong to an earlier phase.
1889	K 25	K 26	L 26		This is an open space to the SW of 1888 to the W edge of the excavation.
1890	K 26	L 26	L 27		Curvilinear structure; could be circular but is large; could also be the apsidal end of a house; paved with stones; one a mortar or door socket.

Table A2.4 Rooms of Level XV

Room	SQ	SQ	SQ	SQ	Observations
1874	J 22	J 21			Partially preserved room at NE corner of excavation; several lines of stones may suggest phasing or earlier stratum.
1875	J 23	J 24			Irregular-shaped open area with wall stubs, back-to-back walls and stone indicating that there were a number of phases represented in the architecture of this Level.
1876	K 21	K 22	K 23		A wide corridor or lane between wall fragments probably representing several building complexes; wall fragments block it indicating several phases represented here.
1877	K 22	L 22	K 23	L 23	This is a partially preserved curvilinear structure; several small wall fragments and a pit or bin impinge upon it.
1878	L 23				An open area contiguous and to the SE of 1877; same interpretation.
1879	K 24	L 24	L 25		A narrow corridor formed by two, almost parallel walls.
1880	K 26	L 26			Open area at S end of excavation in which are a number of brick and stone walls; one partially preserved circular installation and several curved and rectilinear wall segments indicate several phases or strata are represented here.

Table A2.5 Rooms of Level XIV

Room	SQ	SQ	SQ	SQ	Observations
1859	L 25	M 25			Partial rectangular room E of 1856 to W edge of excavation; the W wall of this room has several phases indicated.
1860	I 23	J 23			Small rectangular room S of 1852 formed by W 1222; as drawn this wall seems to rest atop W 1221, 1223; there are discrepancies with the elevations of these walls suggesting several building phases.
Below 1825					Presumably within the confines of these rooms/loci, but below the walls of Level XII; see p. 35 in Level Book.
Below 1826					Same as below 1825.
Below 1826-9					Uncertain meaning.
Below 1838					Uncertain meaning.
Below 1834					Uncertain meaning.
Below 1844					Same as below 1825.
1859	M 24	M 25	M 26		Partially exposed, irregular-shaped room E of 1869, 1872 to E edge of excavation; part of SE complex.
1861	K 20	K 21	K 22	L 21	South end of rectangular building with curved corners. Numerous phases are represented by a series of superimposed and mismatched walls; at least 2 strata here with several phases.
1862	J 21	J 22			Narrow lane to W of curvilinear house, E of complex formed by 1863, 1865, 1866; open onto piazza 1868.
1863	J 22	I 22			Small room, part of series in. complex building that seems to be incompletely preserved on W side.
1864	J 20	J 21	K 21		Open space in NW corner to sounding; N or W complex of rooms.
1865	J 22				Small, irregular-shaped chamber, part of complex on W side of the sounding.
1866	I 23	J 23	K 23		Large, irregular-shaped chamber in the W complex of rooms; a bench may line the E wall externally; it may also be part of superimposed walls of different phases.
1867	J 24	J 25			A partially excavated room with stubs of walls impinging on its integrity; several different phases are obvious here.
E. of 1866?					Same as 1868; noted by FitzGerald, but why he distinguished it from 1868 is uncertain.
1868	L 23	L 24			Irregular-shaped space bordering on a triangular-shaped piazza where 2 lanes between houses diverge; bounded by a curved wall; contains a bin; the southwest wall represents one of a series of superimposed phases.
Below 1869	L 24	L 25			Irregular-shaped room with a small pilaster-like wall jutting into its NE slanted wall; no entrance visible; part of SE complex.
1870	K 25	L 25			Small, almost square room; part of SE complex.
1871	K 26	L 26			Small, irregular-shaped chamber; part of SE complex; the line of stones on NW side of room may be indicative of architectural phasing.
1872	L 26				Small, rectangular-shaped room; part of SE complex; line of stones belongs to something earlier.
1873	M 26	M 27			Partial rectangular room at SW corner of excavation; part of SE complex.
Below 1846					P. 42 Level Book, 1931-3 Season.
Below 1847					P. 42 Level Book, 1931-3 Season.
Below 1848					P. 42 Level Book, 1931-3 Season.
Below 1849					P. 42 Level Book, 1931-3 Season.
Below 1860					P. 49 Level Book, 1931-3 Season.
Below 1872					Earlier phase?

Table A2.6 Rooms of Level XIII

Room	SQ	SQ	SQ	SQ	SQ	Observations
1845	I 24	J 24	K 24			Open area/ room? S of W 1226, W1232 to S edge of excavation.
1846	L 20	L 21	L 22	K 21	K 22	Large, irregular-shaped room, divided by W 1260 and the circular stone-lined pit it abuts. This pit is obviously earlier, W 1207 is built above its western end.
E of 1846	L21	L22				Narrow strip of fill between walls 1210, 1211, 1212 to edge of excavation.
1847	I 21	J 21	J 22	K 22	L 22	Narrow corridor, S of 1846, 1848, 1849; N of 1853 (not on FitzGerald's list in notebook).
1848	K 20	K 21	K 22			Narrow broadroom, width of house with openings to 1846, 1849.
1849	I 20	J 20	J 21	K 20	K 21	Large, almost square room, partially incomplete with opening onto 1848. North half of room has 6 evenly spaced post-holes/wooden pillars.
1851	J 23	K 23				Narrow, almost trapezoidal space between W 1228, 1227, 1230, 1229; very small and may not be a room or even an open space.
1852	I 22	J 22	I 23	J 23		Large, irregular space to S of 1847 corridor, W of excavation border, N of 1860 and E of 1853, 1851. There are a number of walls more or less forming partial structures within.
1853	K 22	K 23	J 23			Trapezoidal room S of 1847, N of 1851.
1854						Listed in notes; not on plan.
1855	L 23	L 24				Small, almost square room bordered by stone walls 1240, 1236, 1241, 1242 1238.
1856	L 24	L 25				Almost rectangular room (NE corner cut off) with no entrance indicated—walls of this room include either benches or earlier wall stubs; W wall of this room may have an external bench or earlier structural phases.
1857	L 26	K 26	K 25	L 25		Rectangular room with bin and internal walls. Obviously there are a number of superimposed building phases here.
1858	L 24	M 24				Room or space between wall fragments W1237, W1239, and N of 1859 to E edge of excavation.

Bibliography

Amiran, R.
1969 *Ancient Pottery of the Holy Land.* Jerusalem: Massada.
1978 *Early Arad: The Chalcolithic Settlement and Early Bronze City.* Jerusalem: Israel Exploration Society.

Andelkovic, B.
1995 *The Relations Between Early Bronze Age I Canaanites and Upper Egyptians.* Belgrade: Faculty of Philosophy, Center for Archaeological Research.

Baird, D., and G. Philip
1994 Preliminary Report on the Third (1993) Season of Excavations at Tell esh-Shuna North. *Levant* 26:111-33.

Banning, E. B. M.
2001 Review of: *Neolithic and Chalcolithic Pottery of the Southern Levant*, by Yosef Garfinkel (1999). *Bulletin of American Schools of Oriental Research* 322:79-81.

Banning, E. B., M. Blackham, and D. Lasby
1998 Excavations at WZ 121: A Chalcolithic Site at Tubna, in Wadi Ziqlab. *Annual of the Department of Antiquities of Jordan* 42:141-59.

Bar-Adon, P.
1980 *The Cave of the Treasure: The Finds from the Caves in Nahal Mishmar.* Jerusalem: Israel Exploration Society.

Bar-Yosef, O.
1992 The Neolithic Period. Pp. 10-39 in A. Ben-Tor, ed. *The Archaeology of Ancient Israel.* New Haven, CT: Yale University Press.

Beck, P.
1985 An Early Bronze Age "Family" of Bowls from Tel Aphek. *Tel Aviv* 12:17-28.

Ben-Dor, I.
1936 Pottery of the Middle and Late Neolithic Periods. Pp. 77-91 and Plates XXIX-XXXIII and XLII in Jericho: City and Necropolis. Report for Sixth and Concluding Season 1936. *Annals of Archaeology and Anthropology* 23:67-100.

Betts, A. V. G., ed.
1992 *Excavations at Tell Um Hammad: The Early Assemblages (EB I-II).* Edinburgh: Edinburgh University Press.

Betts, A. V. G., and S. Helms
1992 Conclusion. Pp. 136-147 in A. V. G. Betts, ed. *Excavations at Tell Um Hammad: The Early Assemblages (EB I-II).* Edinburgh: Edinburgh University Press.

Bienert, H-D., and D. Vieweger
1999 Archaeological Excavations at the Late Neolithic Site of Ash-Shalaf: A Preliminary Report on the 1998 Season. *Annual of the Department of Antiquities of Jordan* 43:49-67.

Blackham, M., K. Fisher, and D. Lasby
1998 Tall Fendi, a Late Chalcolithic Settlement in the Lower Wasi Ziqlab, Jordan. *Annual of the Department of Antiquities of Jordan* 42:161-77.

Bourke, S. J.
1997 The "Pre-Ghassulian" Sequence at Teleilat Ghassul: Sydney University Excavations 1975-1995. Pp. 395-417 in H. G. K. Gebel, Z. Kafafi, and G. O. Rollefson, eds. *The Prehistory of Jordan, II: Perspectives from 1997.* Studies in Early Near Eastern Production, Subsistence, and Environment 4. Berlin: Ex Oriente.
2000 Pella in the Early Bronze Age. Pp. 233-53 in G. Philip and D. Baird, eds. *Breaking with the Past: Ceramics and Change in the Early Bronze Age of the Southern Levant.* Sheffield: Sheffield Academic Press.
2001 The Chalcolithic Period. Pp. 107-62 in B. Macdonald, R. Adams, and P. Bienkowski, eds. *The Archaeology of Jordan.* Sheffield: Sheffield Academic Press.

Braun, E.
1985 *En Shadud: Salvage Excavations at a Farming Community in the Jezreel Valley, Israel.* British Archaeological Reports, International Series 249. Oxford: British Archaeological Reports.
1989a The Transition from the Chalcolithic to the Early Bronze Age in Northern Israel and Transjordan: Is there a Missing Link? Pp. 7-28 in P. de Miroschedji, ed. *L'urbanisation de la Palestine à l'âge du Bronze ancien: bilan et perspectives des recherches actuelles, Actes du Colloque d'Emmaüs: 20-24 Octobre 1986.* Oxford: British Archaeological Reports.
1989b The Problem of the Apsidal House: New Aspects of Early Bronze I Domestic Architecture in Israel, Jordan and Lebanon. *Palestine Exploration Quarterly* 121:1-43.
1990 Basalt Bowls of the EB I Horizon in the Southern Levant. *Paléorient* 16:87-95.
1996a Cultural Diversity and Change in the Early Bronze I of Israel and Jordan: Towards an Understanding of the Chronological Progression and Patterns of Regionalism in Early Bronze Society. Ph.D. dissertation, Tel Aviv University.
1996b Salvage Excavations at the Early Bronze Age Site of Me'ona: Final Report. *'Atiqot* 26-27:1-31.
1997 *Yiftahel: Salvage and Rescue Excavations at a Prehistoric Village in Lower Galilee, Israel.* IAA Reports 2. Jerusalem: Israel Antiquities Authority.
2000 Area G at Afridar, Palmahim Quarry 3 and the Earliest Pottery of Early Bronze I: Part of the Missing Link. Pp. 113-128 in G. Philip and D. Baird, eds. *Breaking with the Past: Ceramics and Change in the Early Bronze Age of the Southern Levant.* Sheffield: Sheffield Academic Press.
2001a "Little Boxes" of the Southern Levant: Some Observations on the Domestic Architecture of the Early Bronze Age. Pp. 31*-39* in A. M. Maeir and E. Baruch, eds. *Settlement, Civilization and Culture: Proceedings of the Conference in Memory of David Alon.* Ramat Gan, Israel: Bar Ilan University.
2001b Proto and Early Dynastic Egypt and Early Bronze I-II of the Southern Levant: Uneasy 14C Correlations. *Radiocarbon* 43:1202-18.

Braun, E., and R. Gophna
1995 Ashqelon Afridar, Area G. *Excavations and Surveys in Israel* 15:97-98.
2004 Excavations at Ashqelon, Afridar-Area G. *Atiqot* 45:185-241.

Braun, E., and I. Milevski
1993 Baja Khorvat `Illin: Una aldea del Bronce Antiguo cerca de Beth Shemesh. *Revista de arqueologia* 142:8-15.

Byrd, B. F., and E. B. Banning
1988 Southern Levantine Pier Houses: Intersite Architectural Patterning during the Pre-Pottery Neolithic B. *Paléorient* 14(1):65-72.

Ciasca, R.
1962 Scavi e esplorazioni: Tell Gat. *Oriens Antiquus* I, Fasc. I:23-39.

Commenge-Pellerin, C.
1990 *La poterie de Safadi (Beersheva) au IVe millénaire avant l'ère chrétienne.* Paris: Association Paléorient.

de Contenson, H.
1960 Three Soundings in the Jordan Valley. *Annual of the Department of Antiquities of Jordan* 4-5:12-98.
1979 A propos des vases en chaux: recherche sur leur fabrication et leur origine. *Paléorient* 5:177-82.

Dayan, Y.
1969 Tel Turmus in the Huleh Valley. *Israel Exploration Journal* 19:65-78.

Dollfus, G., and Z. Kafafi
1986 Preliminary Results of the First Season of the Joint Jordano-French Project at Abu Hamid. *Annual of the Department of Antiquities of Jordan* 30:353-379.
1993 Recent Researches at Abu Hamid. *Annual of the Department of Antiquities of Jordan* 27:241-62.

Dothan, M.
1959 Excavations at Meser 1957: Preliminary Report on the Second Season. *Israel Exploration Journal* 9:13-29.
1970 A Burial Cave Near Tel Esur. *Ezor Menashe* [The region of the tribe of Menashe] 2:1-16 and figures (Hebrew).

Droop, J. P.
1935 Pottery of the Chalcolithic and Neolithic Levels, 1935. Pp. 169-173 and Plates XXXVIII, XL-XLII, XLIV-XLVI and XL in Jericho: City and Necropolis: Fifth Report. *Annals of Archaeology and Anthropology* 22:169-75.

Dunand, M.
1973 *Fouilles de Byblos* V. Texte et planches. Paris: Maisonneuve.

Duncan, J. G.
1930 *Corpus of Dated Palestinian Pottery*. London: British School of Archaeology in Egypt.

Eisenberg, E.
1989 Chalcolithic and Early Bronze I Occupations at Tel Teo. Pp. 29-40 in P. de Miroschedji, ed. *L'urbanisation de la Palestine à l'âge du Bronze ancien: bilan et perspectives des recherches actuelles, Actes du Colloque d'Emmaüs: 20-24 Octobre 1986*. Oxford: British Archaeological Reports.
1997 Tel Shalem: Soundings in a Fortified Site of the Early Bronze Age IB. *'Atiqot* 30:1-24.
1998 Khirbet et Tuwal: Salvage Excavations at an EB I B Settlement in the Bet She'an Valley. *'Atiqot* 35:1-7.

Eisenberg, E., A. Gopher, and R. Greenberg
2001 *Tell Te'o: A Neolithic, Chalcolithic, and Early Bronze Age Site in the Hula Valley.* IAA Reports 13. Jerusalem: Israel Antiquities Authority.

Engberg, R., and G. Shipton
1934 *Notes on the Chalcolithic and Early Bronze Pottery of Megiddo.* Studies in Ancient Oriental Civilizations 10. Chicago: Oriental Institute.

Epstein, C.
1998 *The Chalcolithic Culture of the Golan.* IAA Reports 4. Jerusalem: The Israel Antiquities Authority.

Esse, D. L.
1991 *Subsistence, Trade, and Social Change in Early Bronze Age Palestine.* Studies in Ancient Oriental Civilization 50. Chicago: Oriental Institute.

Feinbrun, N.
1938 New Data on Some Cultivated Plants and Weeds of the Early Bronze Age in Palestine. *Palestine Journal of Botany*. Jerusalem Series 1: 238-41.

Finkelstein, I., and D. Ussishkin
2000 Area J. Pp. 25-74 in I. Finkelstein, D. Ussishkin, and B. Halpern, eds. *Megiddo III: The 1992-1996 Seasons*. Tel Aviv Monograph Series No. 18. Tel Aviv: Institute of Archaeology, Tel Aviv University.

Fischer, P. M.
1993 Tell Abu al-Kharaz: The Swedish Jordan Expedition 1991—Second Season Preliminary Excavation Report. *Annual of the Department of Antiquities of Jordan* 37:279-305.
2000 The Early Bronze Age at Tell Abu al-Kharaz, Jordan Valley: A Study of Pottery Typology and Provenance, Radiocarbon Dates, and Synchronism. Pp. 201-32 in G. Philip and D. Baird, eds. *Ceramics and Change in the Early Bronze Age of the Southern Levant*. Sheffield: Sheffield Academic Press.

FitzGerald, G. M.
1933a Field Diary: 1933 Season (Beth Shan). University of Pennsylvania Museum of Archaeology and Anthropology Archives.
1933b Letter: 1 December 1933 to Horace H. F. Jayne, Director of the University Museum. University of Pennsylvania Museum of Archaeology and Anthropology Archives.
1933c Letter: 31 December 1933 to Horace H. F. Jayne, Director of the University Museum. University of Pennsylvania Museum of Archaeology and Anthropology Archives.

1933d   Beth-Shan Excavations, Season 1933. *First Report to 5th October 1933*. Typescript with corrections, deletions, and hand-written addenda: University of Pennsylvania Museum of Archaeology and Anthropology Archives.

1934   Excavations at Beth-Shan in 1933. *Palestine Exploration Quarterly for 1934*:123-34.

1935   Beth Shan: Earliest Pottery. *The Museum Journal* 24:5-22.

1936   (Part) III: Pottery of the Early Bronze Age. Pp. 91-100 and Plates XXXIV-XXXIX in J. Garstang, I. Ben-Dor, and G. M. FitzGerald, joint authors. *Jericho: City and Necropolis. Report for Sixth and Concluding Season 1936. Annals of Archaeology and Anthropology* 23:67-100.

1939a   *A Sixth-Century Monastery at Beth Shan*. Philadelphia: University of Pennsylvania Museum.

1939b   Pottery of the Early Bronze Age I in *Jericho: City and Necropolis—Report for Sixth and Concluding Season 1936. Annals of Archaeology and Anthropology* 23:91-100.

nd   Index Card File of Finds by Room from the 1932 and 1933 Seasons of Beth Shan (with Stratigraphic Association and Notes in longhand; also annotated by F. James and with drawings of selected objects, probably by one or more, unidentified draftsperson). University of Pennsylvania Museum of Archaeology and Anthropology Archives.

Foerster, G.
1993   Beth-Shean at the Foot of the Mound. Pp. 223-35 in E. Stern, ed. *The New Encyclopedia of Archaeological Excavations in the Holy Land 1-4*. Jerusalem: Israel Exploration Society.

Fritz, V.
1990   *Kinneret: Ergebnisse der Ausgrabungen auf dem Tell el-'Oreme am See Gennesaret 1982-1985* 15 (Abhandlungen des Deutschen Palsstinavereins).

Gal, Z., and C. Covello-Paran
1996   Excavations at 'Afula, 1989. *'Atiqot* 30:25-67.

Garfinkel, Y.
1992   *The Pottery Assemblages of the Sha'ar Hagolan and Rabah Stages of Munhata (Israël)*. Les Cahiers du Centre de Recherche Français de Jerusalem 6. Paris: Association Paléorient.

1999   *Neolithic and Chalcolithic Pottery of the Southern Levant*. Qedem 39. Jerusalem: Hebrew University.

Getzov, R.
1998   Tel Bet Yerah. *Excavations and Surveys in Israel* 18:20-21.

1999   Ha-Gosherim. *Hadashot Arkheologiyot: Excavations and Surveys in Israel* 110:2-3 [English 2*-3*].

Getzov, N., Y. Paz, and R. Gophna
2001   *Shifting Urban Landscapes during the Early Bronze Age in the Land of Israel*. Tel Aviv: Ramot.

Gilead, I., and Y. Goren
1995   Pottery Assemblages from Grar. Pp. 137-222 in I. Gilead, ed. *Grar: A Chalcolithic Site in the Northern Negev*. Beer-Sheva VIII. Beer-Sheva: Ben Gurion University of the Negev Press.

Gopher, A.
1993   Netiv Ha-gedud. Pp. 1150-52 in E. Stern, ed. *The New Encyclopedia of Archaeological Excavations in the Holy Land 1-4*. Jerusalem: Israel Exploration Society.

Gopher, A., and Ts. Tsuk
1996   The Chalcolithic Assemblages: Pottery. Pp. 91-109 in A. Gopher, ed. *The Nahal Qanah Cave: Earliest Gold in the Southern Levant*. Tel Aviv: Tel Aviv University.

Gophna, R., and S. Sadeh
1988-9   Excavations at Tel Tsaf: An Early Chalcolithic Site in the Jordan Valley. *Tel Aviv* 15-16:3-36.

Goren, Y., and S. Zuckermann
2000   An Overview of the Typology, Provenance and Technology of the Early Bronze Age I "Grey Burnished Ware." Pp. 165-1182 in G. Philip and D. Baird, eds. *Breaking with the Past: Ceramics and Change in the Early Bronze Age of the Southern Levant*. Sheffield: Sheffield Academic Press.

Gustavson-Gaube, C.
1985   Tell esh-Shuna North 1984: A Preliminary Report. *Annual of the Department of Antiquities of Jordan* 29:43-87.

1986   Tell esh-Shuna North 1985: A Preliminary Report. *Annual of the Department of Antiquities of Jordan* 30:69-113.

Helms, S.
1991   Introduction; Stratigraphy; The Pottery; Stamped, Incised and Painted Designs on Pottery; Other Finds. Pp. 6-18, 19-54, 55-109, 110-39, 154-67, respectively, in A. V. Betts, ed. *Excavations at Jawa 1972-1986.* Edinburgh: Edinburgh University Press.
1992   Introduction; Stratigraphy; Architecture; The Pottery Typology. Pp. 5-14, 15-29, 30-38, 39-121, respectively, in A. V. Betts, ed. *Excavations at Tell Um Hammad: The Early Assemblages (EB I-II).* Edinburgh: Edinburgh University Press

Hennessy, J. B.
1969   Preliminary Report on a First Season of Excavations at Teleilat Ghassul. *Levant* 1:1-24.

Holland, T. A.
1986   Jericho and the Proto-Urban Period. *Alesco Studies in the History and Archaeology of Palestine.* 2:17-25. Aleppo University, Palestine Archaeological Center.

Kafafi, Z. A.
2001   *Jebel Abu Thawwab (Er-Rumman), Central Jordan: The Late Neolithic and Early Bronze Age I Occupations.* Berlin: Ex Oriente.

Kaplan, J.
1969   'Ein el Jarba: Chalcolithic Remains in the Plain of Esdraelon. *Bulletin of the American Schools of Oriental Research* 194:2-37.

Kempinski, A., and W-D. Niemeier, eds.
1992   *Excavations at Kabri 6: Preliminary Report of 1991 Season.* Tel Kabri Expedition.

Kenyon, K.
1960   *Archaeology in the Holy Land.* 3rd ed. New York: Praeger.
1979   *Archaeology in the Holy Land.* 4th ed. London: Ernest Benn.

Kenyon K. M., and T. A. Holland
1983   *Excavations at Jericho: The Pottery Phases of the Tell and Other Finds 5.* London: British School of Archaeology in Jerusalem.

Koeppel, R.
1940   *Teleilat Ghassul* II. Rome: Pontifical Biblical Institute.

Leonard, A. K.
1992   *The Jordan Valley Survey, 1953: Some Unpublished Soundings Conducted by James Mellaart.* Annual of the American Schools of Oriental Research 50. E. M. Meyers and W. G. Dever, eds., Winona Lake, IN: Eisenbrauns.

Levy, T. E., D. Alon, P. Smith, Y. Yekutieli, Y. Rowan, P. Goldberg, N. Porat, E. C. M. van den Brink A. J. Witten, J. Golden, C. Grigson, L. Dawson, A. Holl, J. Moreno, and M. Kersel
1997   Egyptian-Canaanite Interaction at Nahal Tillah, Israel (ca. 4500-3000 B.C.E.): An Interim Report on the 1994-1995 Excavations. *Bulletin of American Schools of Oriental Research* 307:1-52.

Loud, G.
1948   *Megiddo II: Seasons of 1935-1939.* Chicago: University of Chicago Press.

Lovell, J.
1999   The Late Neolithic and Chalcolithic Periods in the Southern Levant: New Data from the Site of Teleilat Ghassul, Jordan. Ph. D. dissertation, University of Sydney.

Lovell, J., Z. Kafafi, and G. Dollfus
1997   A Preliminary Note on the Ceramics from the Basal Levels of Abu Hamid. Pp. 395-417 in H. G. K. Gebel, Z. Kafafi, and G. O. Rollefson, eds. *The Prehistory of Jordan, II: Perspectives from 1997.* Studies in Early Near Eastern Production, Subsistence, and Environment 4. Berlin: Ex Oriente.

Macdonald, E.
1932   Prehistoric Fara. Pp. 1-21 in *Beth-Pelet* II. London: British School of Archaeology in Egypt.

Maeir, A. M.
1997   The Material Culture of the Central Jordan Valley during the Middle Bronze II period: Pottery and Settlement Patterns. Ph. D. dissertation, Hebrew University of Jerusalem.

Mallon, A.
1932   La civilisation du IIIe millénaire dans la Vallée du Jourdain. *Syria* 13:333-44.

Mallon, A. S. J., S. J. Koeppel, and R. Neuville
1934   *Teleilat Ghassul* I. Rome: Pontifical Biblical Institute.

Macalister, R. A. S.
1902   Report on the Excavation of Gezer. *Palestine Exploration Fund Quarterly Statement* (for 1902) 35:347-63.
1912   *The Excavation of Gezer I-III* London: John Murray.

Mazar, A.
1993   Beth-Shean: Tel Beth-Shean and the Northern Cemetery. Pp. 214-23 in E. Stern, ed. *The New Encyclopedia of Archaeological Excavations in the Holy Land 1-4.* Jerusalem: Israel Exploration Society.
1994   Tel Bet She'an-1992/1993. *Excavations and Surveys in Israel* 14:56-60.

Mazar, A., A. Ziv-Esudri, and A. Cohen-Weinberger
2000   Pp. 255-78 in G. Philip and D. Baird, eds. *Breaking with the Past: Ceramics and Change in the Early Bronze Age of the Southern Levant.* Sheffield: Sheffield Academic Press.

McNicoll, A. W., P. C. Edwards, J. Hanbury-Tenison, J. B. Hennessy, T. F. Potts, H. R. Smith, A. Wallmsley, and P. Watson
1992   *Pella in Jordan* 2. Mediterranean Archaeology Supplement 2. Sydney: Meditarch.

Mellaart, J.
1956   The Neolithic Site of Ghrubba. *Annual of the Department of Antiquities of Jordan* 3:24-40.

Meyerhof, E. L.
1989   *The Bronze Age Necropolis at Kibbutz Hazorea, Israel.* British Archaeological Reports, International Series 534. Oxford: British Archaeological Reports.

Milevski, I.
1992   Nota sobre sistemas de almacenamiento en Palestina y el Próximo Oriente. *Aula Orientalis* 10:69-85.

de Miroschedji, P.
1971   *L'époque pré-urbaine en Palestine.* Cahiers de la Revue Biblique 13. Paris: Gabalda.

de Miroschedji, P., and M. Sadek
2000   Tell es-Sakan 2000. *Orient Express* 2000(4):97-101.

Moore, A. M. T.
1973   The Late Neolithic in Palestine. *Levant* 5:36-68.

Orni, E., and E. Efrat
1980   *Geography of Israel.* 4th rev. ed. Jerusalem: Israel Universities Press.

Parr, P. J.
1956   A Cave at Arqub el Dhahr. *Annual of the Department of Antiquities of Jordan* 3:61-73.
2000   Proto-Urban Jericho: The Need for Reappraisal. Pp. 389-98 in L. E. Stager, J. A. Greene, and M. D. Coogan, eds. *The Archaeology of Jordan and Beyond: Essays in Honor of James A. Sauer*, Winona Lake, IN: Eisenbrauns.

Petrie, W. M. F.
1891   Chronology of Pottery. *Palestine Exploration Fund Quarterly Statement for 1891*:68.
1921   *Corpus of Prehistoric Pottery and Palettes.* London: Bitish School of Archaeology in Egypt.

Perrot, J.
1972   Préhistoire Palestinienne—prémices. Columns 286-446 in L. Pirot, A. Robert, H. Cazelles, and A. Feuillet, eds. *Dictionnaire de la bible. Supplément, Vol. 8*. Paris: Letouzey et Ané.
1993   'Enan. Pp. 389-392 in E. Stern, ed. *The New Encyclopedia of Archaeological Excavations in the Holy Land 1-4.* Jerusalem: Israel Exploration Society.

Perrot, J., and D. Ladiray
1980   *Tombes à ossuaires de la région côtière palestinienne au IVe millénaire avant l'ère chrétienne.* Mémoires et travaux du Centre de Recherches Préhistoriques Français de Jérusalem 1. Paris: Association Paléorient.

Rollefson, G. O.
1998   `Ain Ghazal (Jordan): Ritual and Ceremony III. *Paléorient* 24:43-58.

Rollefson, G. O., Z. Kafafi, and A. H. Simmons
1990   The Neolithic Village of `Ain Ghazal, Jordan: Preliminary Report on the 1998 Season. Pp. 95-116 in W. E. Rast, ed. *Preliminary Reports of ASOR Sponsored Excavations 1982-89.* BASOR Supplement No. 27.

Rollefson, G. O., A. H. Simmons, and Z. Kafafi
1992 Neolithic Cultures at 'Ain Ghazal, Jordan. *Journal of Field Archaeology* 19:443-70.

Rowe, A.
1930 *The Topography and History of Beth-Shan with Details of the Egyptian and Other Inscriptions Found on the Site.* Philadelphia: University of Pennsylvania Museum.

Roux, V., and M-A. Courty
1997 Les bols élaborés au tour d'Abu Hamid: rupture technique au 4e millénaire avant J.-C. dans le Levant-Sud. *Paléorient* 23(1):25-43.

Sadeh, S., and R. Gophna
1991 Observations on the Chalcolithic Ceramic Sequence in the Jordan Valley. *Mitekufat Haeven* 4:135-48.

Shalev, S., and E. Braun
1997 The Metal Ojects from Yiftahel II. Pp.92-96 in E. Braun *Yiftahel: Salvage and Rescue Excavations at a Prehistoric Village in Lower Galilee, Israel.* Jerusalem: Israel Antiquities Authority.

Stekelis, M.
1972 *The Yarmukian Culture of the Neolithic Period.* Jerusalem: Magnes.

Tal, O.
1998 Tel Hamid: The Lower Terrace. *Hadashot Arkheologiyot* 108:125-27 (Hebrew).

Tsuneki, A., and Y. Miyake
1998 *Excavations at Tell Umm Qseir in the Middle Khabur Valley, North Syria: Report of the 1996 Season.* Studies for West Asian Archaeology, 1.Tsukuba, Japan: University of Tsukuba.

Tubb, J. N., G. Dorrell, and F. J. Cobbing
1996 Interim Report on the Eighth Season (1995) of Excavations at Tell es-Sa'idiyeh, Jordan. *Palestine Exploration Quarterly* 128:16-40.
1997 Interim Report on the Ninth Season (1996) of Excavations at Tell es-Sa'idiyeh, Jordan. *Palestine Exploration Quarterly* 129:54-77.

van den Brink, E. C. M., Y. Rowan, and E. Braun
1999 Pedestaled Basalt Bowls of the Chalcolithic: New Variations. *Israel Exploration Journal* 49(3-4):161-83.

de Vaux, R., and A. M. Steve
1948 La seconde campagne de fouilles à Tell el-Far'ah, près Naplouse. *Revue Biblique* 55:544-80.
1949 La deuxième campagne de fouilles à Tell el-Far'ah, près Naplouse. *Revue Biblique* 56:102-38.

de Vaux, R.
1961 Les fouilles de Tell el-Far'ah: rapport préliminaire sur les 7e, 8e, 9e campagnes, 1958-1960. *Revue Biblique*: 68:557-92.

Winn, S. M. M., and J. Yakar
1984 The 1982 Excavations at Tel Kinrot: The Early Bronze Age Settlement. *Tel Aviv* 11:20-47.

Wheeler, M.
1982 Loomweights and Spindle Whorls. Pp. 622-37 in K. Kenyon and T. A. Holland. *Excavations at Jericho IV.* London: British School of Archaeology in Jerusalem.
1983 Greenstone Amulets. Pp. 781-87 in K. Kenyon and T. A. Holland. *Excavations at Jericho V.* London: British School of Archaeology in Jerusalem.

Wright, G. E.
1937 *The Pottery of Palestine From the Earliest Times to the End of the Early Bronze Age.* New Haven, CT: American Schools of Oriental Research.
1958 The Problem of the Transition between the Chalcolithic and Bronze Ages. *Eretz-Israel* 5: 37*-45*.
1971 The Archaeology of Palestine from the Neolithic through the Middle Bronze Age. *Journal of the American Oriental Society* 91:276-93.

Yannai, E., and Z. Grosinger
2000 Preliminary Summary of Early Bronze Age Strata and Burials at 'Ein Assawir, Israel. Pp. 153-64 in G. Philip and D. Baird, eds. *Breaking with the Past: Ceramics and Change in the Early Bronze Age of the Southern Levant.* Sheffield: Sheffield Academic Press.

Yannai, E., Z. Horovitz, D. Lazar, Z. Grosinger, and F. Sontag
In press *'Ein Assawir: Excavations at a Protohistoric Site and Adjacent Cemeteries in the Coastal Plain, Israel.* IAA Reports. Jerusalem: Israel Antiquities Authority.

Figures

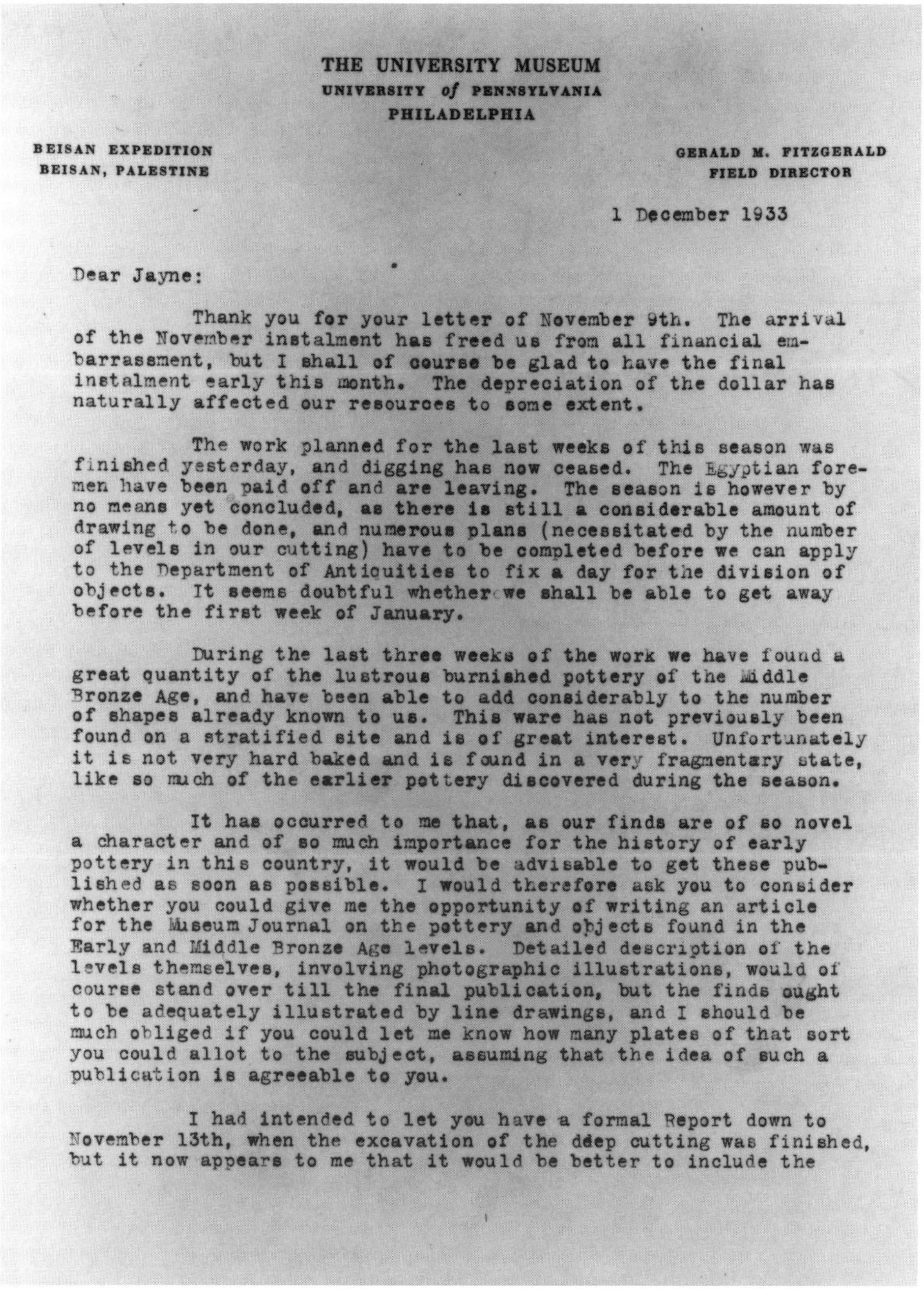

THE UNIVERSITY MUSEUM
UNIVERSITY *of* PENNSYLVANIA
PHILADELPHIA

BEISAN EXPEDITION
BEISAN, PALESTINE

GERALD M. FITZGERALD
FIELD DIRECTOR

1 December 1933

Dear Jayne:

Thank you for your letter of November 9th. The arrival of the November instalment has freed us from all financial embarrassment, but I shall of course be glad to have the final instalment early this month. The depreciation of the dollar has naturally affected our resources to some extent.

The work planned for the last weeks of this season was finished yesterday, and digging has now ceased. The Egyptian foremen have been paid off and are leaving. The season is however by no means yet concluded, as there is still a considerable amount of drawing to be done, and numerous plans (necessitated by the number of levels in our cutting) have to be completed before we can apply to the Department of Antiquities to fix a day for the division of objects. It seems doubtful whether we shall be able to get away before the first week of January.

During the last three weeks of the work we have found a great quantity of the lustrous burnished pottery of the Middle Bronze Age, and have been able to add considerably to the number of shapes already known to us. This ware has not previously been found on a stratified site and is of great interest. Unfortunately it is not very hard baked and is found in a very fragmentary state, like so much of the earlier pottery discovered during the season.

It has occurred to me that, as our finds are of so novel a character and of so much importance for the history of early pottery in this country, it would be advisable to get these published as soon as possible. I would therefore ask you to consider whether you could give me the opportunity of writing an article for the Museum Journal on the pottery and objects found in the Early and Middle Bronze Age levels. Detailed description of the levels themselves, involving photographic illustrations, would of course stand over till the final publication, but the finds ought to be adequately illustrated by line drawings, and I should be much obliged if you could let me know how many plates of that sort you could allot to the subject, assuming that the idea of such a publication is agreeable to you.

I had intended to let you have a formal Report down to November 13th, when the excavation of the deep cutting was finished, but it now appears to me that it would be better to include the

Figure 1.1 Letter from G. M. Fitzgerald to Director of Museum, 1933.

THE UNIVERSITY MUSEUM
UNIVERSITY *of* PENNSYLVANIA
PHILADELPHIA

BEISAN EXPEDITION
BEISAN, PALESTINE

GERALD M. FITZGERALD
FIELD DIRECTOR

the last stage of the work in a single Report, and I will let you have this as soon as possible.

I imagine that you are not at present making any plans for the resumption of digging next year.

We have had a few showers and the weather has turned extremely cool; the chillier members of the expedition are shivering night and day.

Yours sincerely,

Gerald M. Fitzgerald

Figure 1.1 cont.

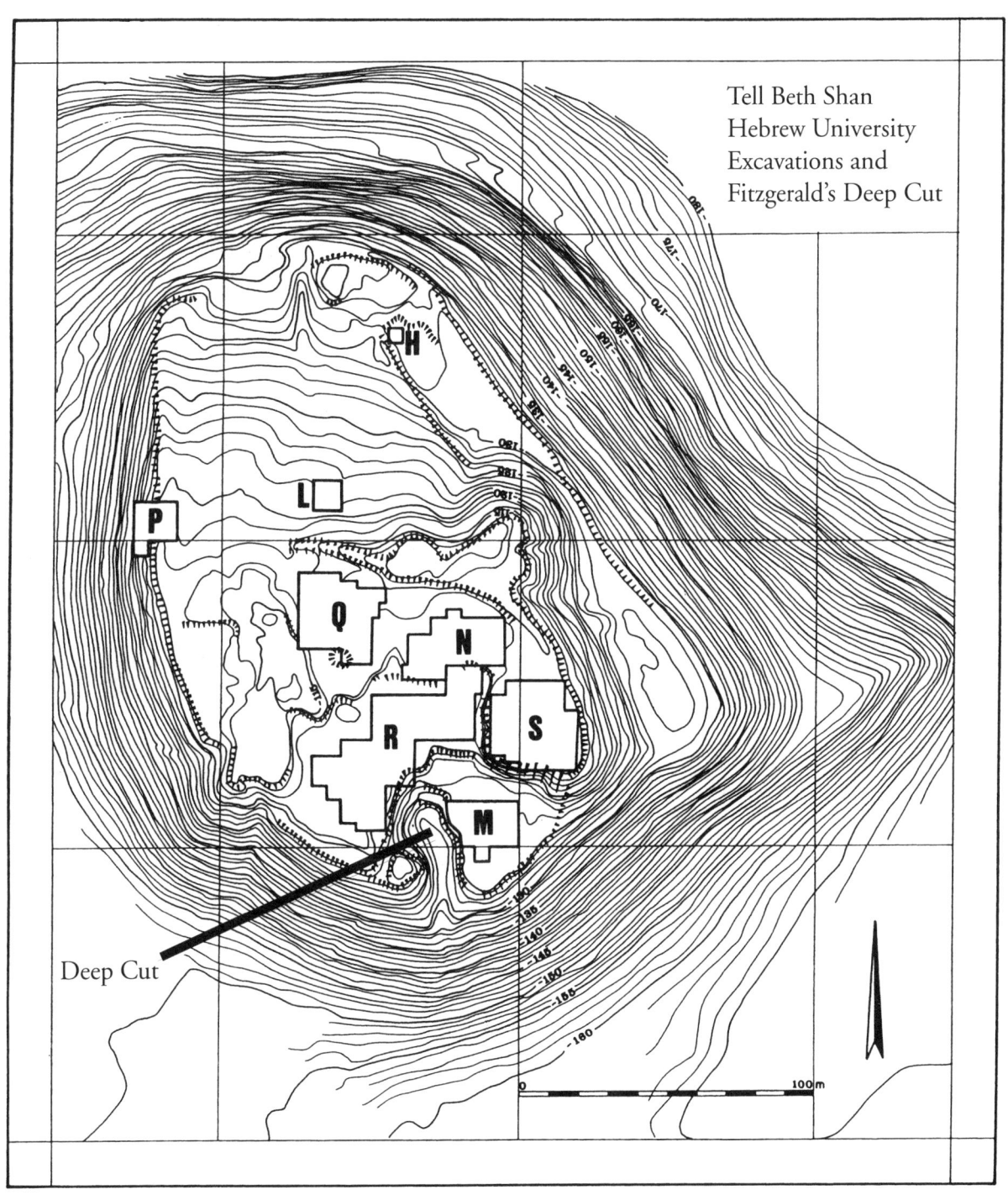

Figure 1.2 Topographic plan of Tell Beth Shan with excavation areas. Courtesy of A. Mazar and the Institute of Archaeology, The Hebrew University of Jerusalem.

Figure 1.3 Northwest Area of Level XII, looking north with the very top of the Deep Cut in the foreground.

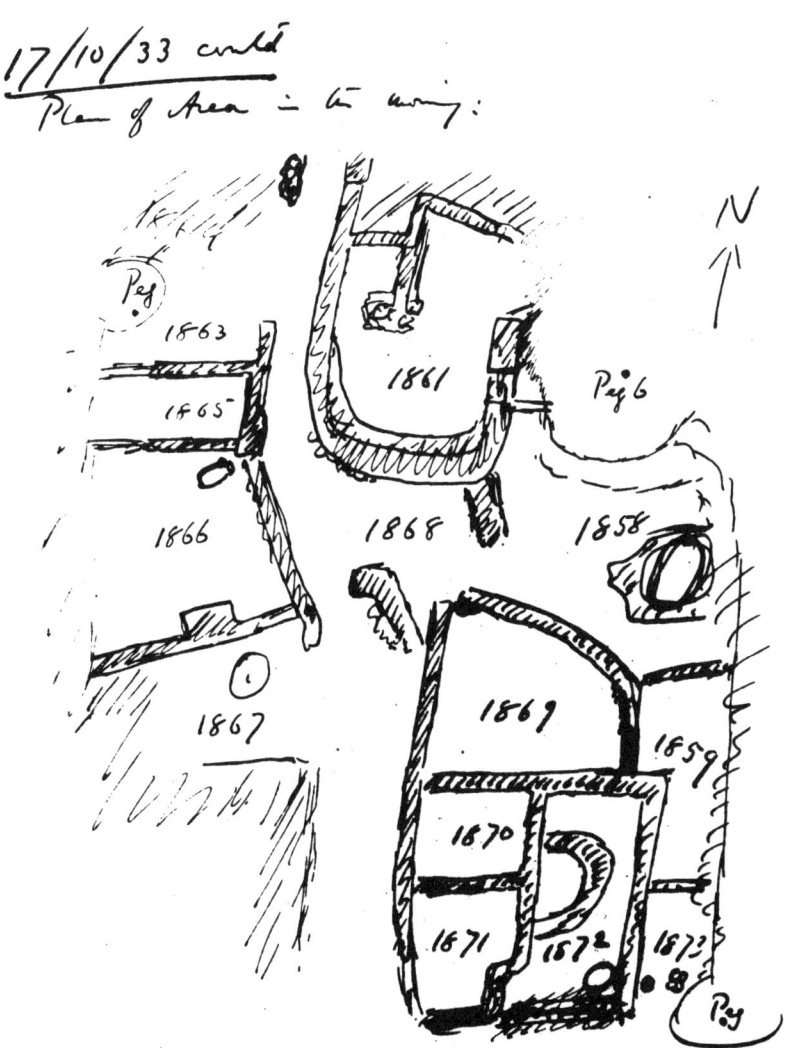

Figure 1.4 Page 252 from FitzGerald's 1933 field diary.

Figure 1.5 The expedition's permanent camp ca. 1924. Note the tell in the right middle ground behind the dig house.

Figure 1.6 The staff of the 1933 season (FitzGerald is center; others are unidentified).

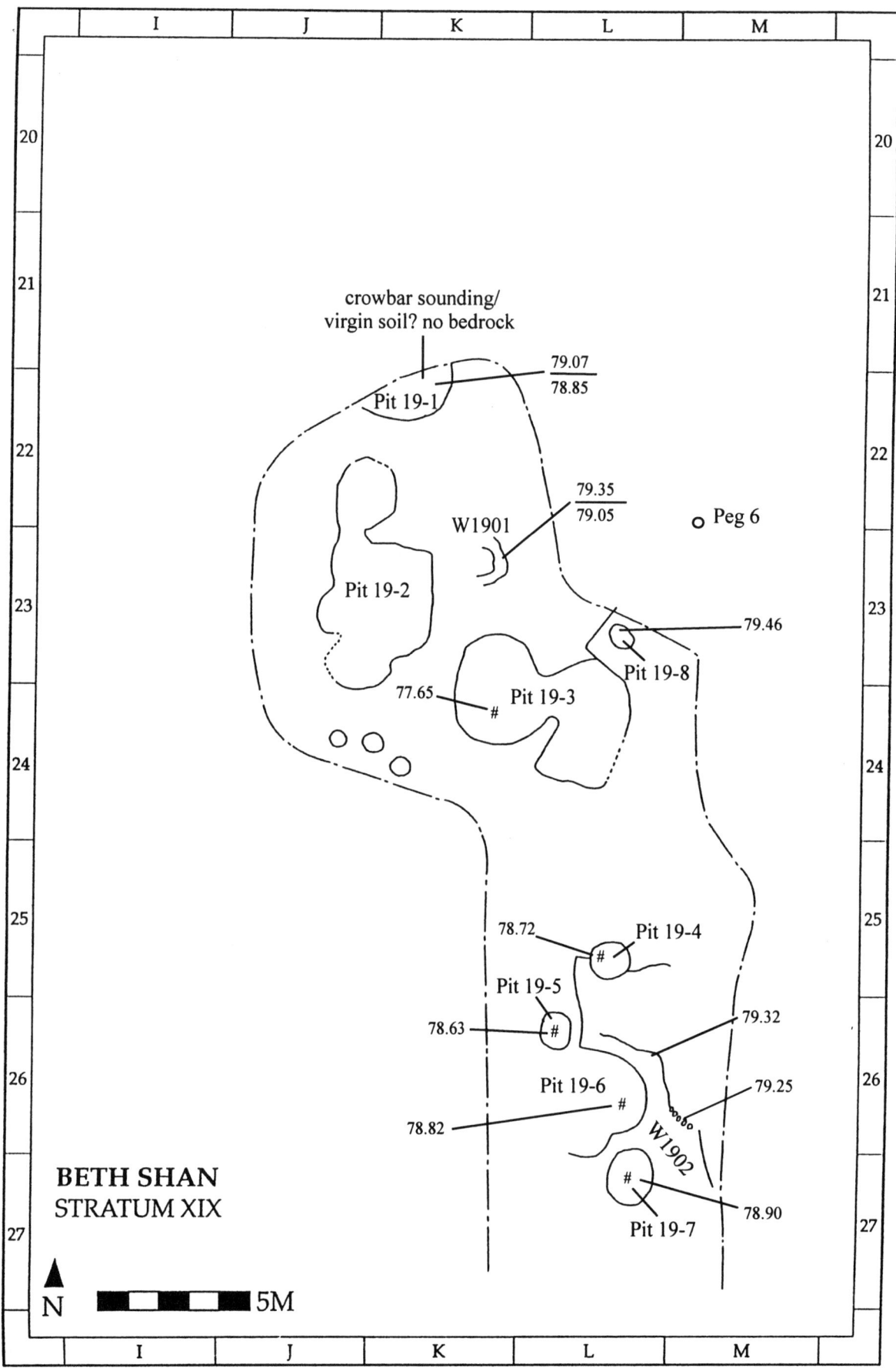

Figure 2.1 Plan of Stratum XIX.

Figure 2.2 Close-up view of Pit 19-2 (Stratum XIX) (Field Neg. #2925).

Figure 2.3 Close-up view of Pit 19-3 (Stratum XIX) (Field Neg. #2923).

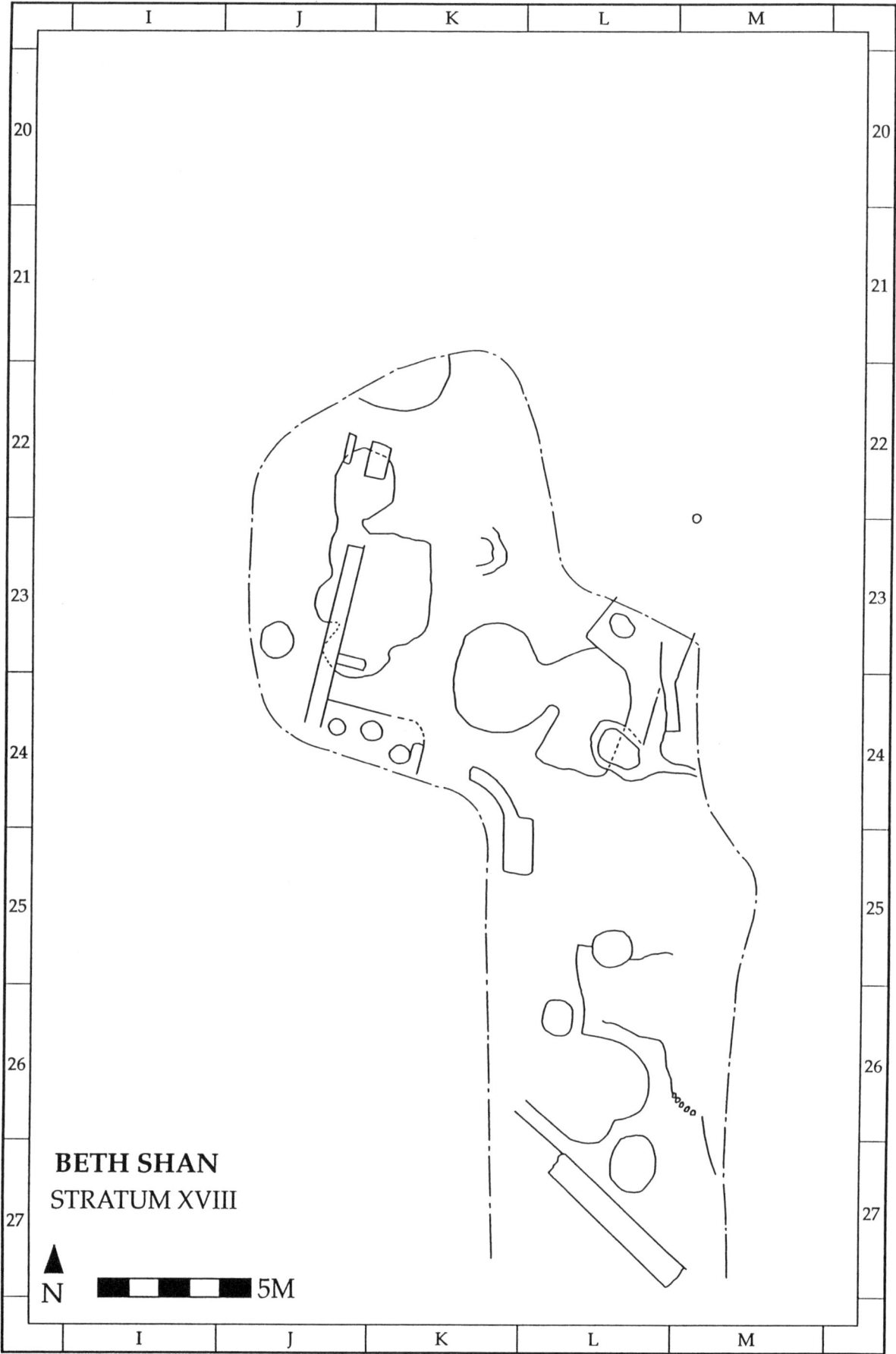

Figure 2.4 FitzGerald's Plan of Level XVIII.

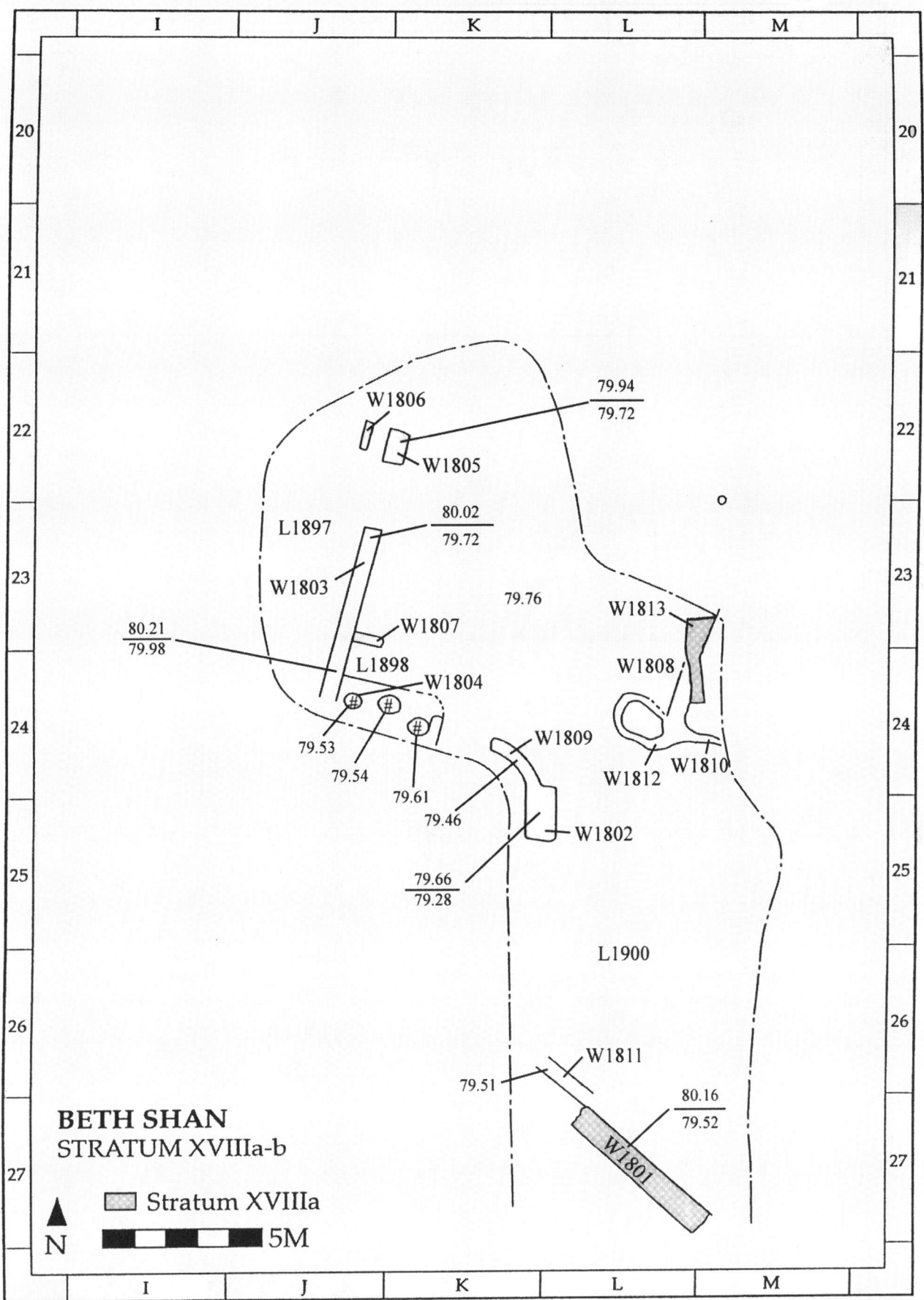

Figure 2.5 Annotated Plan of Stratum XVIII b-a.

Figure 2.6 View of structures of Stratum XVIII, facing south (Field Neg. #2924).

Figure 2.7 View of Strata XVIII with the partially excavated pits of Stratum XIX (Field Neg. #2922B).

Figure 2.8 Close-up of Room 1897. Stratum XVIII with pits of Stratum XIX in the foreground (Field Neg. #2922A).

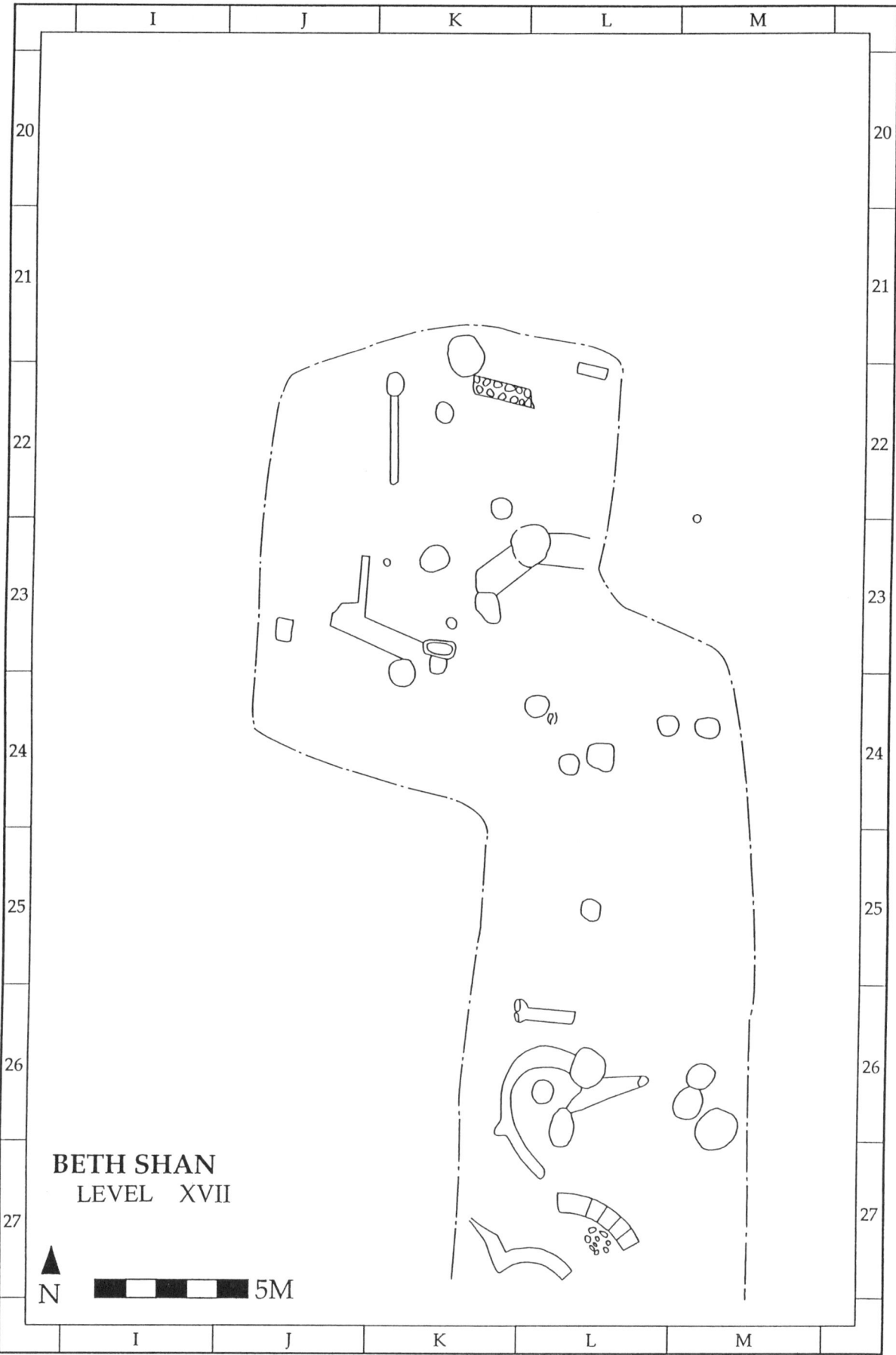

Figure 2.9 FitzGerald's Plan of Level XVII.

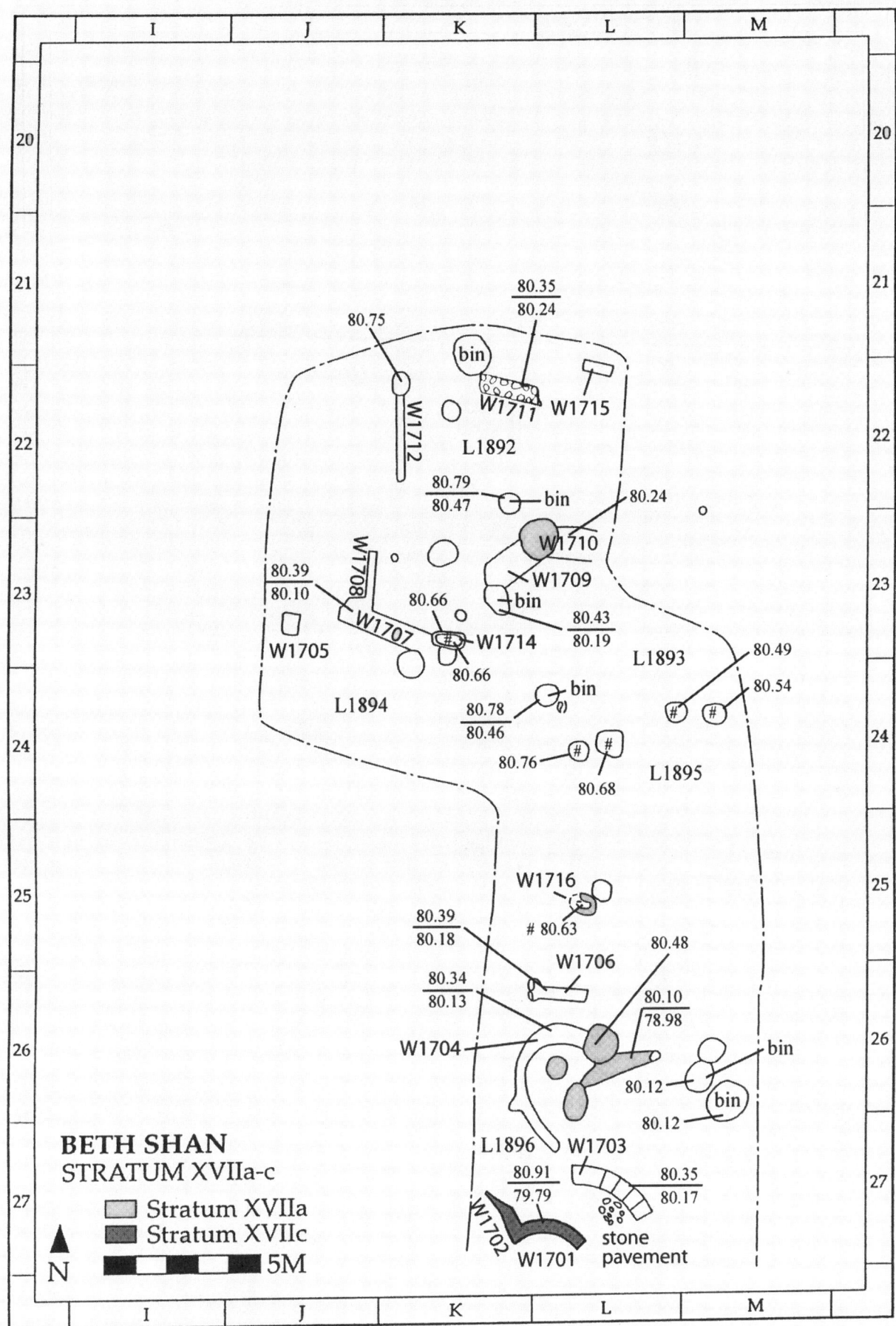

Figure 2.10 Annotated Plan of Stratum XVII, phases c-a.

Figure 2.11 Detail of Stratum XVII, facing north (Field Neg. #2917).

Figure 2.12 Detail of Room 1893 (Stratum XVII) (Field Neg. #2912).

Figure 2.13 "Plano-convex" bricks from Stratum XVII (Field Neg. #2920).

Figure 2.14 Detail of Wall 1704, facing north northwest (Stratum XVII) (Field Neg. #2918).

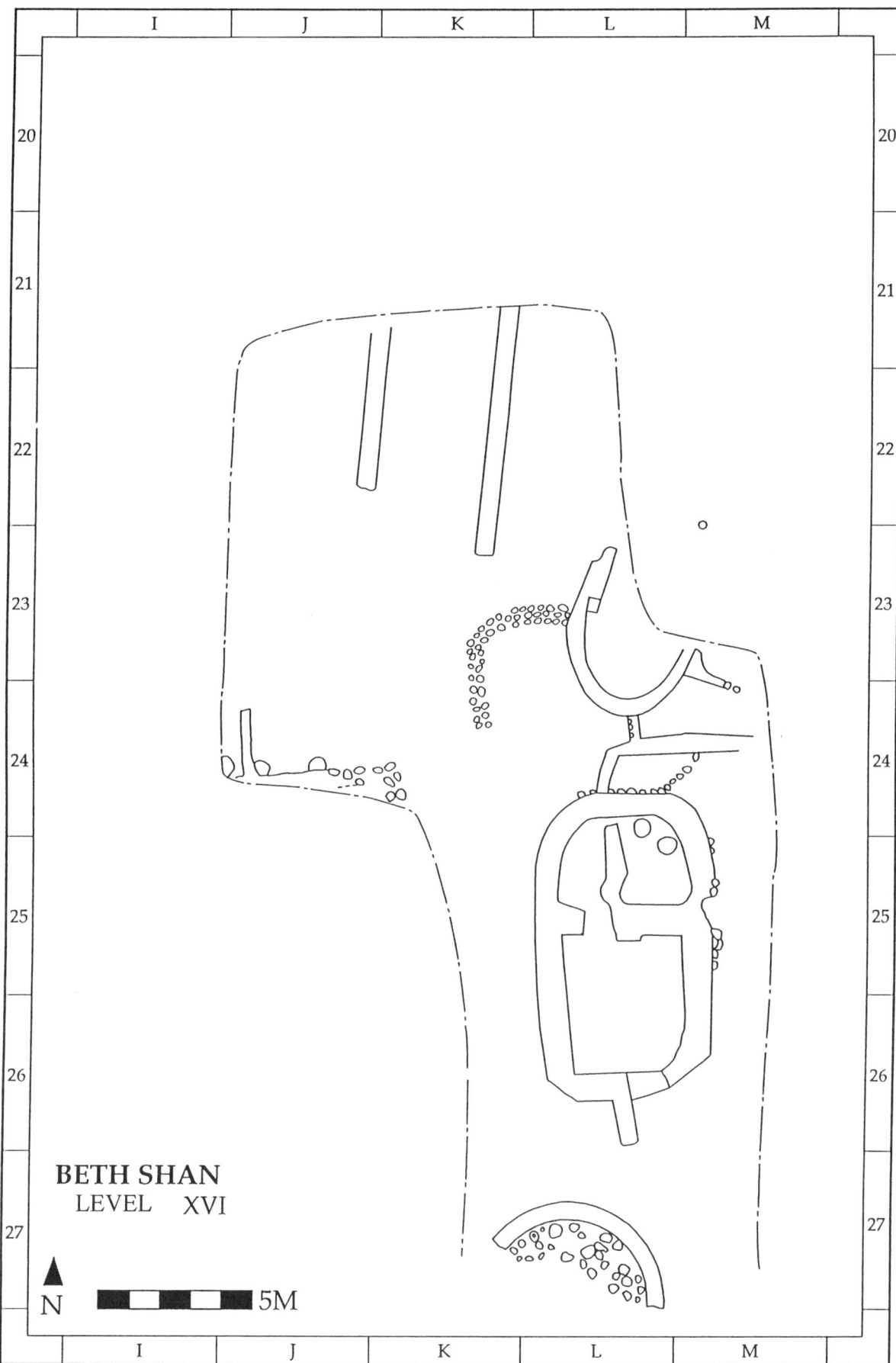

Figure 2.15 FitzGerald's Plan of Level XVI.

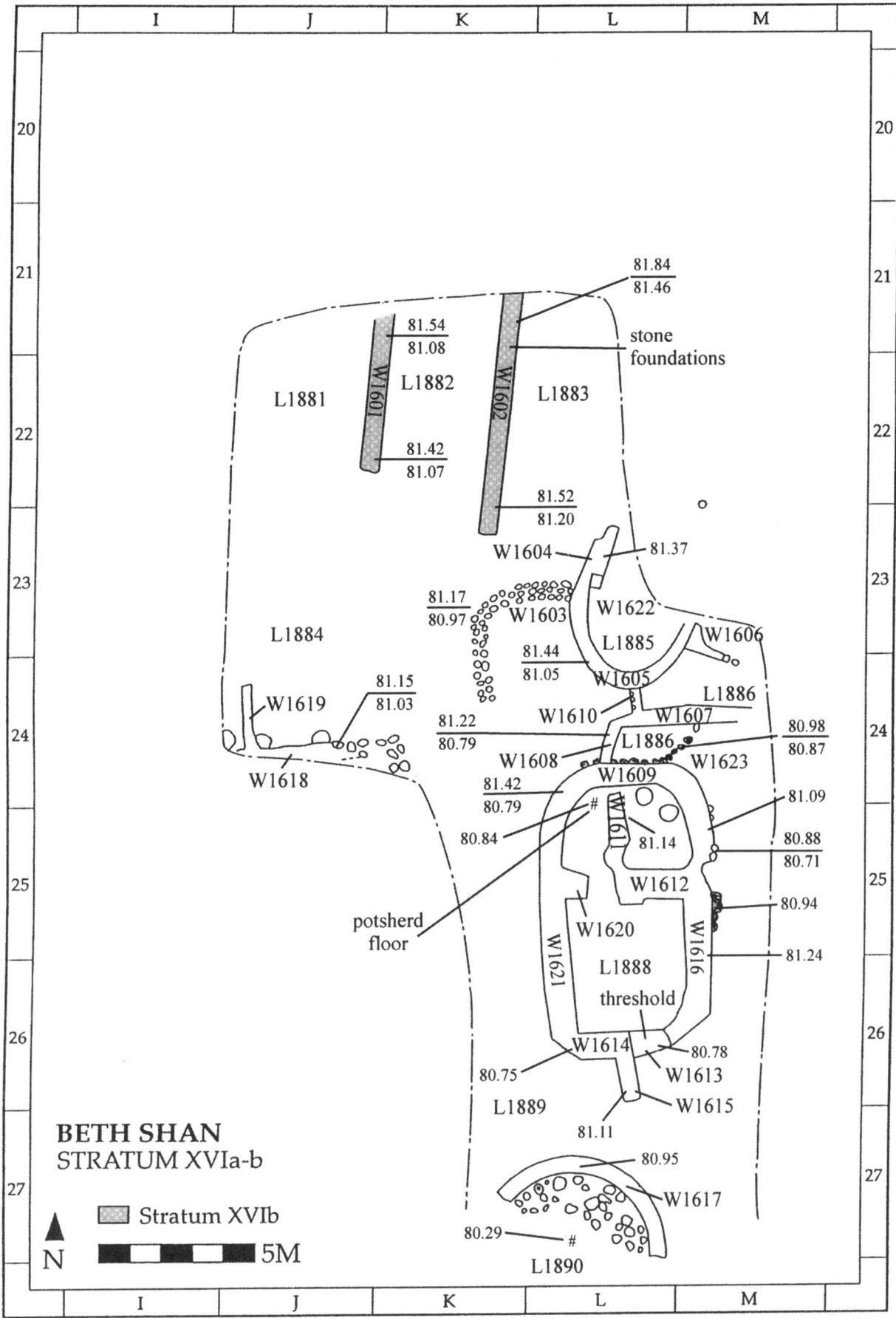

Figure 2.16 Annotated Plan of Stratum XVI, phases b-a.

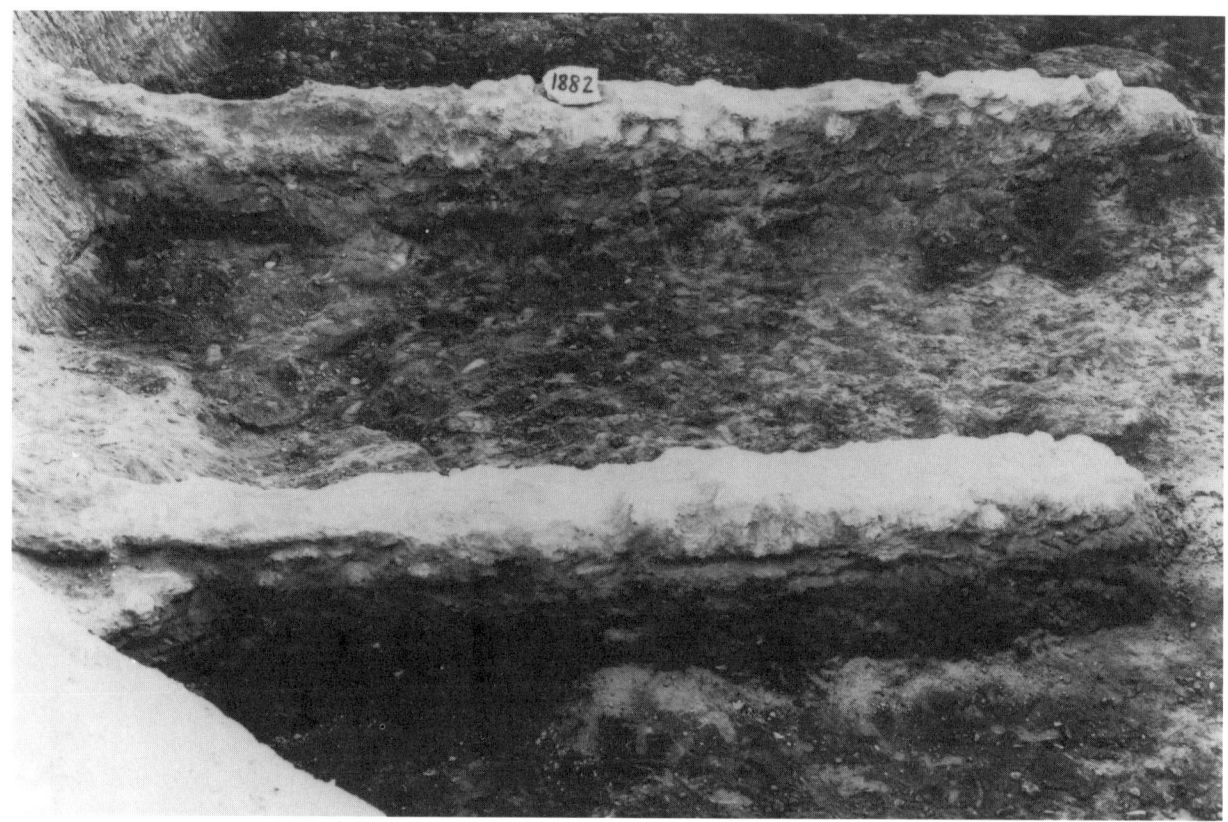

Figure 2.17 Detail of Room 1882 (Stratum XVI) (Field Neg. #2906).

Figure 2.18 Detail of Rooms 1885 and 1886 (Stratum XVI) (Field Neg. #2903).

Figure 2.19 View of the curvilinear house of Stratum XVI (Field Neg. #2901).

Figure 2.20 Potsherd floor in Room 1887 (Stratum XVI) (Field Neg. #2902).

Figure 2.21 Detail of Room 1890, facing south (Stratum XVI) (Field Neg. #2905).

Figure 2.22 Detail of Walls 1618 and 1619 (Stratum XVI) (Field Neg. #2904).

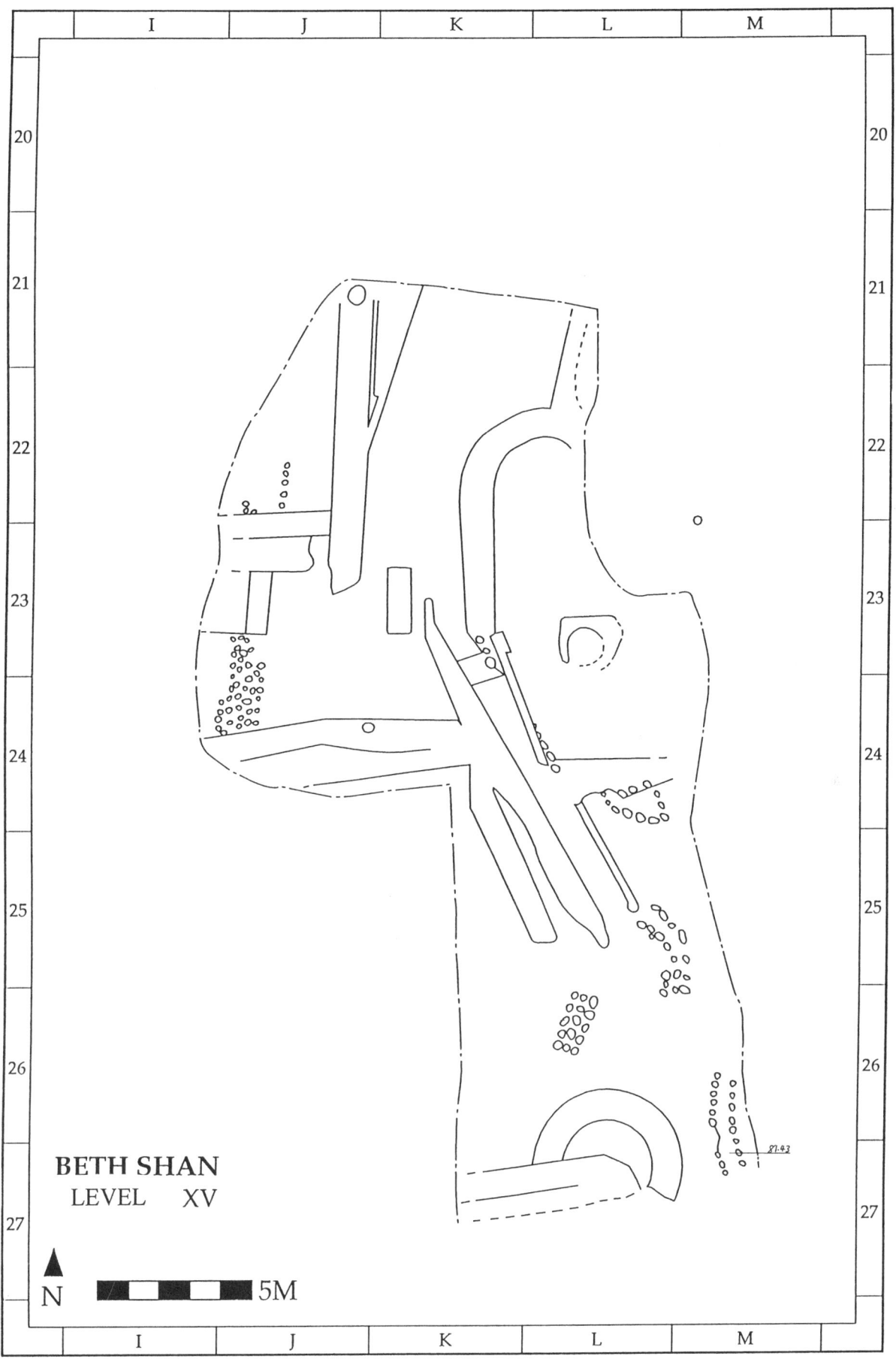

Figure 2.23 FitzGerald's Plan of Level XV.

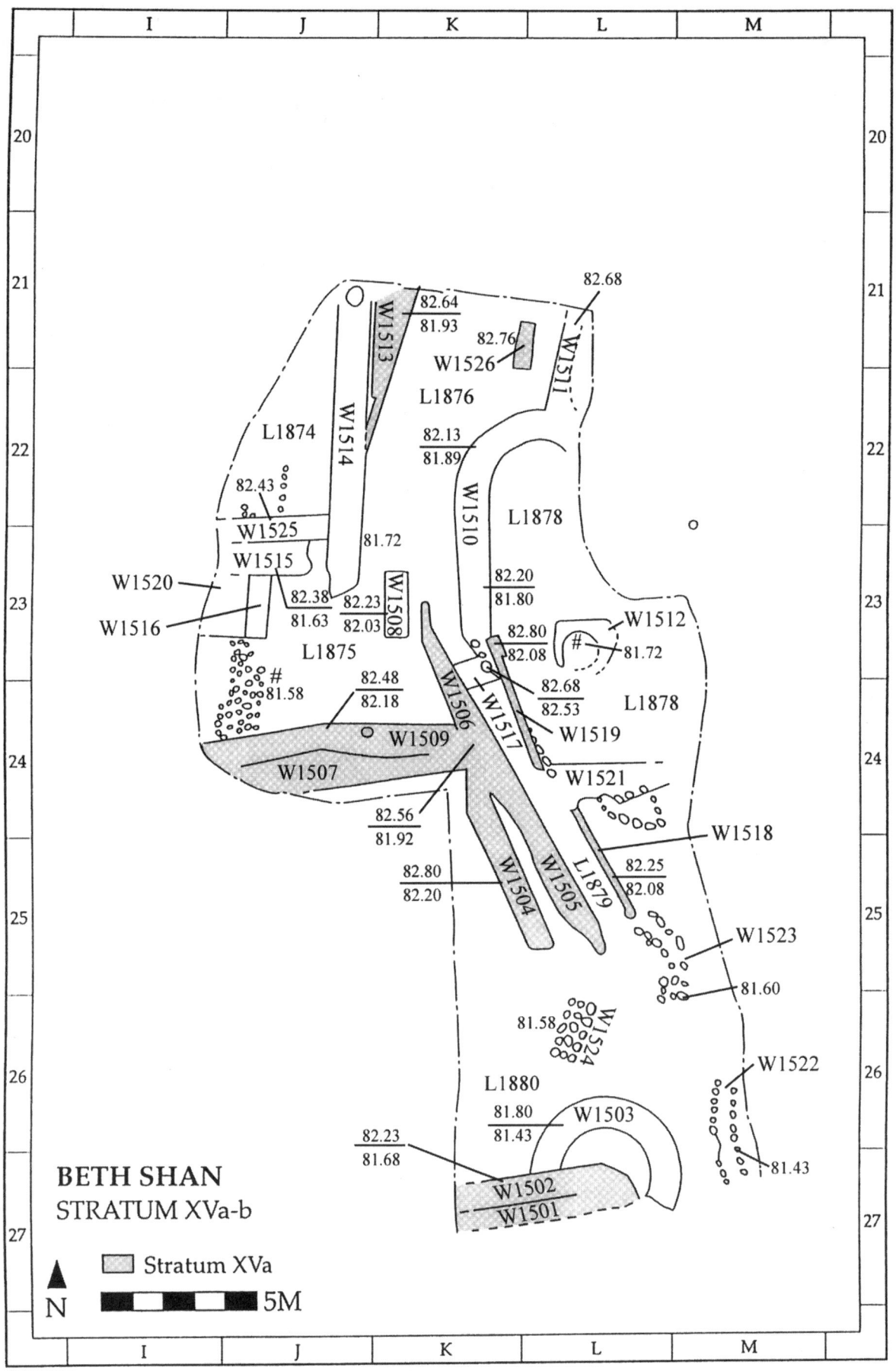

Figure 2.24 Annotated Plan of Stratum XV, phases b-a.

Figure 2.25 Detail of Room 1874 in foreground, facing south (Stratum XV) (Field Neg. #2897).

Figure 2.26 The north end of Stratum XV, facing north. Room 1878 is formed by the curvilinear wall at the right margin of the photo (Field Neg. #2899).

Figure 2.27 Northeast end of the Deep Cut in Stratum XV with curvilinear Room 1878 in background, facing east (Field Neg. #2900).

Figure 2.28 Stratum XV, facing south with Room 1878 in foreground (Field Neg. #2898).

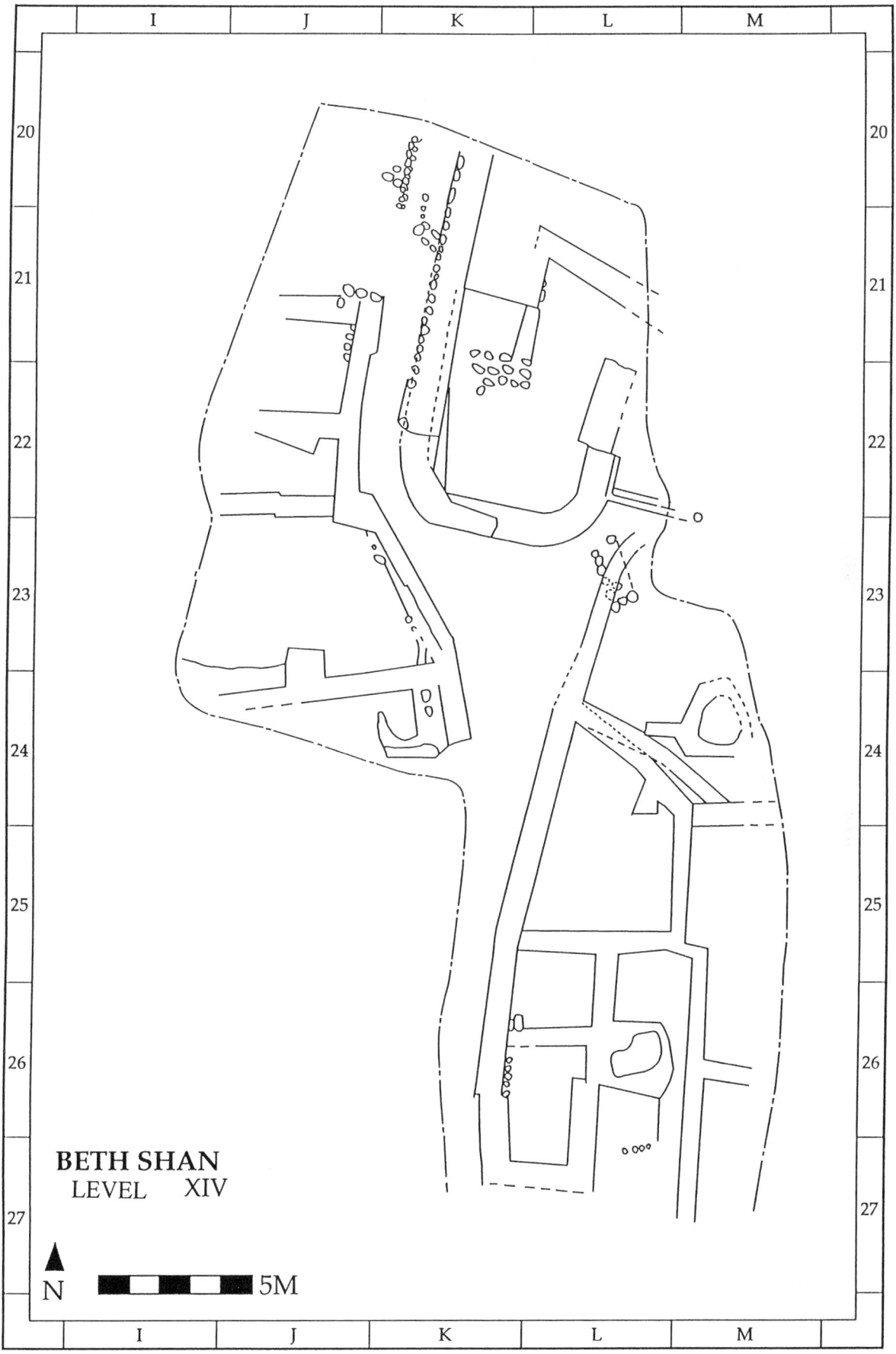

Figure 2.29 FitzGerald's Plan of Level XIV.

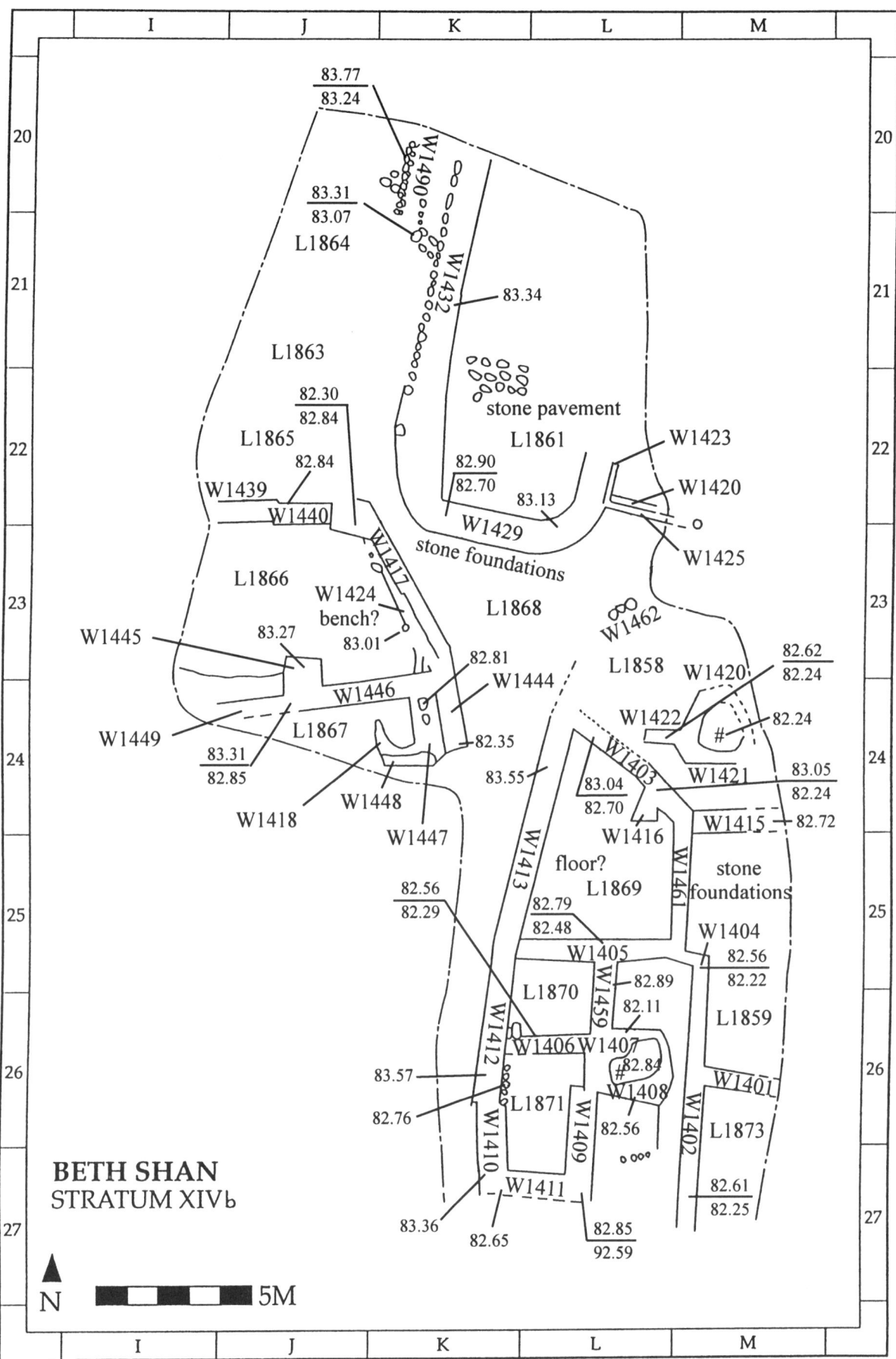

Figure 2.30 Annotated Plan of Stratum XIV, phase b.

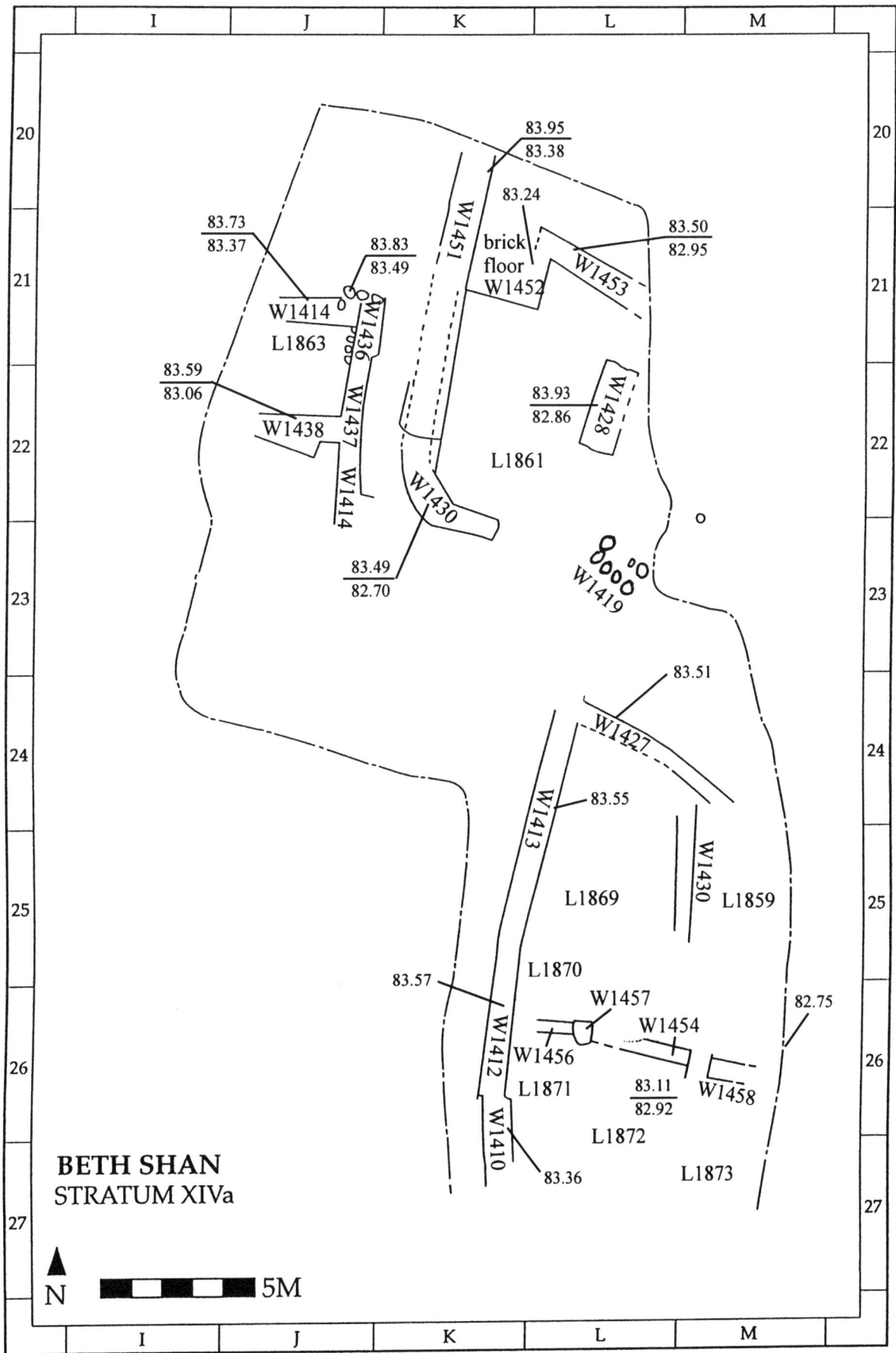

Figure 2.31 Annotated Plan of Stratum XIV, phase a.

Figure 2.32 View of Level XIV (Field Neg. #2894).

Figure 2.33 Detail of the rooms of Level XIV at the south end of the Deep Cut (Field Neg. #2896).

Figure 2.34 View of Rooms 1866 and 1867 (Stratum XIV) (Field Neg. #2884).

Figure 2.35 View of Stratum XIV, facing west. Note the inverted modern basket in the right foreground.

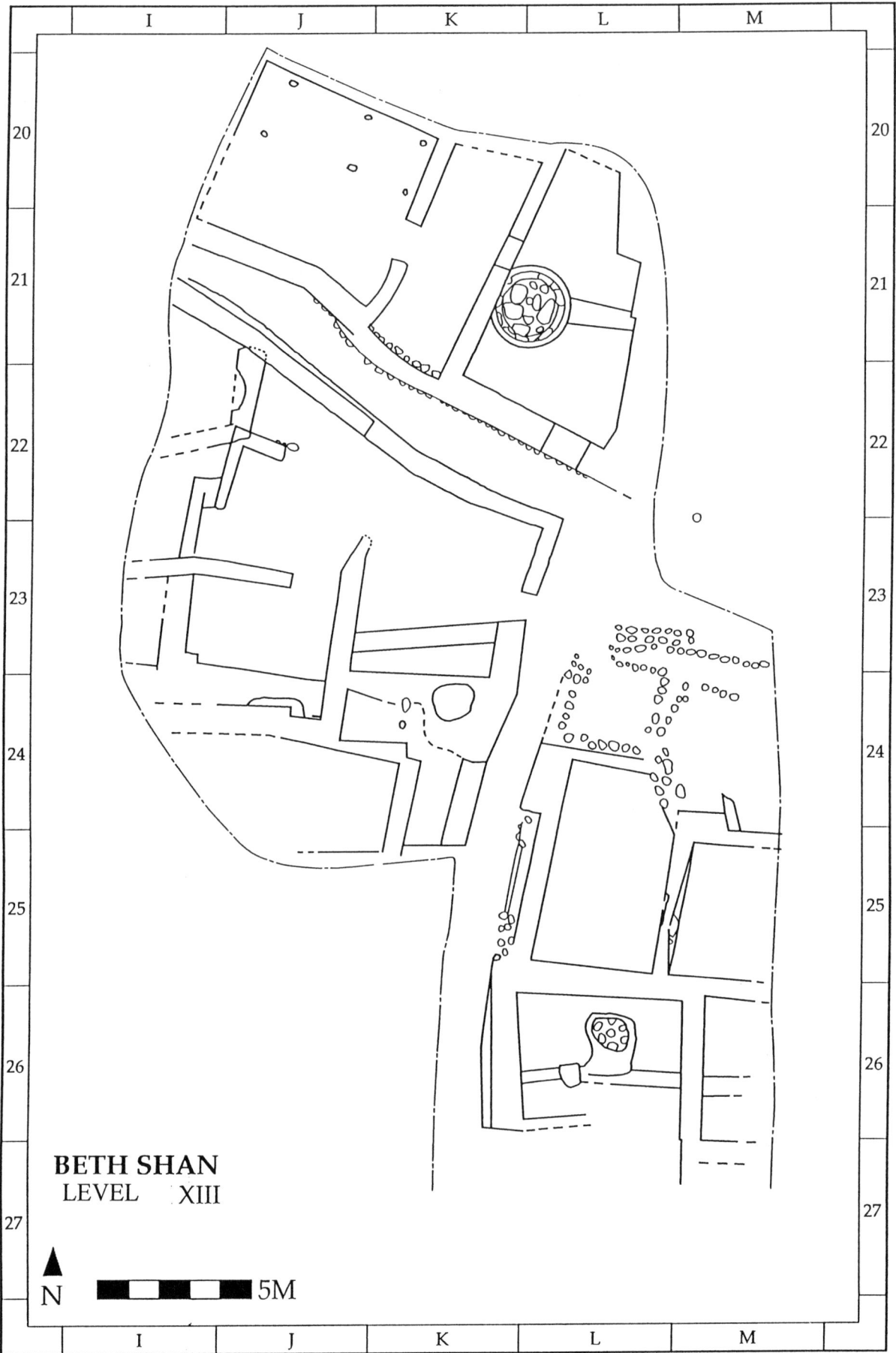

Figure 2.36 FitzGerald's Plan of Level XIII.

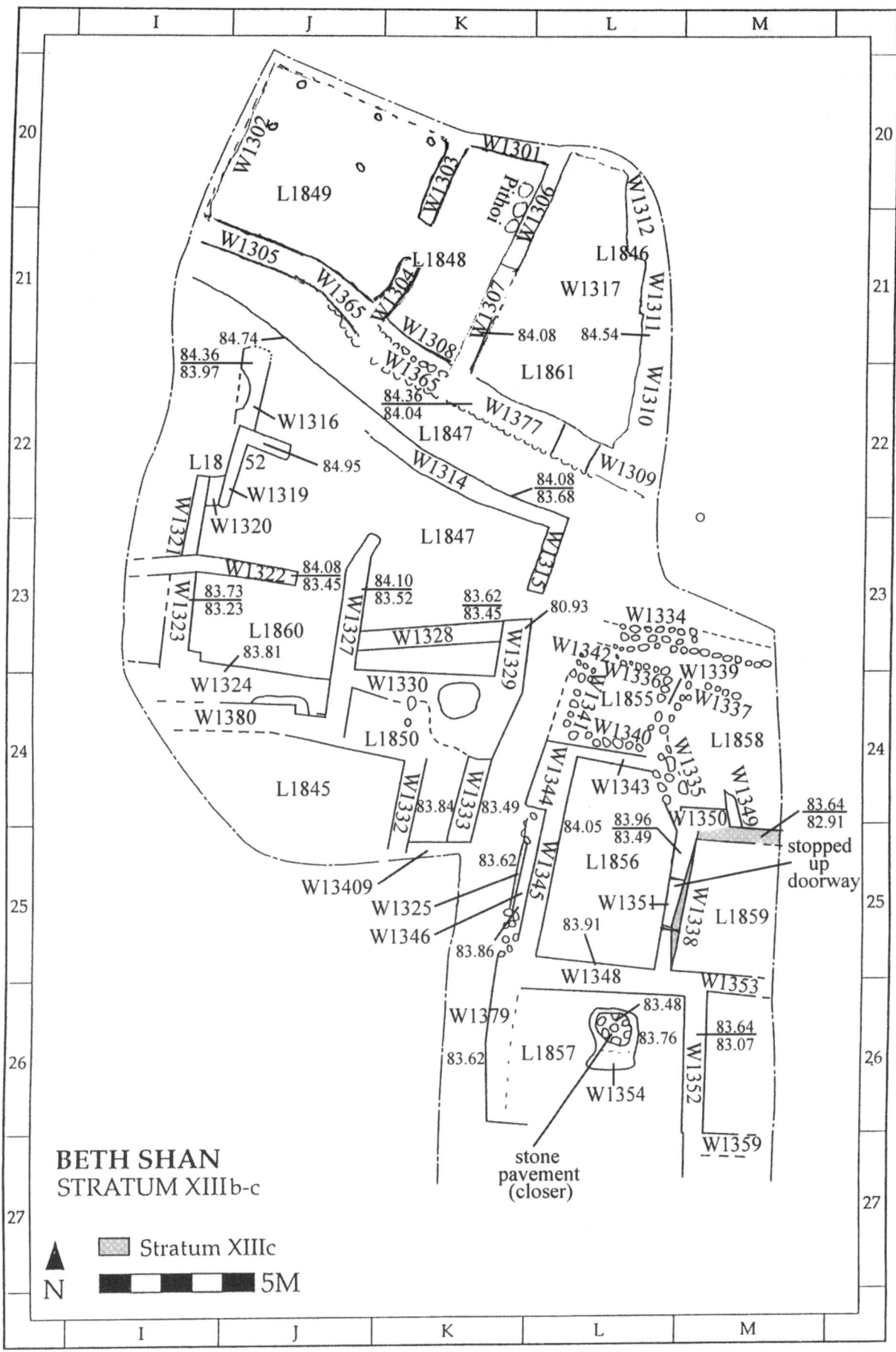

Figure 2.37 Annotated Plan of Stratum XIII, phases b-c.

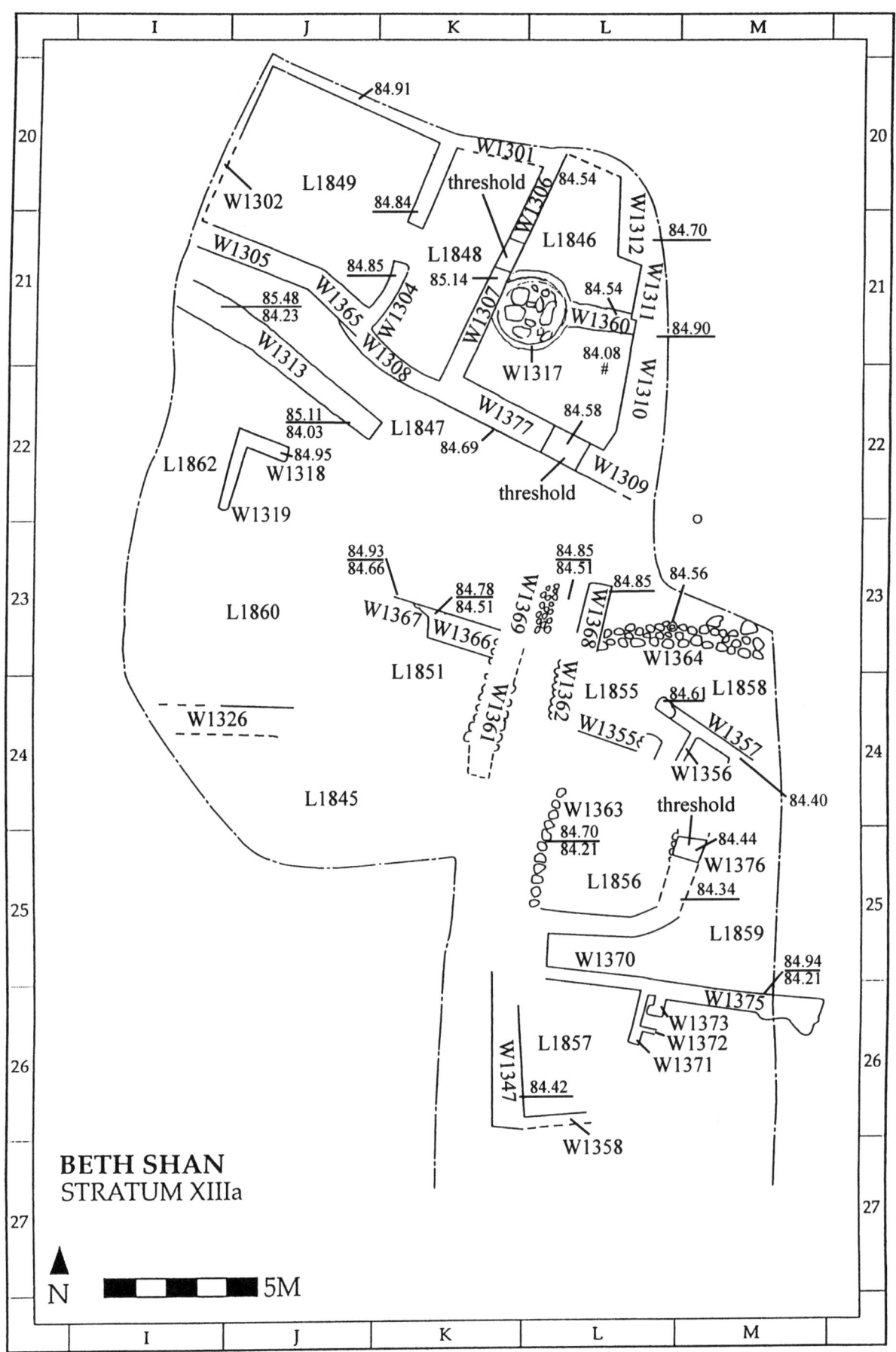

Figure 2.38 Annotated Plan of Stratum XIII, phase a.

Figure 2.39 Detail of Room 1846 (Stratum XIII) (Field Neg. #2872).

Figure 2.40 Northern building in Stratum XIII, facing west (Field Neg. #2873).

Figure 2.41 Mudbricks from Room 1848 (Field Neg. #2893).

Figure 2.42 Detail of a stone-paved bin in Room 1857 (Stratum XIII) (Field Neg. #2885).

Figure 2.43 Detail of pottery *in situ* on the floor of Room 1848 (Stratum XIII) (Field Neg. #2870).

Figure 2.44 East-west lane in the northern precinct of Stratum XIII, facing west (Field Neg. #2871).

Figure 2.45 Room 1856, facing east (Stratum XIII) (Field Neg. #2886).

Figure 2.46 View of buildings in the southeast precinct of Stratum XIII, facing northeast with Stratum XIV buildings below (Field Neg. #2888).

Figure 2.47 View of buildings in the southeast precinct of Stratum XIII, facing south (Field Neg. #2887).

Figure 3.1 Pottery of Stratum XIX.

# on facing page	Museum #	Description	Field #
1	34-21-354	Gray buff outside and in, red paint.	33-11-100a
2	Unknown	Gray buff outside and in, red paint.	Unknown
3	34-21-352	Buff outside and in, red paint.	33-11-77
4	34-21-348	Buff outside and in, red wash outside.	33-11-297
5	34-21-349	Buff pink outside and in.	33-11-99c
6	34-21-356	Brown outside and in.	33-11-93
7	34-21-350	Dark gray outside, orange core, brown inside, fire clouded.	33-11-102a
8	34-21-368	Orange buff outside and in, red slipped.	33-11-97
9	34-21-361	Brown fabric outside, dark gray core, gray inside, red slip outside.	33-11-294b
10	34-21-362	Buff fabric outside and in.	33-11-294c
11	34-21-365	Buff and buff pink, outside and in.	33-11-93 (7)
12	34-21-359	Buff pink, brown paint. Drawing is at 1:2 scale.	33-11-71
13	34-21-366	Dark gray to red outside, gray core, gray inside.	33-11-98a
14	34-21-374	Brown, red outside.	33-11-73b
15	34-21-371	Buff outside and in, red slip.	33-11-74a
16	34-21-372	Buff outside and in, red slip.	33-11-72b

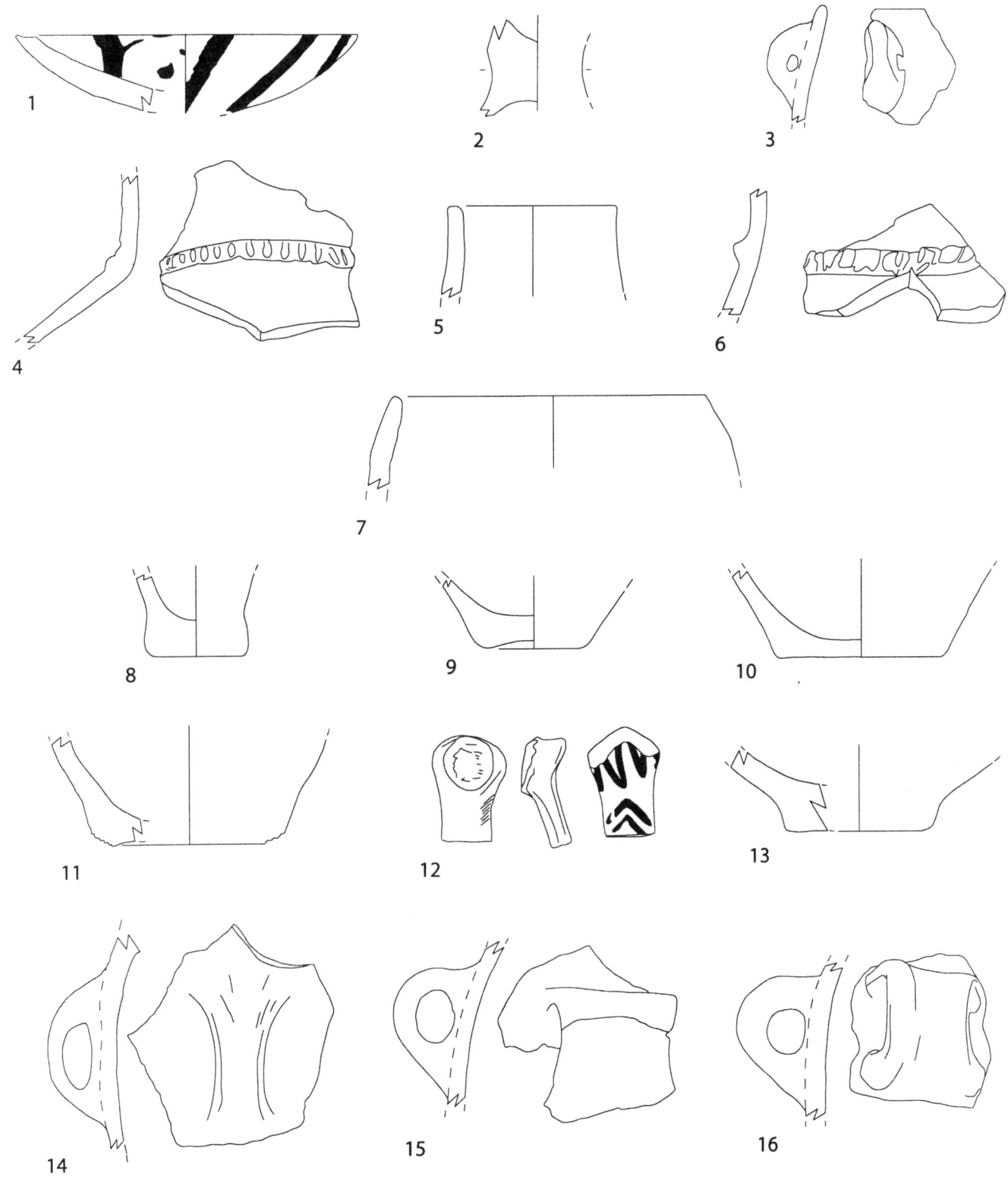

Figure 3.2 Pottery of Stratum XVIII.

# on facing page	Museum #	Description	Field #
1	34-21-247	Buff outside and in.	33-11-152
2	IAA	Buff gray outside and in, red paint.	33-11-245
3	34-21-693	Brown ware, light brown slip, red wash	33-10-371
4	34-21-251	Buff gray outside and in, fire clouded.	33-11-261
5	34-21-219	Gray outside and in, finely levigated, red slip.	33-11-107
6	34-21-220	Gray buff outside and in, red painted.	33-11-178
7	34-21-227	Gray buff outside and in, red painted.	33-11-180
8	34-21-222	Gray buff inside and out, red slip.	33-11-218
9	34-21-201	Gray buff inside and out, red painted.	33-11-220
10	34-21-209	Orange to gray outside, gray core and inside, red painted outside, dripped inside.	33-11-118c
11	34-21-204	Brown and gray outside and in.	33-11-196b
12	34-21-205	Buff inside and out, red paint.	33-11-224b
13	34-21-221	Gray outside and in, red slipped outside and in.	33-11-132a
14	34-21-228	Orange outside and in, red slipped outside and in.	33-11-89

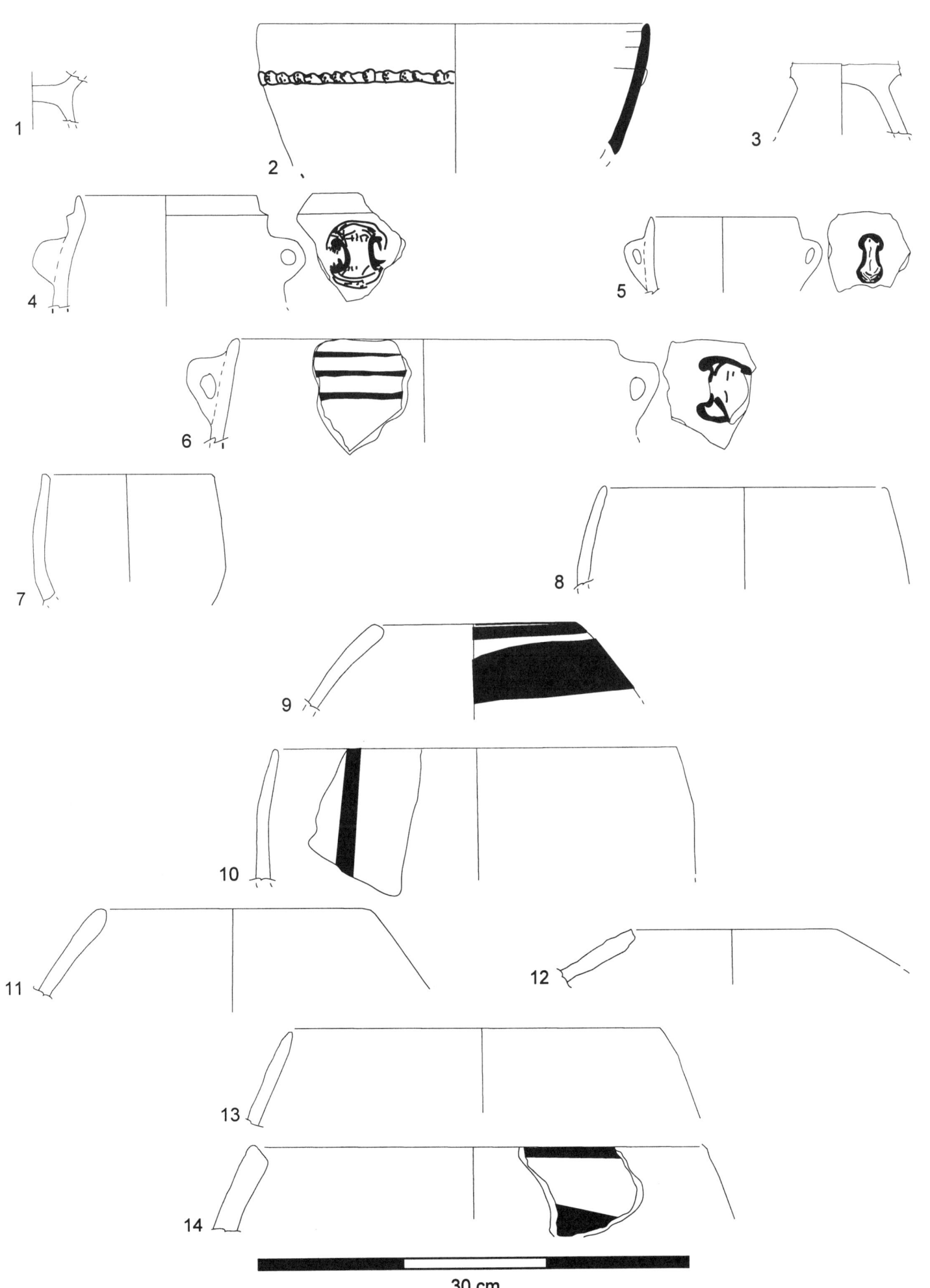

Figure 3.3 Pottery of Stratum XVIII.

# on facing page	Museum #	Description	Field #
1	Unknown	Gray outside and in, red slipped outside and in.	Unknown
2	34-21-223	Gray outside and in, red slipped outside and in.	33-11-140(1)
3	34-21-226	Gray outside and in, red slipped outside and in.	33-11-195
4	34-21-229	Buff outside and in.	33-11-117b
5	34-21-212	Gray outside and in, red painted.	33-11-142c
6	34-21-215	Burnished	33-11-260a
7	34-21-207	Coarse brown ware, light brown slip, red wash.	33-11-192(1)
8	34-21-208	Buff outside and in, red painted.	33-11-179a
9	34-21-210	Gray outside, orange in, red slipped outside.	33-11-160a
10	34-21-211	Gray outside and in, red slipped	33-11-260c
11	34-21-216	Buff outside and in, red slipped.	33-11-121a
12	34-21-313	Gray outside and in, thin black slip, polished.	33-11-123a
13	34-21-199	Brown inside and out, red slip.	33-11-176b
14	34-21-200	Gray outside and in, red slipped outside.	33-11-259
15	34-21-198	Buff to orange outside and in, brown core.	33-11-270

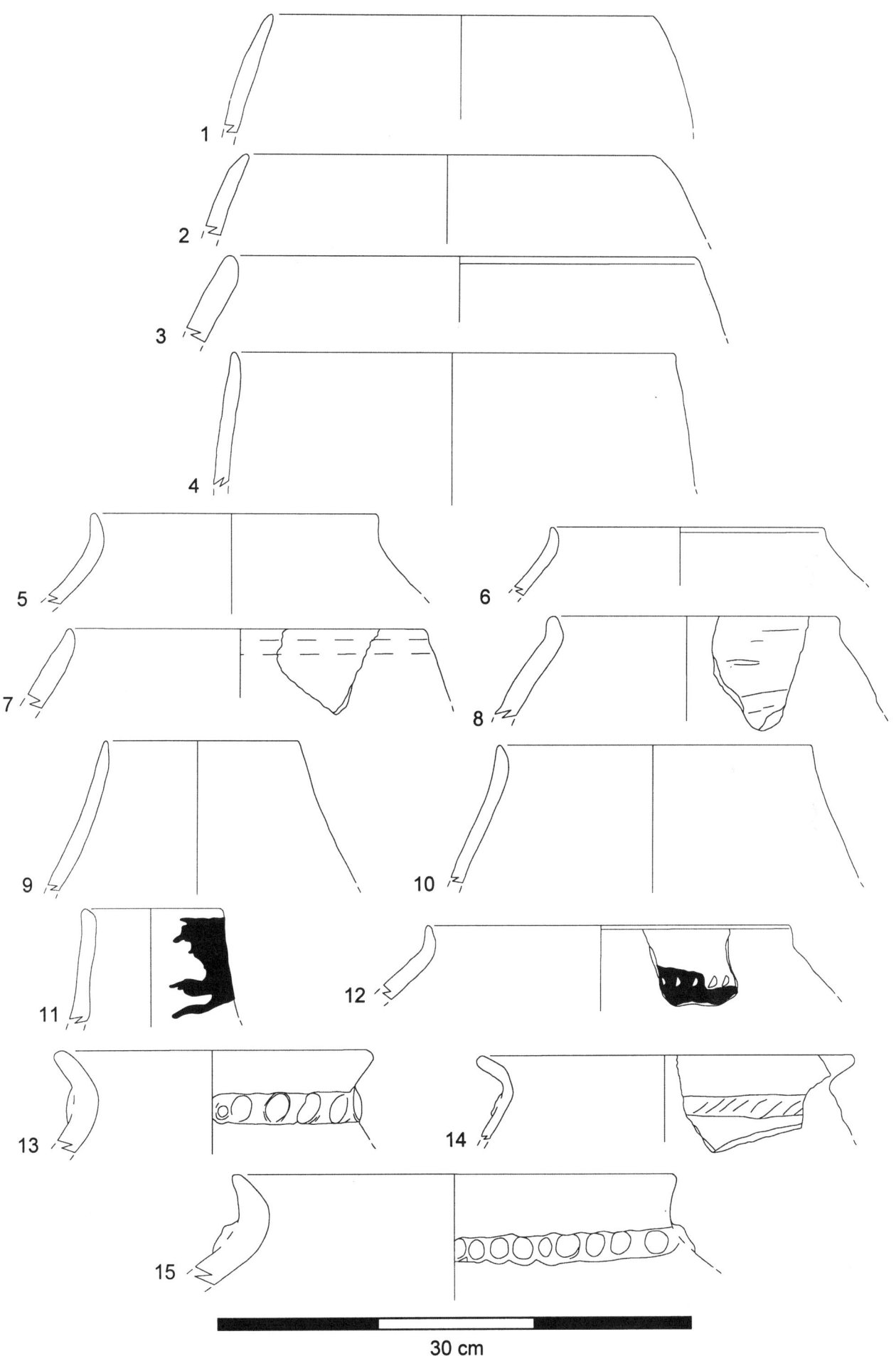

Figure 3.4 Pottery of Stratum XVII.

# on facing page	Museum #	Description	Field #
1	34-21-260	Gray outside and in, red painted.	33-11-197
2	34-21-254	Gray and buff outside and in.	33-11-144
3	34-21-353	Gray and orange outside and in.	33-11-104
4	34-21-255	Gray outside, buff inside, red slipped outside.	33-11-80
5	34-21-371	Gray buff outside and in, red slipped outside.	33-11-74a
6	34-21-253	Buff outside and in.	33-11-202(2)
7	34-21-250	Orange outside and in.	33-11-243
8	34-21-249	Orange outside and in, red slipped outside.	33-11-265a
9	34-21-240	Orange buff outside and in, red slipped outside.	33-11-120b
10	34-21-242	Gray and red outside and inside.	33-11-133
11	34-21-244	Buff pink outside, buff inside.	33-11-156a
12	34-21-241	Buff gray outside and in, gray core.	33-11-227a
13a	34-21-246a	Buff gray outside and in, brown paint.	33-11-191a
13b	34-21-246b	Buff gray outside and in, brown paint.	33-11-191b
14	34-21-235	Buff outside and in, red painted outside.	33-11-266b
15	34-21-233	Buff outside, gray core, buff gray inside, red painted outside.	33-11-199a
16	34-21-230	Buff outside and in, string-cut base.	33-11-200a
17	34-21-237	Brown outside and in, red painted outside.	33-11-199b
18	34-21-231	Buff gray outside and in.	33-11-113a
19	34-21-236	Gray outside and in.	33-11-201a
20	34-21-360	Gray buff outside and inside.	33-11-294a

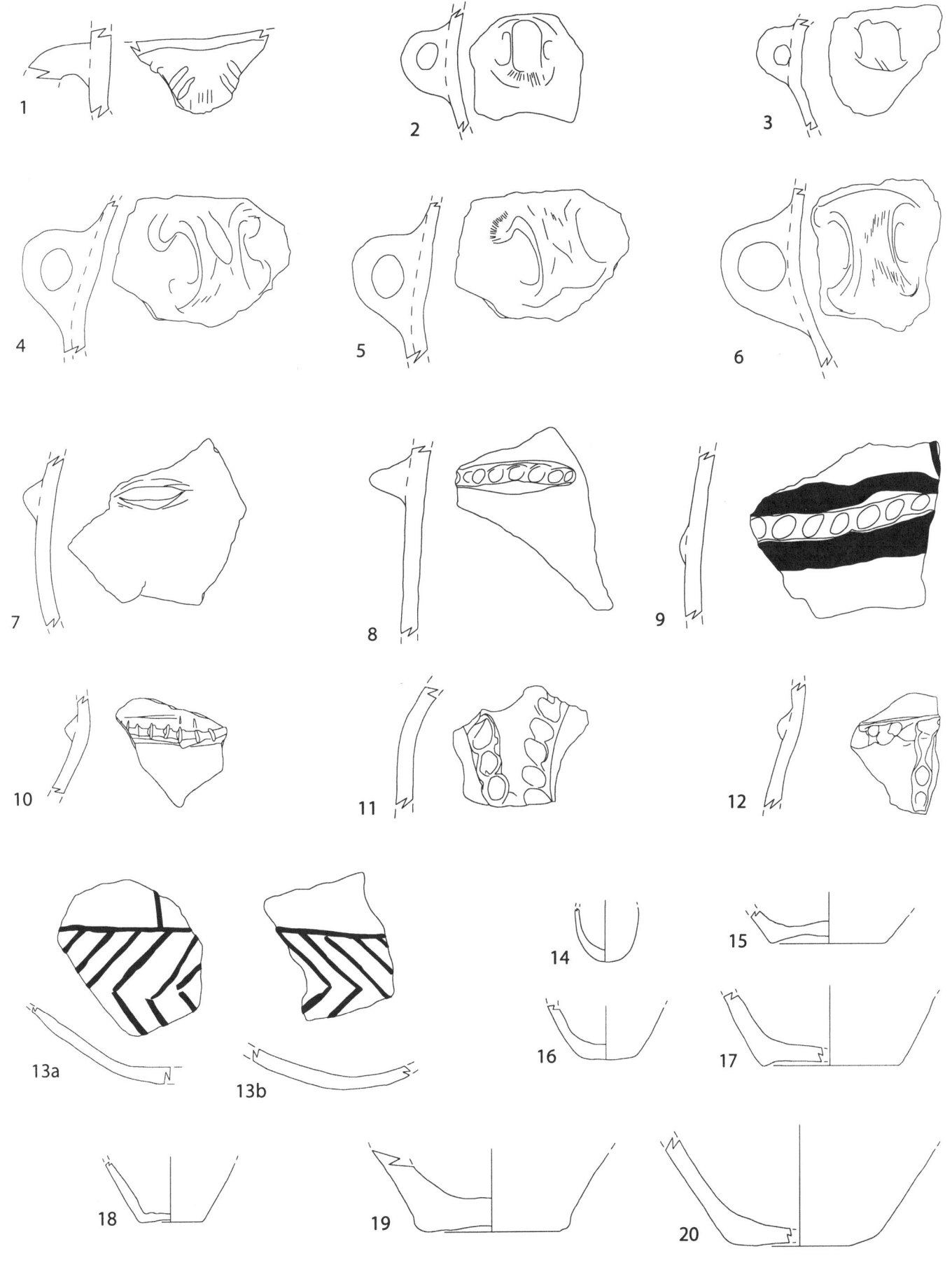

Figure 3.5 Pottery of Stratum XVII.

# on facing page	Museum #	Description	Field #
1	34-21-109	Gray and buff outside and in, burnished outside and in.	33-11-31a
2	34-21-10	Buff orange outside and in, string cut-base.	33-10-1095a
3	34-21-104	Buff outside and in.	33-11-207
4	34-21-110	Gray outside and in, burnished, self slip.	33-11-314a
5	34-21-122	Gray outside and in, red slipped.	33-11-280
6	34-21-121	Gray outside and in.	33-10-1096
7	34-21-106	Gray and pink outside, gray in.	33-10-1101a
8	34-21-248	Buff outside and in.	33-11-161
9	34-21-101	Buff outside and in, red slipped outside.	33-11-206
10	34-21-103	Red outside and in.	33-11-51
11	34-21-98	Buff, gray orange inside, red slipped outside.	33-11-317a
12	34-21-99	Buff gray outside and in, red paint, slash design	33-11-315b
13	34-21-102	Orange outside and in, red slipped outside.	33-11-50
14	34-21-107	Buff outside and inside, red streaky slip	33-11-31b

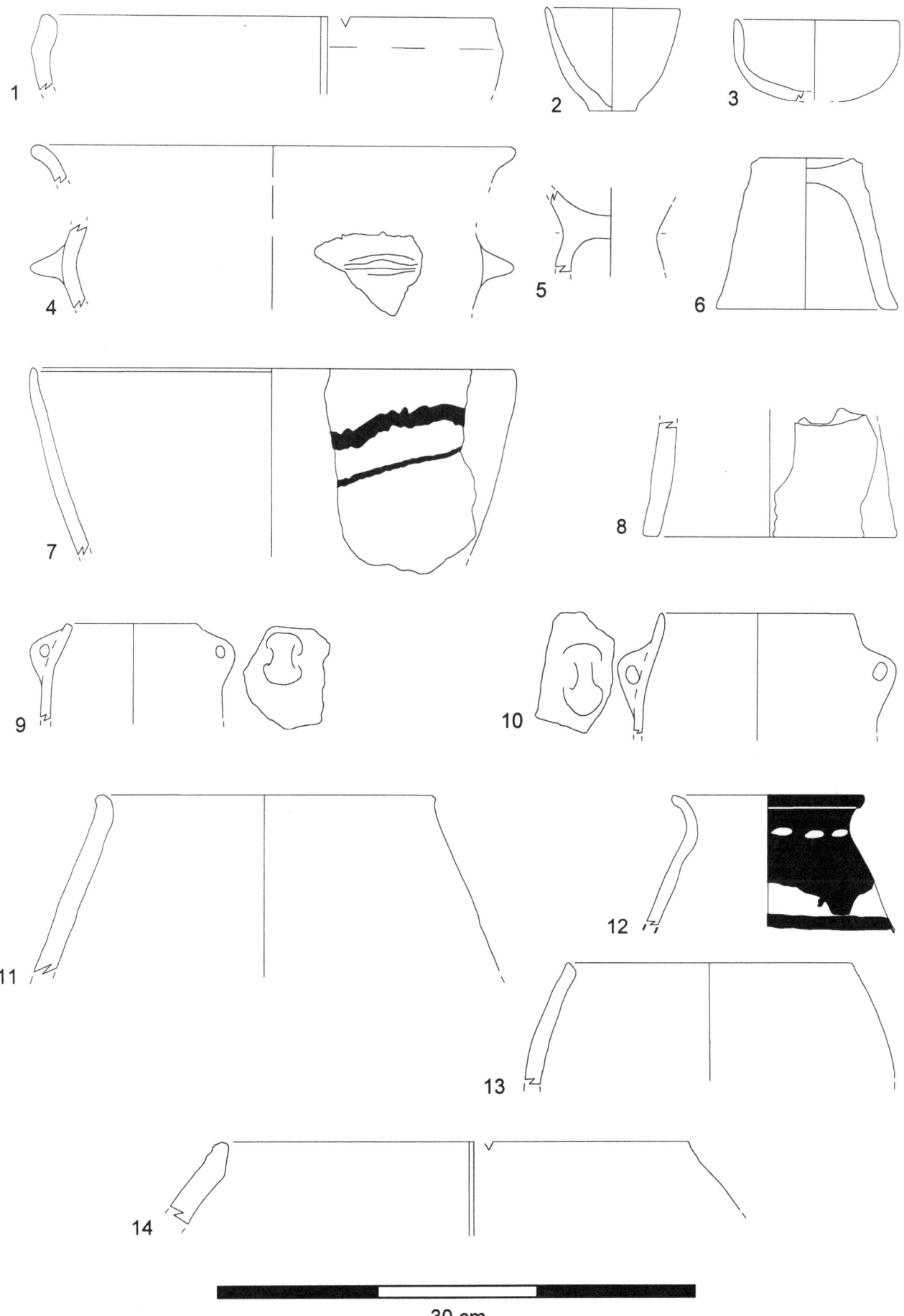

Figure 3.6 Pottery of Stratum XVII.

# on facing page	Museum #	Description	Field #
1	34-21-100	Orange buff outside, gray core, gray outside.	33-10-820
2	34-21-94	Buff outside and in, gray core.	33-11-303b
3	34-21-92	Gray and pink outside and in.	33-11-29
4	34-21-96	Buff brown outside and in.	33-11-281b
5	34-21-93	Buff outside and in, gray core, red painted.	33-11-42a
6	34-21-87	Brown outside and in.	33-10-842a
7	34-21-89	Buff brown outside and in.	33-10-1098b
8	34-21-118	Buff outside and in, red wash.	33-10-1043a

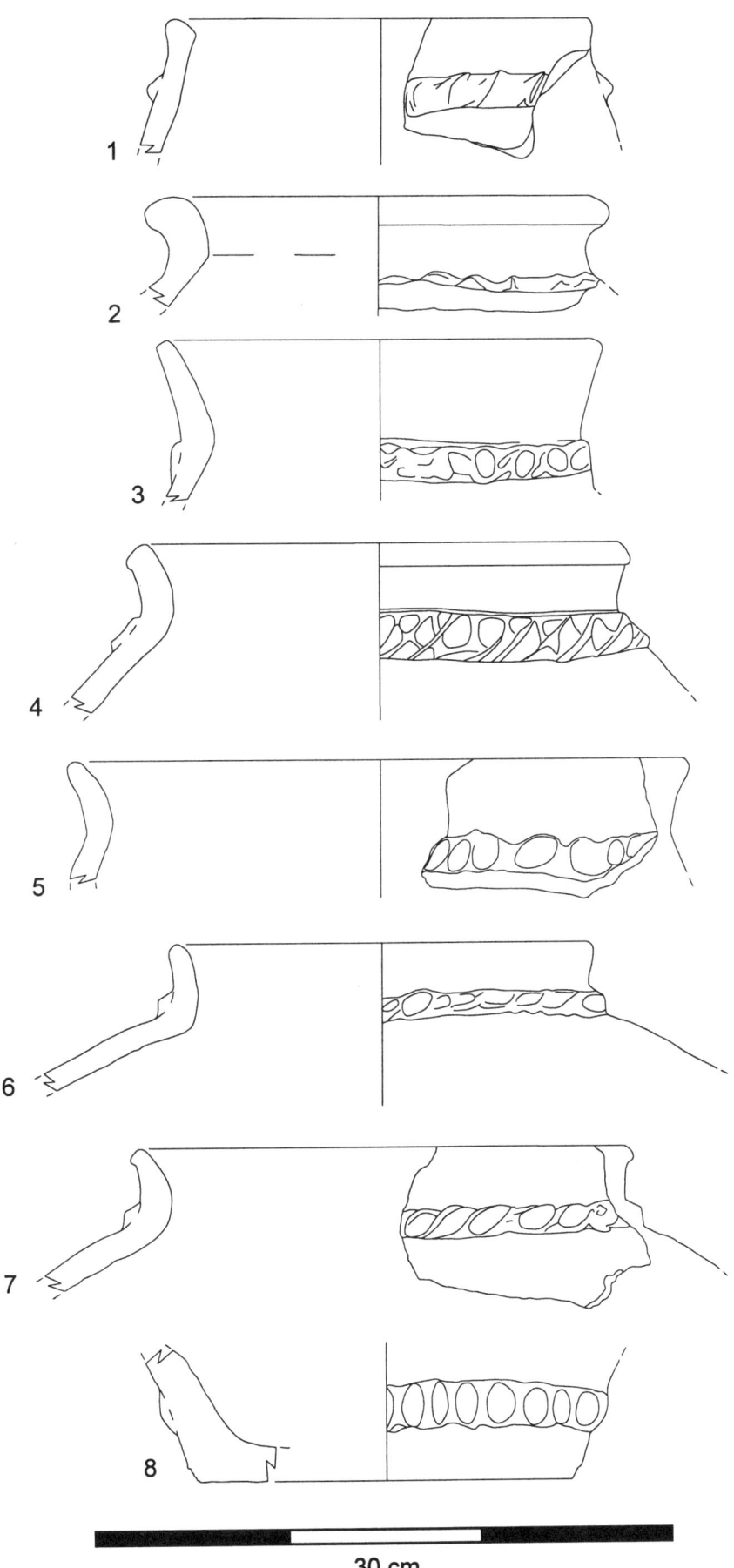

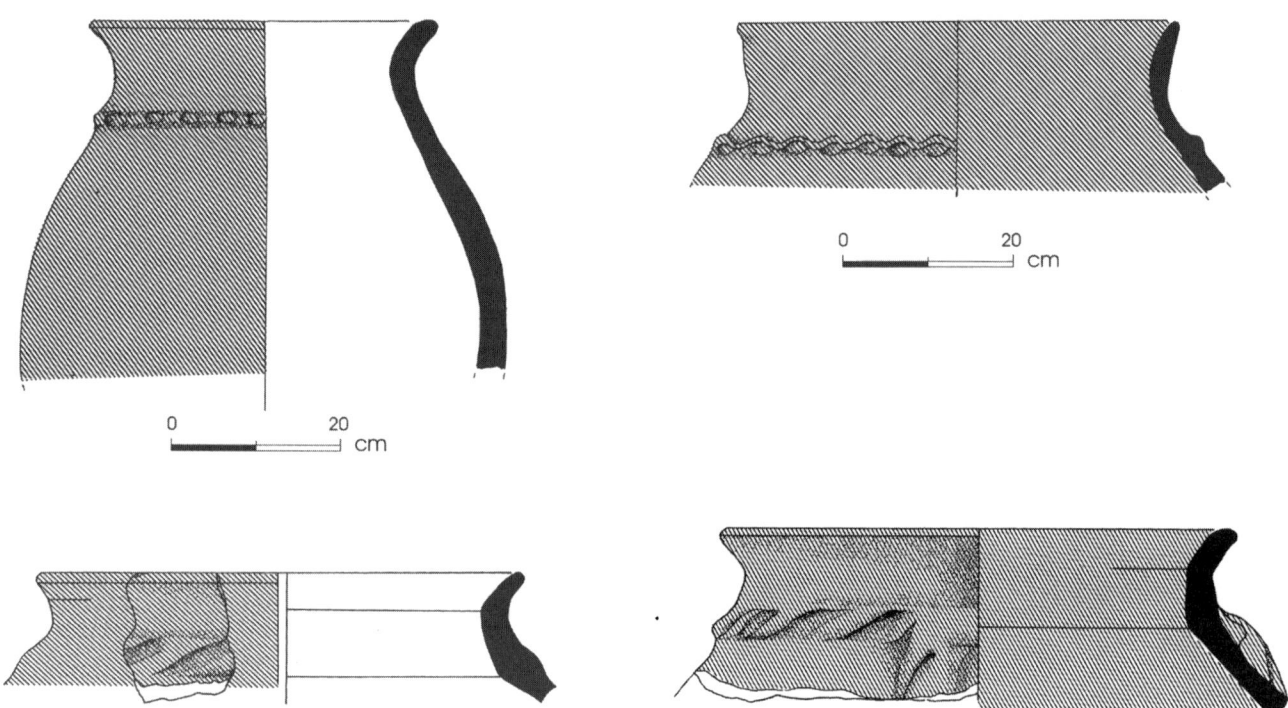

Figure 3.7 Pithoi fragments from Yiftah'el II (EB I; after Braun 1997: fig. 9.17:1, 4, 7, fig. 9.18:4).

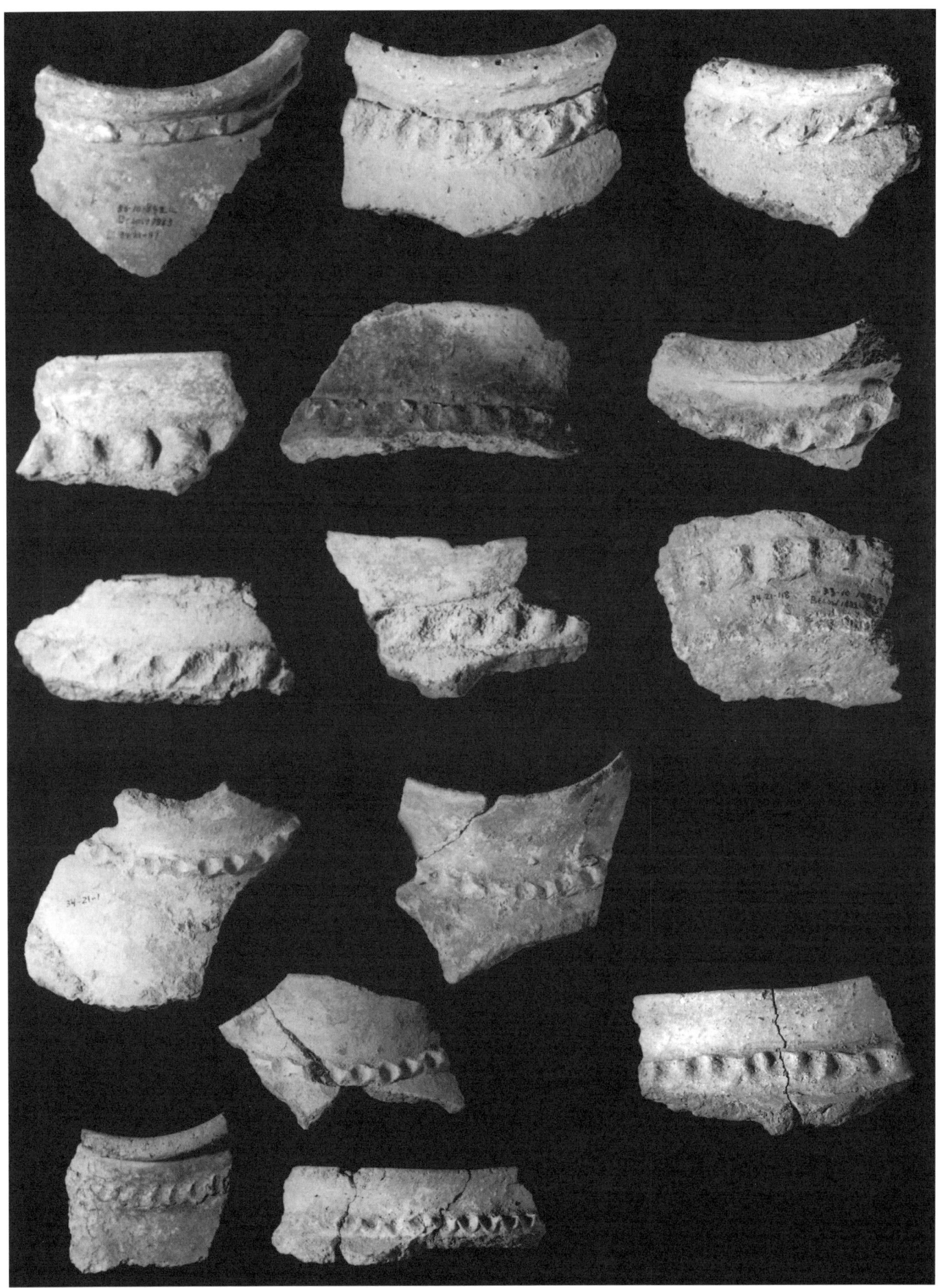

Figure 3.8 Selected Early EB I Pithoi fragments from Strata XVII-XVI from Beth Shan.

Figure 3.9 Pottery of Stratum XVII.

# on facing page	Museum #	Description	Field #
1	34-21-86	Orange buff outside and in.	33-11-39
2	34-21-114	Buff outside and in, red slipped.	33-11-210
3	34-21-119	Buff outside and in, gray core.	33-11-278
4	34-21-120	Gray outside and in, red slipped and polished.	33-11-52
5	34-21-135	Buff orange outside and in.	33-11-284
6	34-21-115	Brown outside, gray inside.	33-10-1103
7	34-21-137	Buff outside and in, gray core, thin red to black slip, slightly polished.	33-11-25
8	34-21-130	Buff gray outside and in, gray core.	33-10-817b
9	34-21-131	Buff outside and in, red blipped out.	33-11-24a
10	34-21-136	Buff orange outside, buff inside, gray core.	33-11-310
11	34-21-124	Pink outside and in, gray core.	33-10-1042a
12	34-21-132	Red outside and in.	33-11-51a
13	34-21-127	Buff outside and in, gray core.	33-11-45
14	34-21-126a	Buff outside and in, gray core.	33-10-1100a
15	34-21-125	Orange outside and in, gray core, red slipped.	33-11-311a

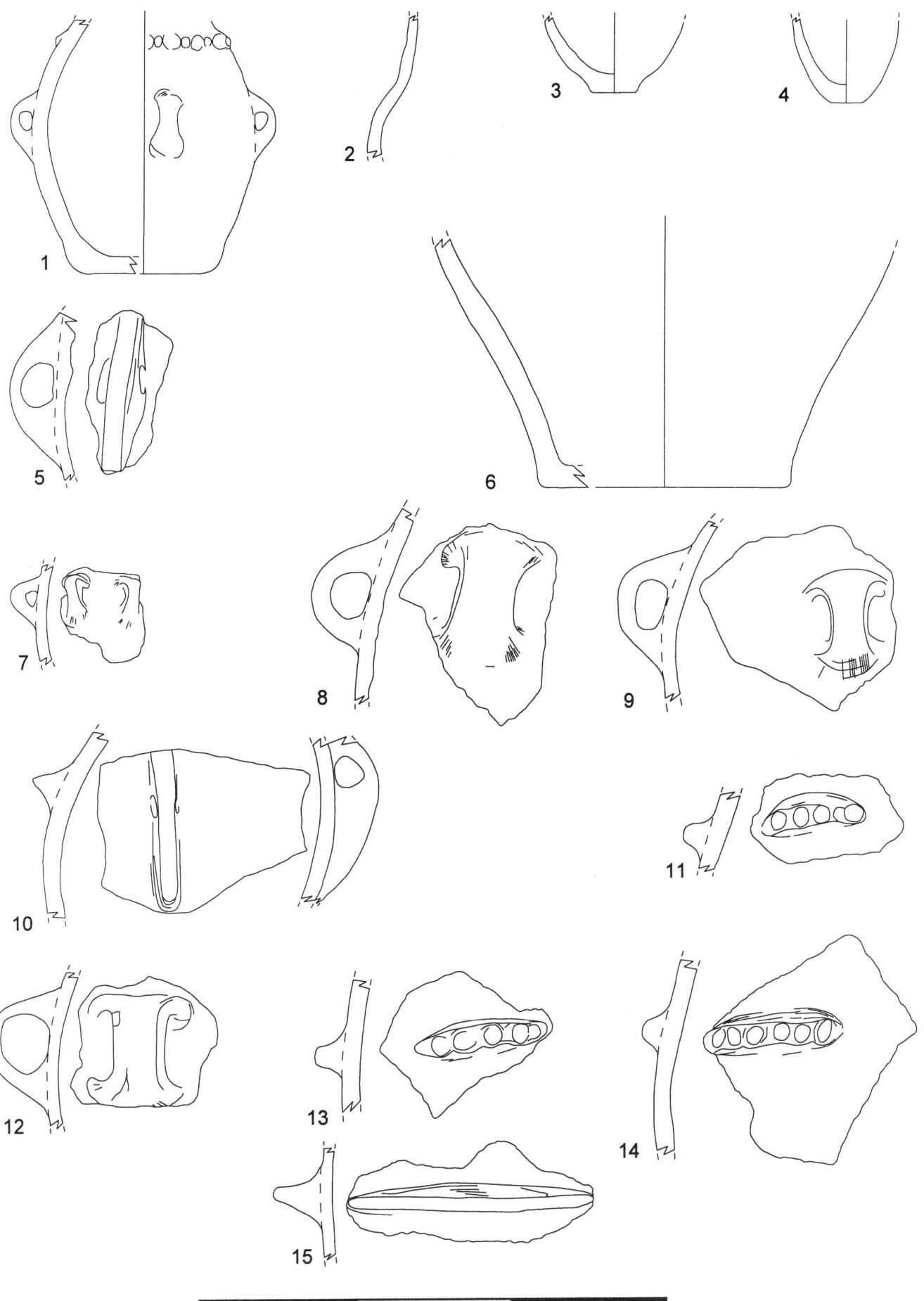

30 cm

Figure 3.10 Pottery of Stratum XVI.

# on facing page	Museum #	Description	Field #
1	34-21-16	Gray outside and in, self slip, burnished.	33-10-1072
2	34-21-21	Gray outside and in.	33-10-798
3	34-21-12	Buff orange outside and in.	33-10-908
4	34-21-28	Yellow brown outside, orange outside and core	33-10-1003
5	34-21-36	Orange buff outside and in, gray core, red slip outside.	33-10-911
6	34-21-15	Gray buff, outside and in, red slipped and polished	33-10-824
7	34-21-663	Gray buff outside and in, red slipped and polished.	33-10-87a
8	34-21-4	Pink outside and in, gray core.	33-10-1002
9	34-21-1	Brown buff outside and in.	33-10-1056
10	34-21-2	Buff outside and in, gray core.	33-10-915b

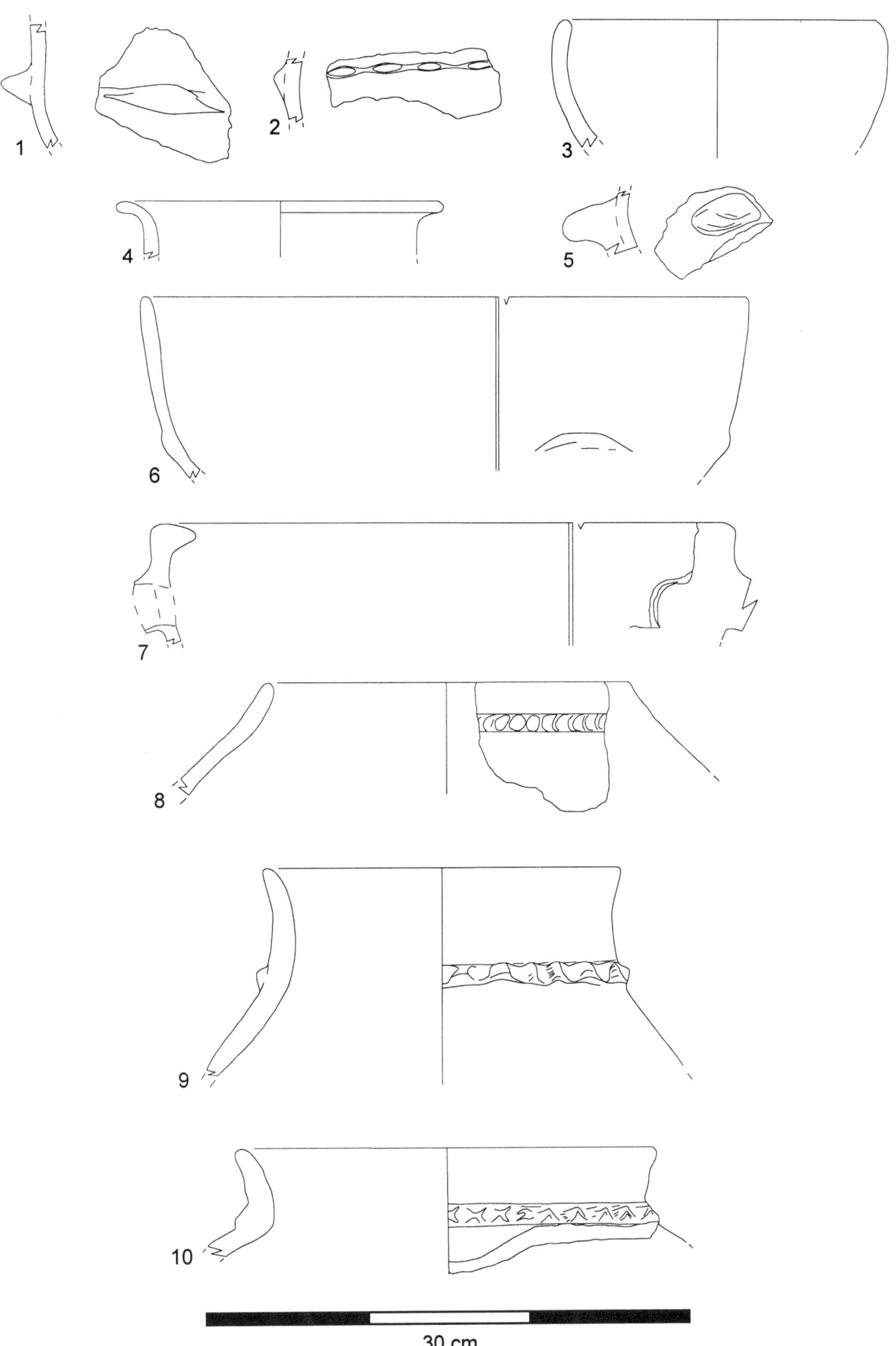

Figure 3.11 Pottery of Stratum XVI.

# on facing page	Museum #	Description	Field #
1	34-21-212	Buff brown, outside and in	33-11-179b
2	34-21-35?	Buff gray, outside and in	33-11-1026
3	34-21-27	Buff outside and in, gray core, red slipped outside.	33-10-905
4	34-21-26	Gray outside and core, brown inside.	33-10-913
5	34-21-6	Gray brown outside and in.	33-10-977
6	34-21-11	Brown outside and in, black core, red streaky wash.	33-10-1001b
7	34-21-5	Buff outside and in, gray core, red slipped and burnished outside.	33-10-824
8	34-21-7	Buff outside and in, gray core, red slipped outside.	33-10-823b
9	34-21-8	Buff outside and inside, gray core, red streaky wash.	33-10-827
10	34-21-14	Buff outside and inside, gray core.	33-10-1028

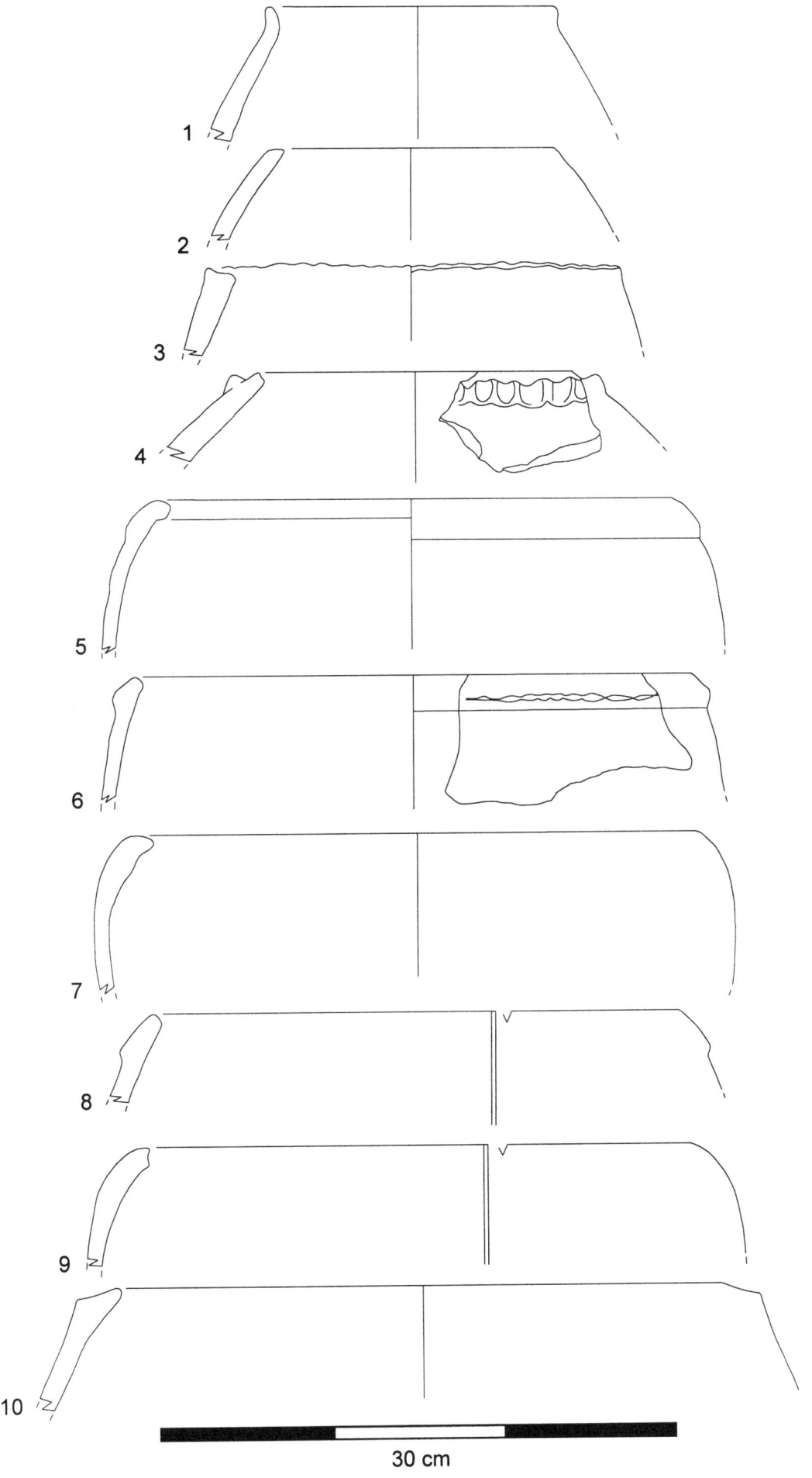

Figure 3.12 Pottery of Stratum XVI.

# on facing page	Museum #	Description	Field #
1	34-21- 37	Buff outside, orange in, red slipped outside.	33-10-829a
2	34-21-40	Orange buff outside and in, gray core.	33-10-797b
3	34-21-38	Brown outside and in.	33-10-1009
4	34-21-30	Buff outside, buff gray inside and core.	33-10-1080
5	34-21-39	Orange and gray outside and in.	3-10-1062a
6	34-21-42	Brown outside and in.	33-10-1051a
7	34-21-41	Buff orange outside and in, red slipped outside	33-10-1081
8	34-21-33	Gray buff outside and in.	33-10-1050
9	34-21-34	Gray outside and in.	33-10-1059
10	34-21-35	Gray outside and in.	33-10-1074

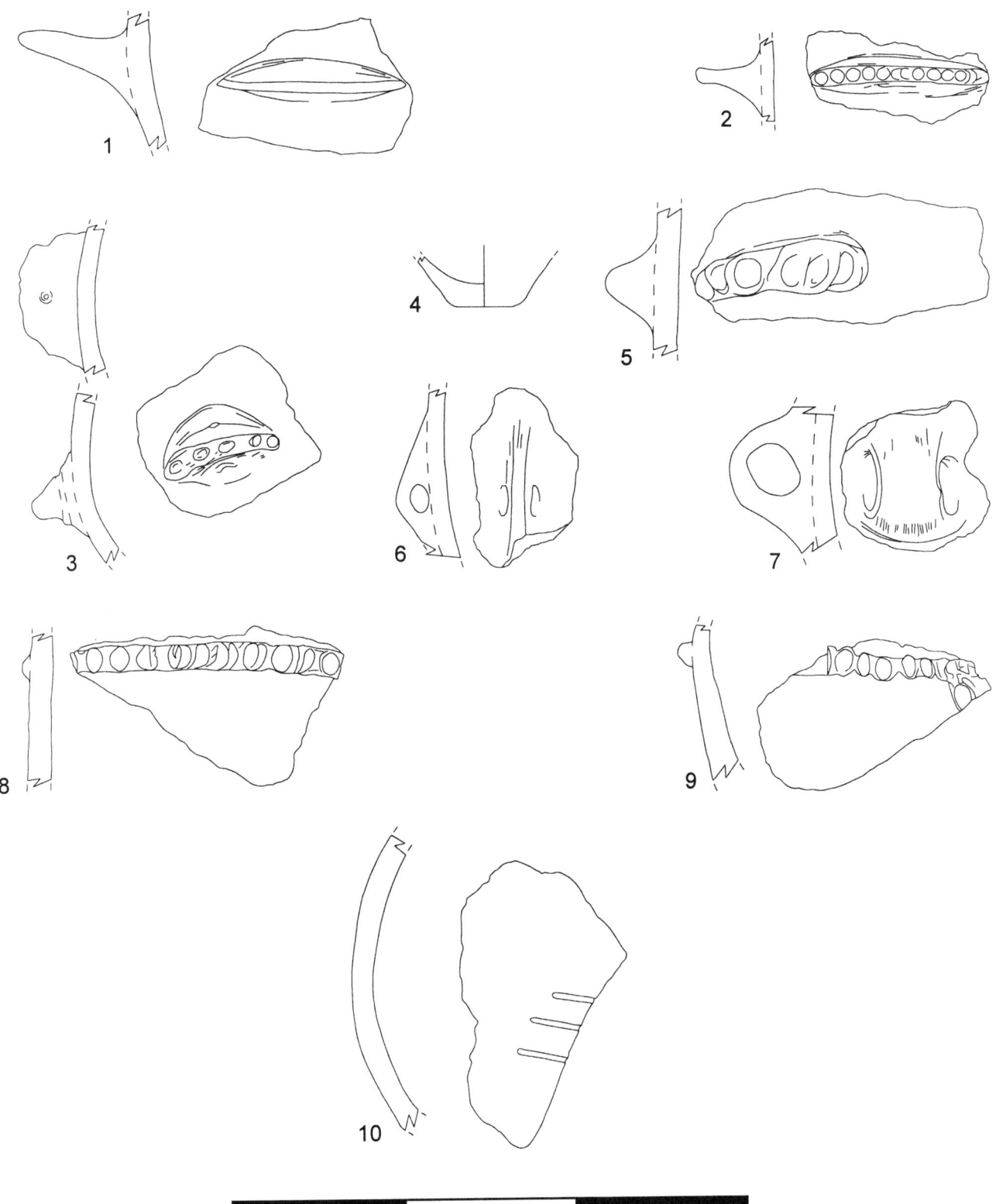

Figure 3.13 Pottery of Stratum XV.

# on facing page	Museum #	Description	Field #
1	34-20-900	Gray outside and in, self slip, burnished.	33-10-940
2	34-20-895	Buff gray outside and in, red slip.	33-10-938a
3	34-20-897	Brown gray outside and in.	33-10-872b
4	34-20-931	Buff outside and in, red slipped, burnished.	33-10-889c
5	34-20-894	Gray, burnished.	33-10-928
6	34-20-947	Gray outside and in, self slip, burnished, fenestrated	33-10-846
7	34-20-898	Gray outside and in, self slip, burnished.	33-10-859a
8	34-21-214	Buff outside and in, red slipped outside.	33-11-179b
9	IAA	Buff ware, red painted, coarse fabric.	33-10-865

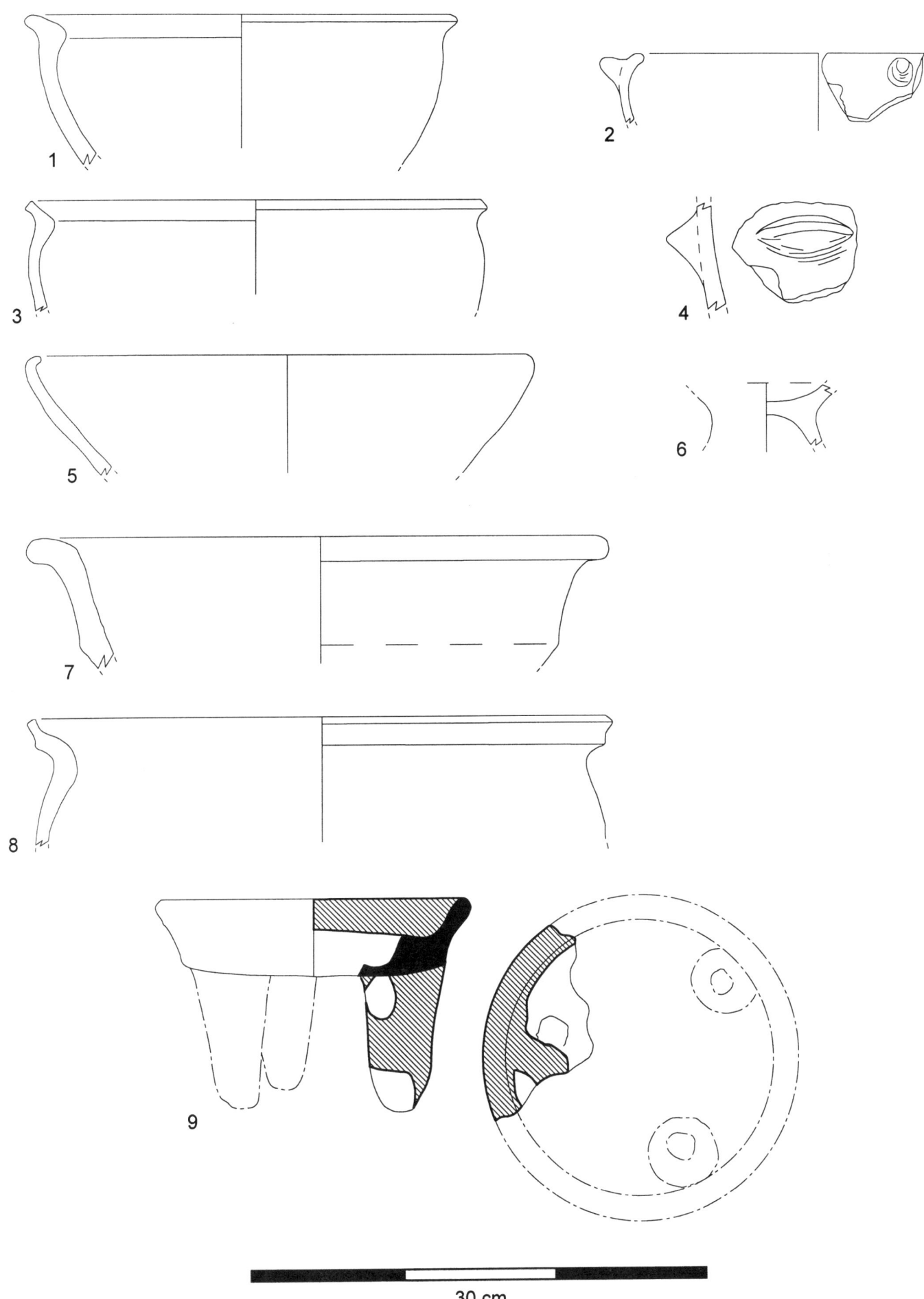

Figure 3.14 Pottery of Stratum XV.

# on facing page	Museum #	Description	Field #
1	34-20-892	Buff outside and in.	33-10-895
2	34-20-899	Buff outside and in, red slipped.	33-10-953
3	34-20-909	Buff outside and in, black core, red slipped outside.	33-10-926
4	34-20-911	Buff gray outside and in, gray core, red painted.	33-10-941a
5	34-20-906	Buff outside and in, gray core, red slip.	33-10-860a
6	34-20-643	Buff outside and in, red slipped outside.	33-10-565b
7	34-20-904	Buff outside and in, gray buff core, red painted.	33-10-452a
8	34-20-905	Buff outside and in, red painted.	33-10-72a
9	34-20-910	Buff orange outside and in, gray core, red painted.	33-10-932a
10	34-20-903	Buff orange outside and in, red slipped outside.	33-10-931c

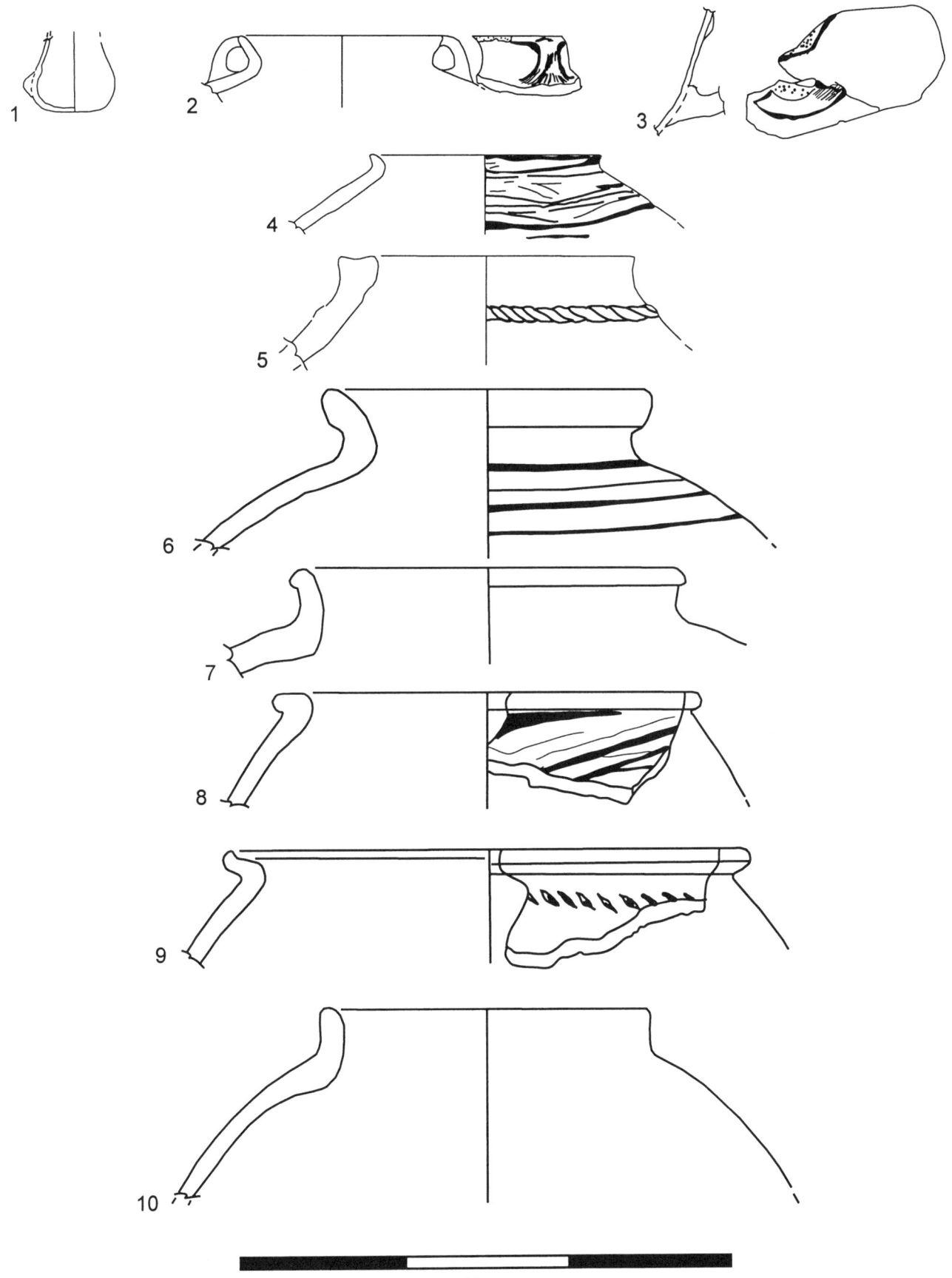

Figure 3.15 Pottery of Stratum XV.

# on facing page	Museum #	Description	Field #
1	34-20-915	Buff outside and in, red slipped.	33-10-869
2	34-20-913	Buff, gray core.	33-10-833c
3	34-20-914	Buff orange outside and in, red painted.	33-10-876a
4	34-20-912	Gray buff outside and in.	33-10-921b
5	34-20-932b	Gray buff outside and in, red slipped.	33-10-832b
6	34-20-929	Gray buff outside and in, red painted.	33-10-947a
7	34-20-934	Gray outside and in, red slipped.	33-10-890
8	34-20-935	Gray buff outside and in, red slipped.	33-10-929b
9	34-20-??	Buff outside and in, red slipped.	33-10-450
10	34-20-923	Buff gray outside and in, gray core, red slipped.	33-10-925
11	34-21-918	Red brown outside and in.	33-10-939
12	34-20-920	Buff gray, gray core, red painted.	33-10-864a

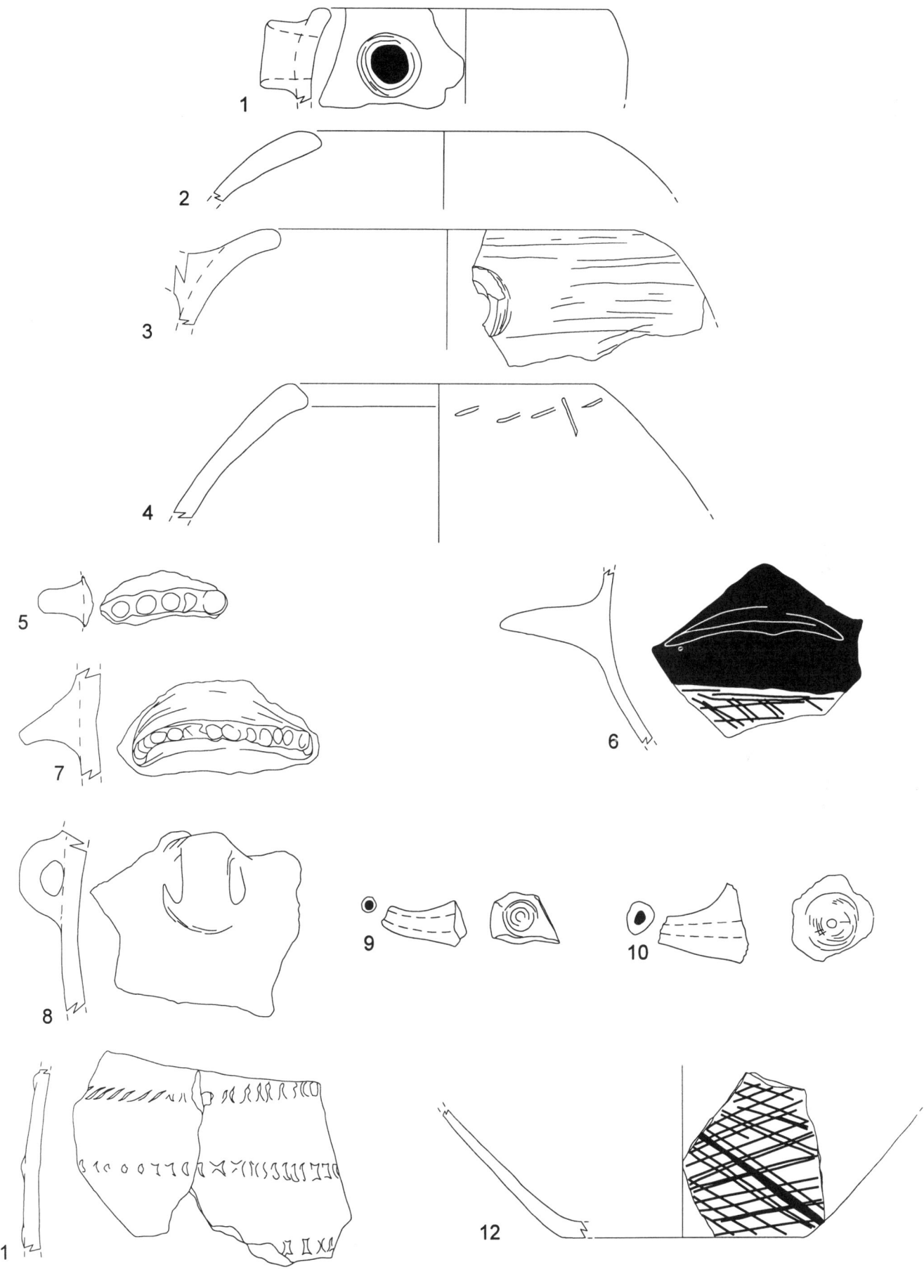

30 cm

Figure 3.16 Pottery of Stratum XIV.

# on facing page	Museum #	Description	Field #
1	34-20-813	Orange outside and in, red painted.	33-10-469
2	34-20-822a	Gray buff outside and in, dark red, burnished outside and in.	33-10-625a
3	34-20-778	Buff orange outside and in, red slipped.	33-10-271
4	34-20-817	Buff gray outside and in, red slipped.	33-10-703b
5	34-20-820	Buff gray outside and in, red slipped, burnished.	33-10-507b
6	34-20-816	Buff outside and in, red slipped and pattern burnished.	33-10-279
7	34-20-811	Buff gray outside and in, red painted outside, spattered red paint inside	33-10-444
8	34-20-779	Gray outside and in, red slipped	33-10-494
9	34-20-781	Gray outside and in.	33-11-287
10	34-20-639	Buff outside and in, gray core.	33-10-273
11	34-20-783	Brown gray, outside and in, red slipped outside.	33-10-315

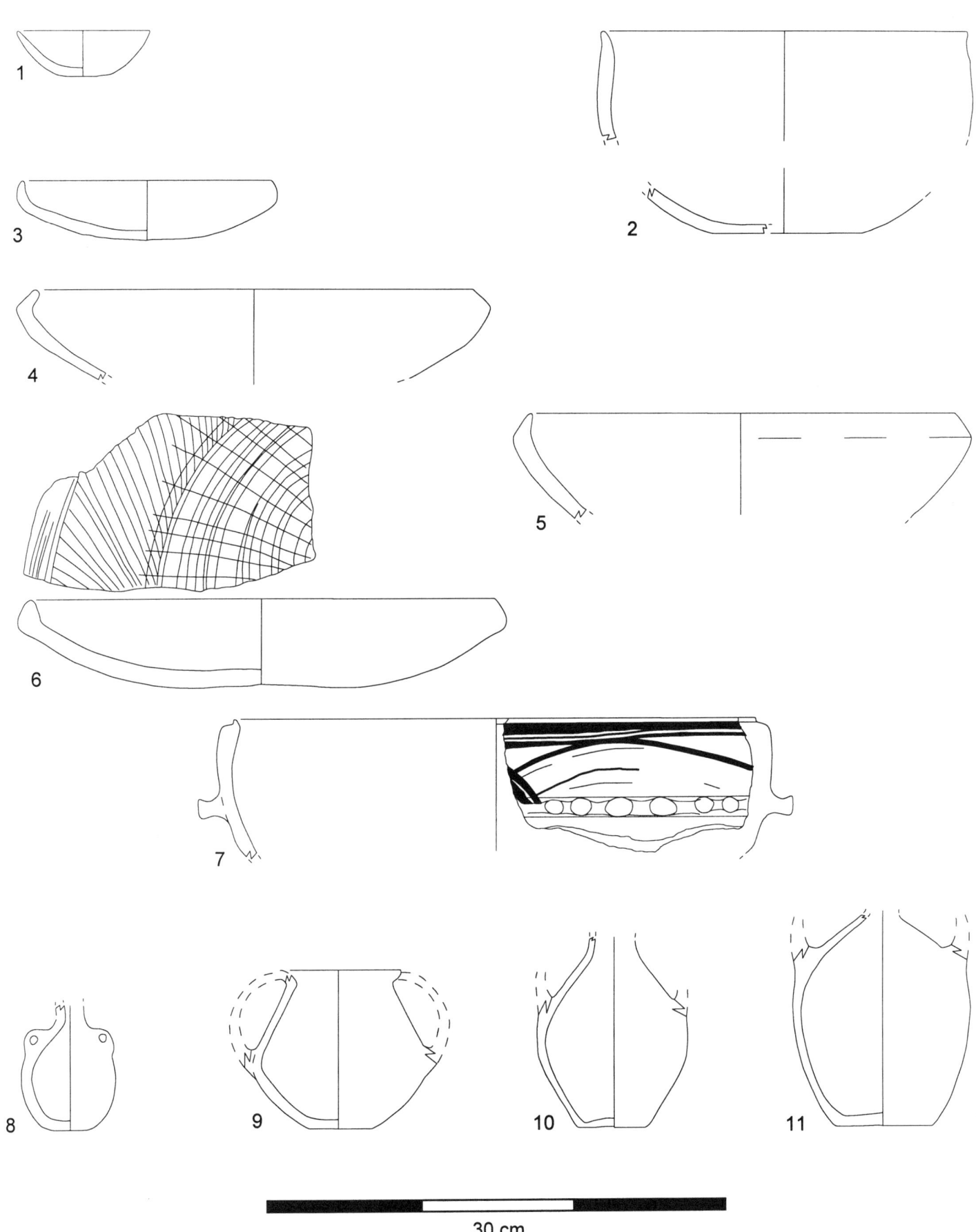

Figure 3.17 Pottery of Stratum XIV.

# on facing page	Museum #	Description	Field #
1	34-20-794	Buff outside and in, gray core, red painted.	33-10-694c
2	34-20-788	Gray outside and in.	33-10-739a
3	34-20-789	Brown outside and in, gray core, red painted.	33-10-450a
4	34-20-787	Brown outside and in, gray core.	33-10-503b
5	34-20-784	Orange outside and in, gray core, red slipped outside.	37-10-685
6	34-20-795	Gray buff outside and in, red painted.	31-10-449a
7	34-20-793	Buff outside and in, red painted.	33-10-966c
8	34-20-843	Buff outside and in, gray core, red slipped.	33-10-804
9	34-20-786	Brown outside and in.	33-10-739b
10	34-20-812	Orange buff outside and in, red slipped outside.	33-10-466
11	34-20-849	Brown gray outside, gray in, red slipped outside.	33-10-398
12	34-20-837	Brown outside and in, red painted.	33-10-447b
13	34-20-840	Buff brown outside and in, brown core, red painted.	33-10-682b

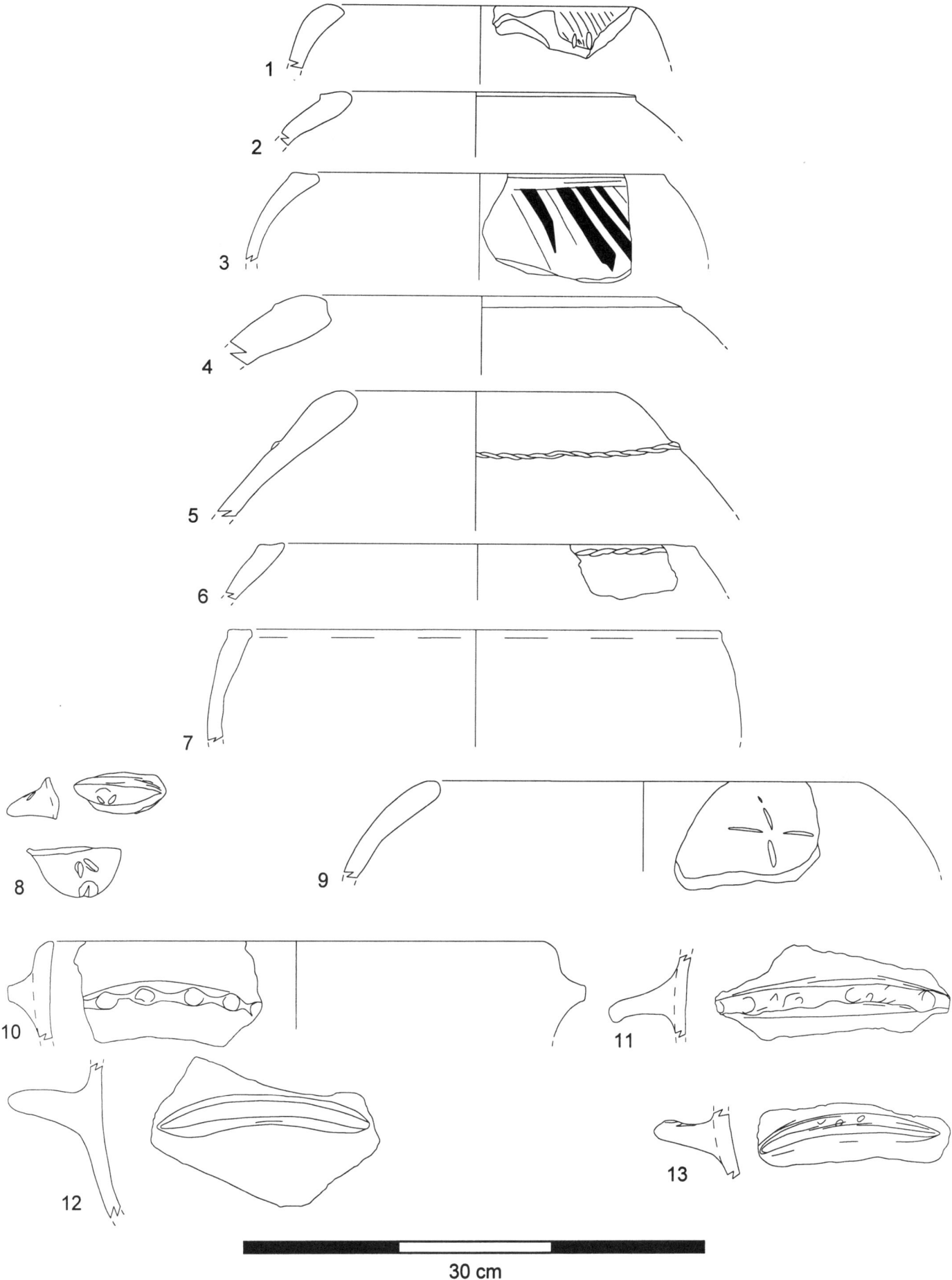

Figure 3.18 Pottery of Stratum XIV.

# on facing page	Museum #	Description	Field #
1	34-20-805	Buff outside and in, gray core, red painted.	33-10-623b
2	34-20-809	Buff outside and in, red painted.	33-10-805b
3	34-20-806	Buff outside and in, red slip.	33-10-623a
4	34-20-807	Gray brown outside and in, red slipped outside and inside of rim.	33-10-635a
5	34-20-801	Buff outside and in, gray core, red painted outside and inside rim.	33-10-746b
6	34-20-804	Buff outside and in, red painted.	33-10-604a
7	34-20-797	Gray buff outside and in, gray core, red wash	33-10-513
8	34-20-808	Buff outside and in, gray core, red slip.	33-10-445
9	34-20-798	Buff outside and in, gray buff core, red wash.	33-10-745
10	34-20-854	Buff outside and in, gray core, red paint.	33-10-732
11	34-20-857	Buff outside and in, red paint.	33-10-669
12	34-20-850	Gray outside and in, red slipped outside.	33-10-707a
13	34-20-856	Gray buff outside and in, red slip.	33-10-678b
14	34-20-855	Buff outside and in, gray painted ("grain wash")	33-10-603
15	34-20-853	Buff outside and in, gray core, red painted.	33-10-471a
16	34-20-810	Gray buff, orange outside and in, gray core.	33-10-763
17	34-20-814	Gray buff, gray core, red slipped outside	33-10-278b

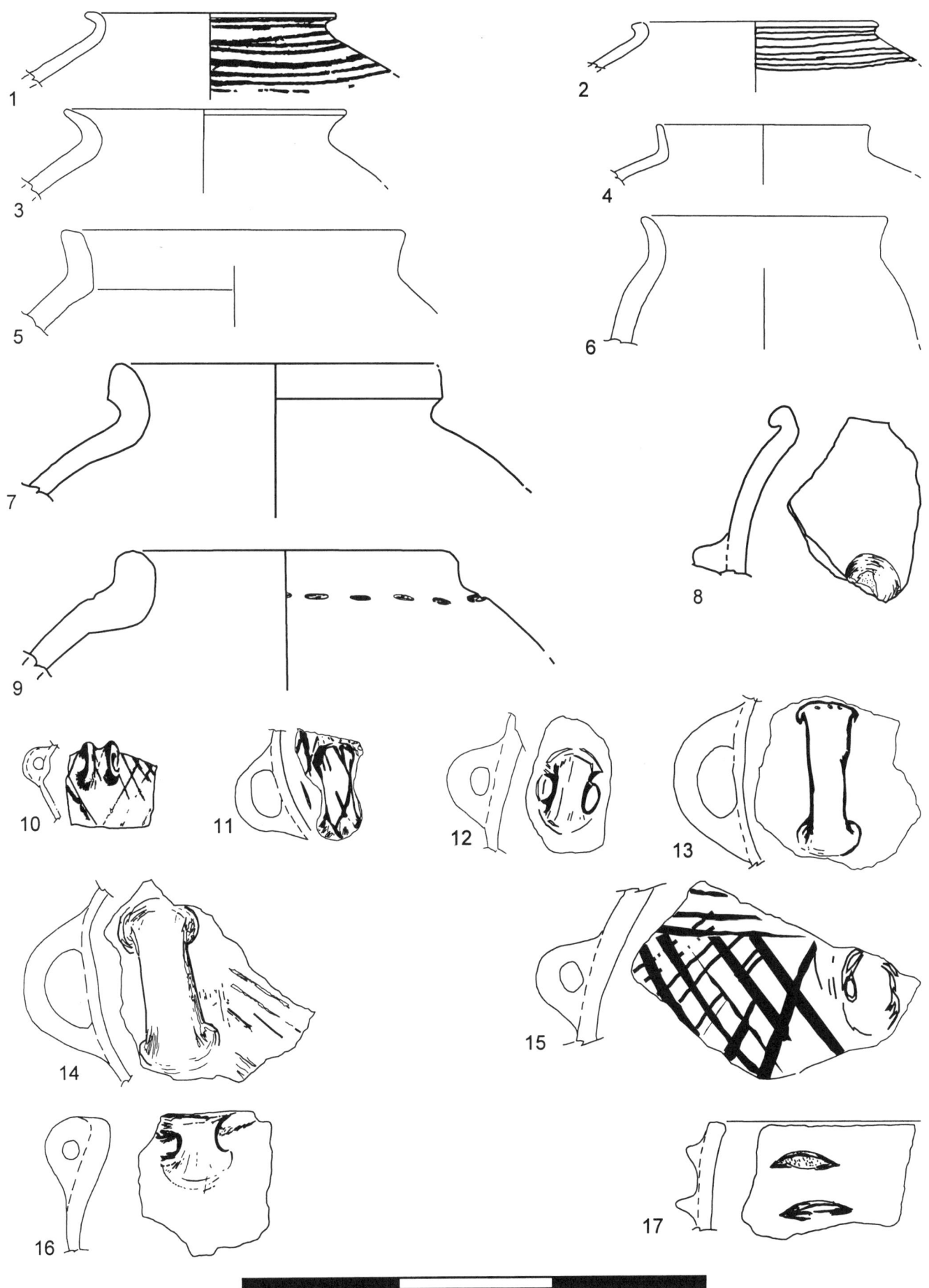

Figure 3.19 Pottery of Stratum XIV.

# on facing page	Museum #	Description	Field #
1	34-20-834	Buff outside and in, gray core.	33-11-714
2	IAA (PDA: 34-1223)	Buff gray outside and in, red painted.	33-10-1036

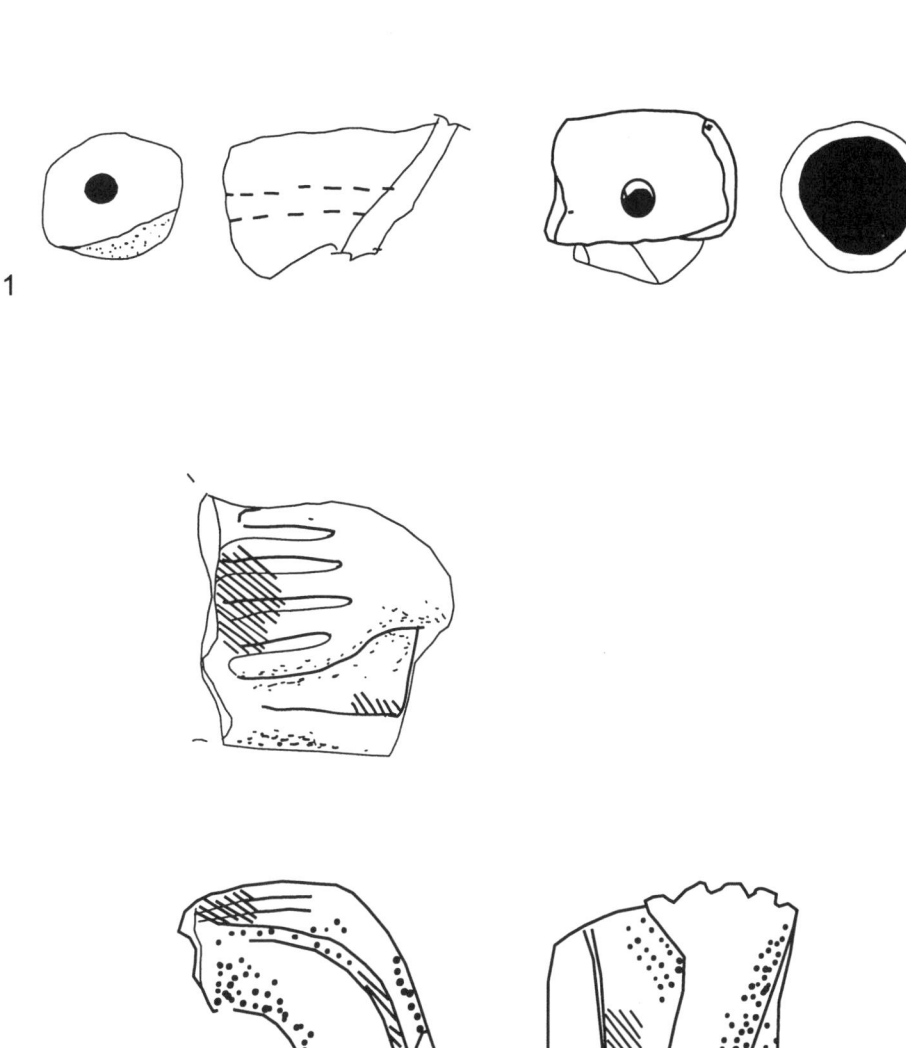
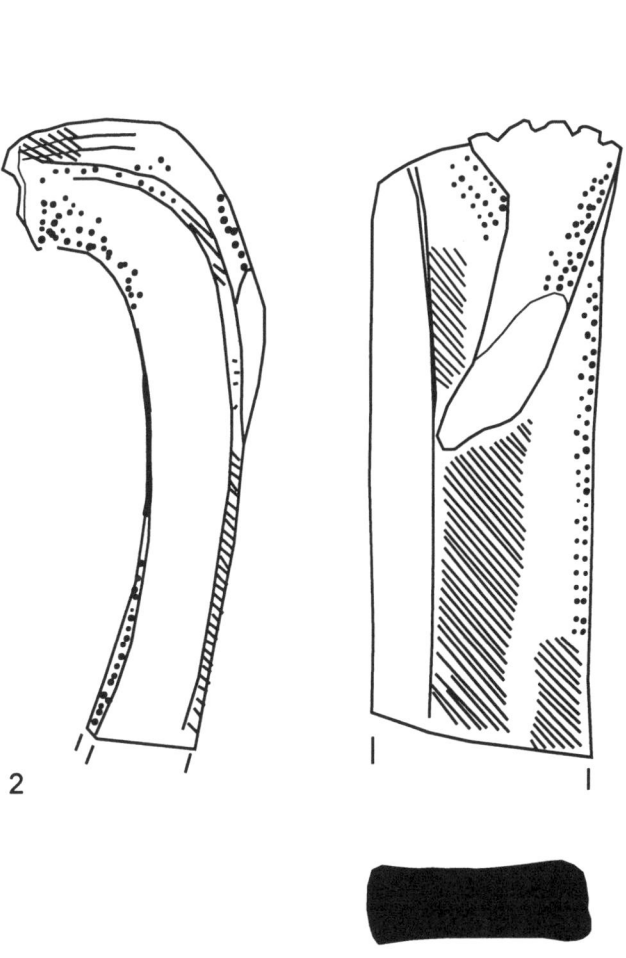

10 cm

Figure 3.20 Pottery of Stratum XIII.

# on facing page	Museum #	Description	Field #
1	34-20-666	Buff orange outside and in, gray core, red slipped outside.	33-10-758a
2	34-20-668	Gray buff outside and in.	33-10-573
3	34-20-674	Gray buff outside and in, red slipped outside.	33-10-782b
4	34-20-671	Buff outside and in, gray core, red slipped outside.	33-10-150
5	34-20-665	Gray outside and in, red slipped outside.	33-10-366a
6	34-20-660	Gay outside and in.	33-10-197a
7	34-20-670	Buff orange outside and in, red slipped outside.	33-10-198b
8	34-20-634	Gray buff outside and in, fire clouded inside, red wash..	33-10-545
9	34-20-661	Gray outside and in.	33-10-405b
10	34-20-654	Buff gray outside and in, red slipped outside.	33-10-195
11	34-20-655	Buff outside and in, dark brown paint.	33-10-782a

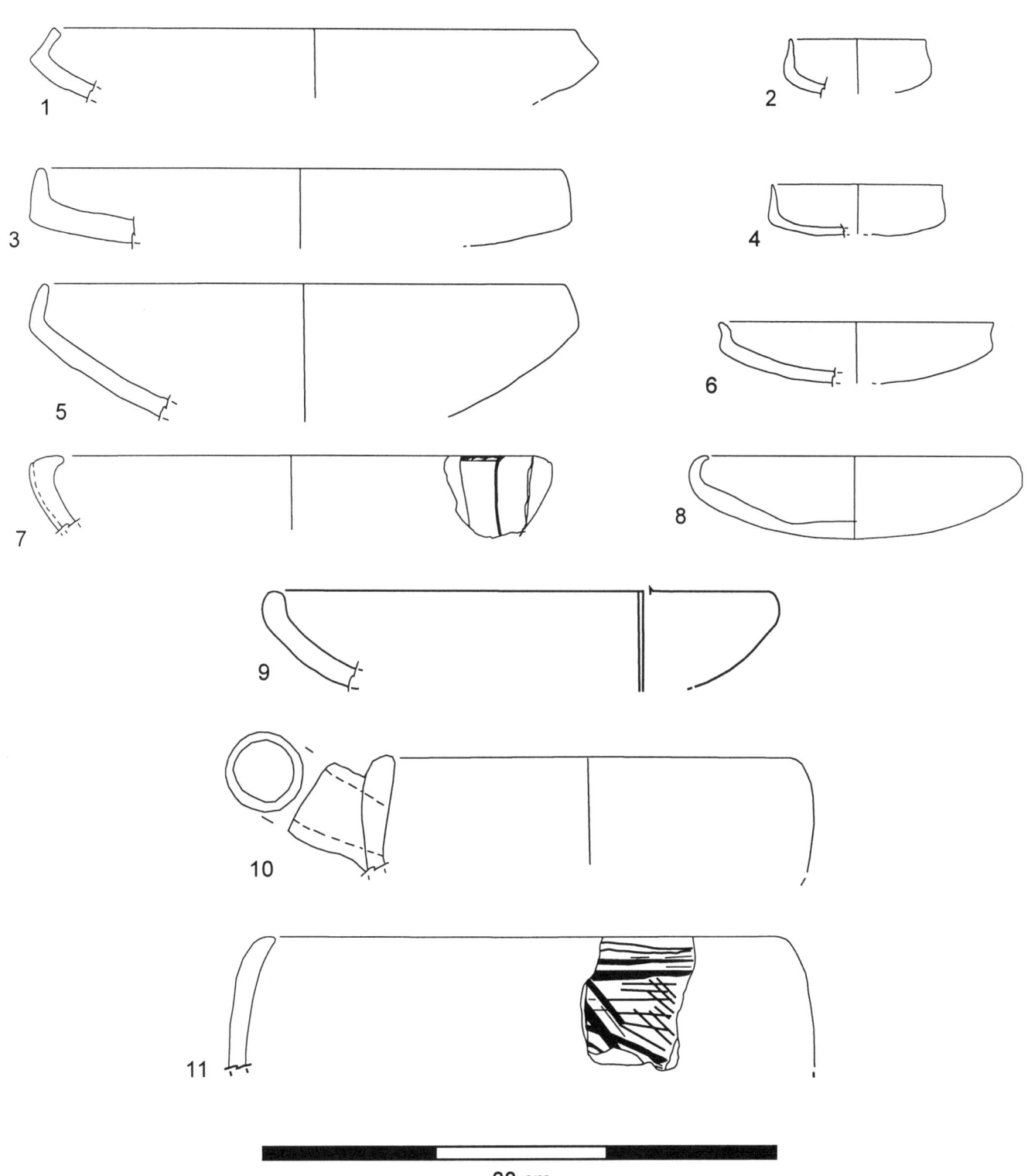

30 cm

Figure 3.21 Pottery of Stratum XIII.

# on facing page	Museum #	Description	Field #
1	34-20-637	Orange outside and in, red slipped.	33-10-382
2	34-20-636	Gray buff outside and in, gray core, red slipped.	33-10-135
3	34-20-640	Brown outside and in, red slipped outside.	33-10-338
4	34-20-657	Brown outside and in, red painted.	33-10-423
5	34-20-694	Red outside and in.	33-10-353
6	34-20-658	Brown outside, buff inside, brown core, red slipped.	33-10-80
7	34-20-692	Buff green outside and in, gray core, red slipped.	33-10-136
8	34-20-690	Buff outside and in, red slipped outside.	33-10-218
9	34-20-700	Orange outside, brown inside.	33-10-754
10	34-20-684	Buff gray outside and in, red slipped.	33-10-415a
11	34-20-683	Gray buff outside and in, gray core.	33-10-355
12	34-20-681	Buff orange outside and in, red slipped outside.	33-10-615
13	34-20-678	Buff outside and in, gray core, red slipped.	33-10-550a
14	IAA	Red brown outside and in.	33-10-899
15	34-20-688	Buff outside and in.	33-10-216
16	34-20-686	Gray outside and in, red slipped and burnished outside.	33-10-324
17	34-20-689	Buff outside and in, red slipped or washed.	33-10-415b
18	34-20-696	Gray buff outside and in, red painted.	33-10-152c

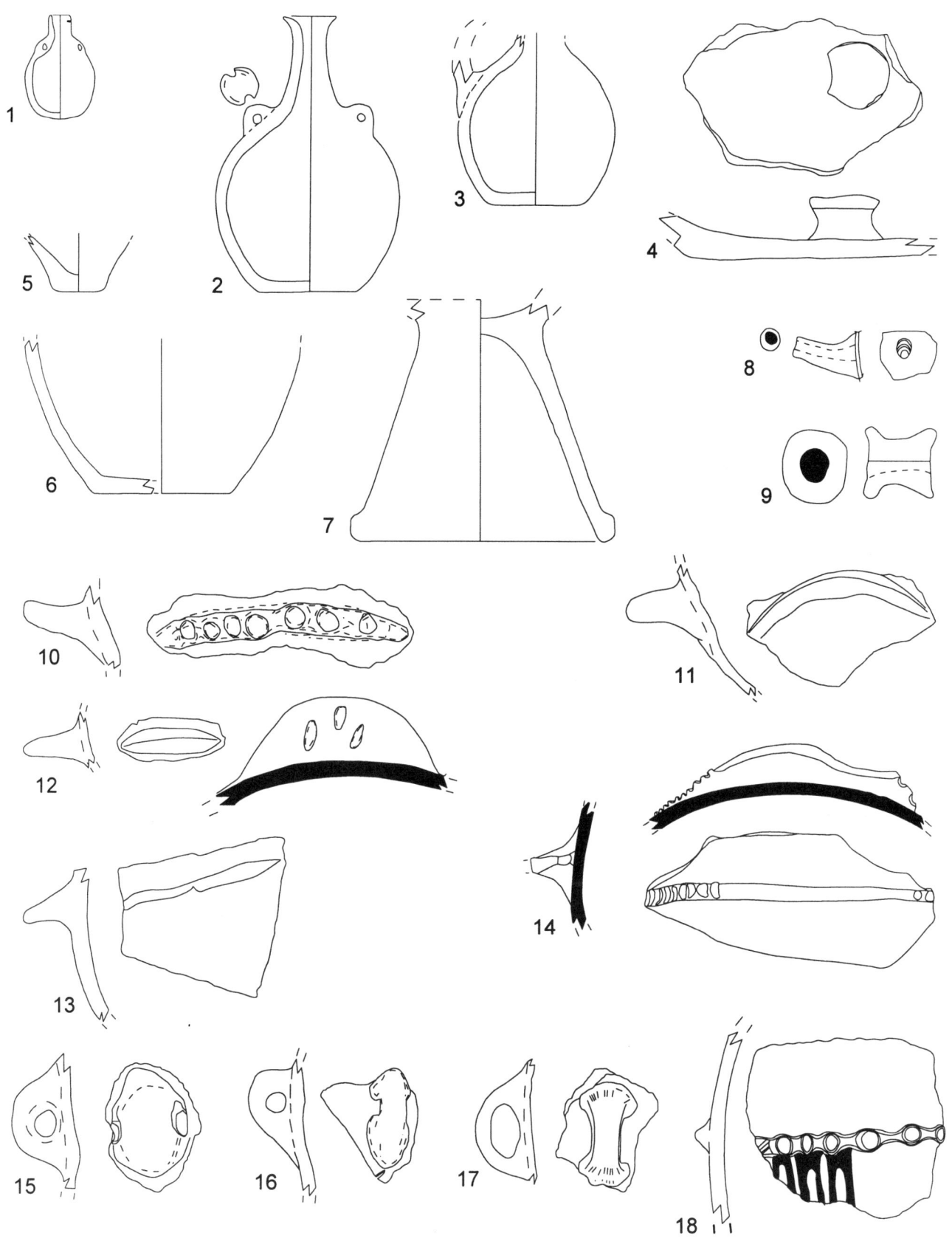

Figure 3.22 Pottery of Stratum XIII.

# on facing page	Museum #	Description	Field #
1	34-20-649	Intrusive EB II-III	33-11-837b
2	34-20-650	Gray buff outside and in, red painted.	33-10-583
3	34-20-642	Buff outside and in, red slipped outside.	33-10-565a
4	IAA	Buff gray outside and in, red slipped outside.	Unknown
5	34-20-647	Gray and black outside and in, red slipped outside.	33-10-220
6	34-20-646	Buff gray outside and in, red slipped outside.	33-10-784b
7	34-20-651	Brown gray outside and in, red slipped outside.	33-10-416d
8	IAA	Brown and gray outside and in, red slipped outside.	Unknown

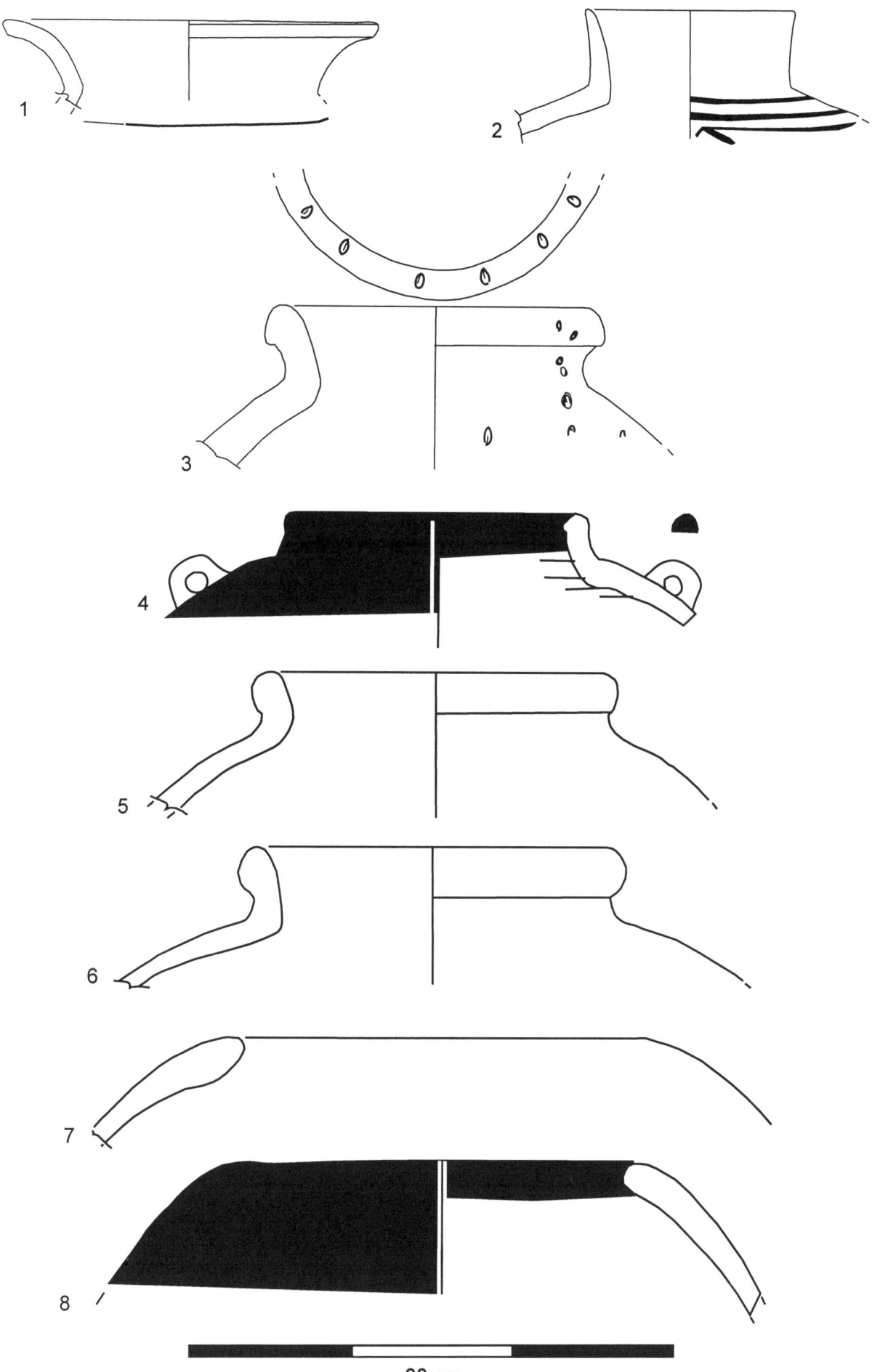

Figure 3.23 Base with vestigial ring, typical of Chalcolithic workmanship.

Figure 3.24 Base of a string-cut bowl, typical of Chalcolithic workmanship.

Figure 3.25 Wheel-made Chalcolithic bowl with typical base, internal view.

Figure 3.26 Wheel-made Chalcolithic bowl with typical base, external view.

Figure 3.27 Late EB I storage jar, possibly of Egyptianized morphology, *in situ* in Room 1866 (Field Neg. #2895).

Figure 3.28 FitzGerald's photo of selected ceramics from the pits below Level XVIII (Stratum XIX) (Field Neg. #2987).

Figure 3.29 FitzGerald's photo of selected ceramics from Level XVIII (Field Neg. #2985).

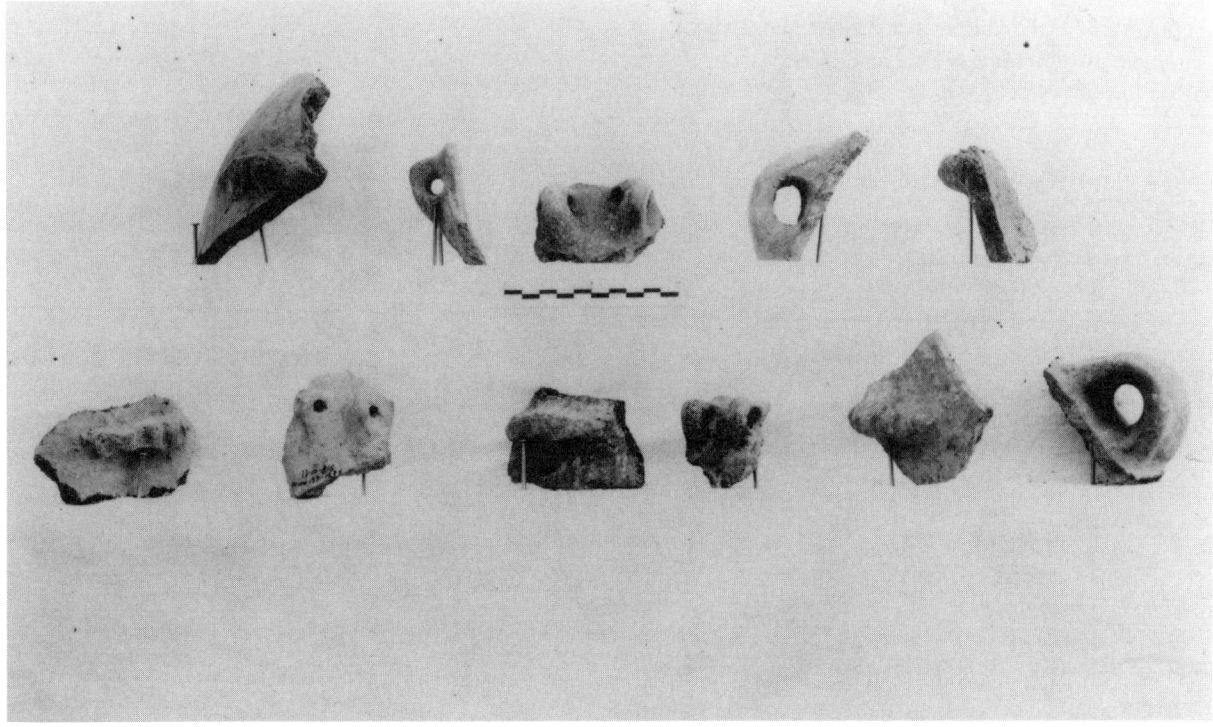

Figure 3.30 FitzGerald's photo of selected ceramics from Level XVII (Field Neg. #2989).

Figure 3.31 FitzGerald's photo of selected ceramics from Level XVII (Field Neg. #2984).

Figure 3.32 FitzGerald's photo of selected ceramics from Level XVI (Field Neg. #2983).

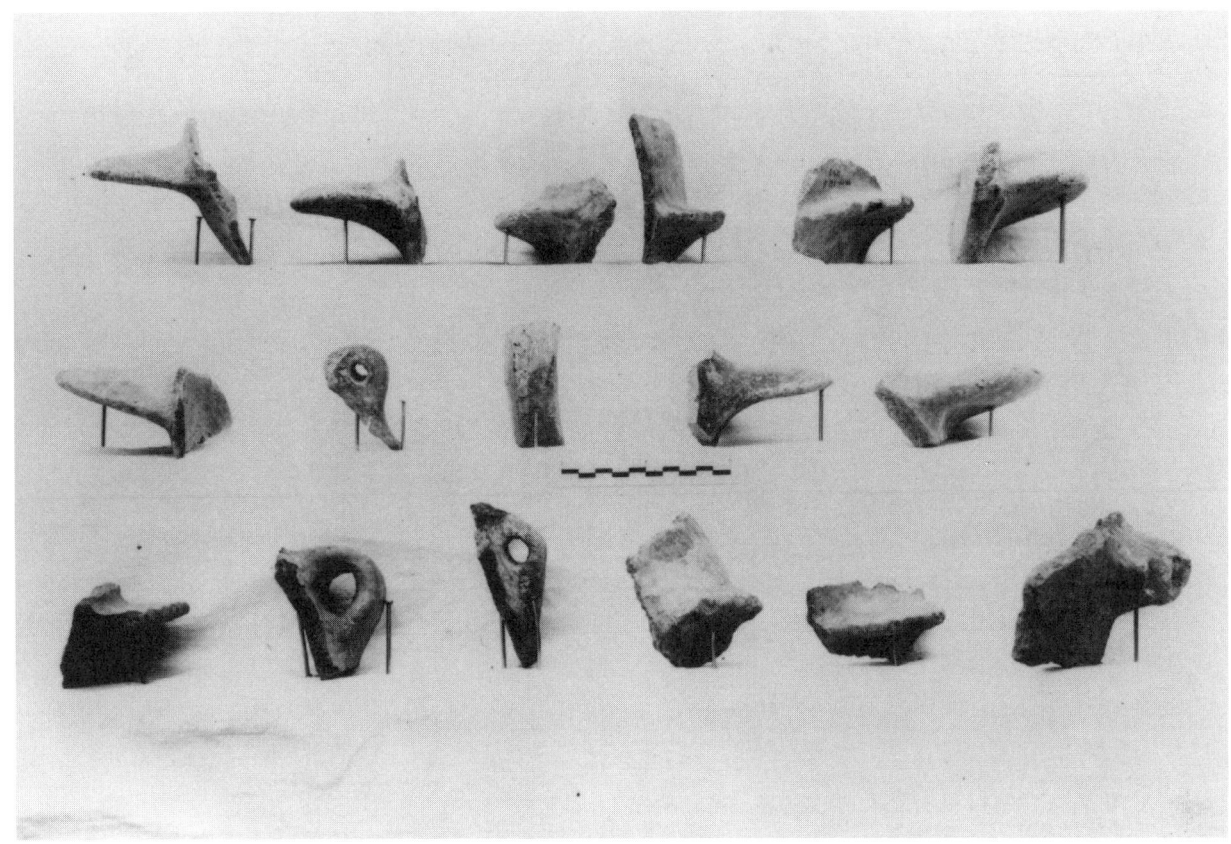

Figure 3.33 FitzGerald's photo of selected ceramic handles from Levels XVI and XV (Field Neg. #2988).

Figure 3.34 FitzGerald's photo of selected ceramics from Level XV (Field Neg. #2982).

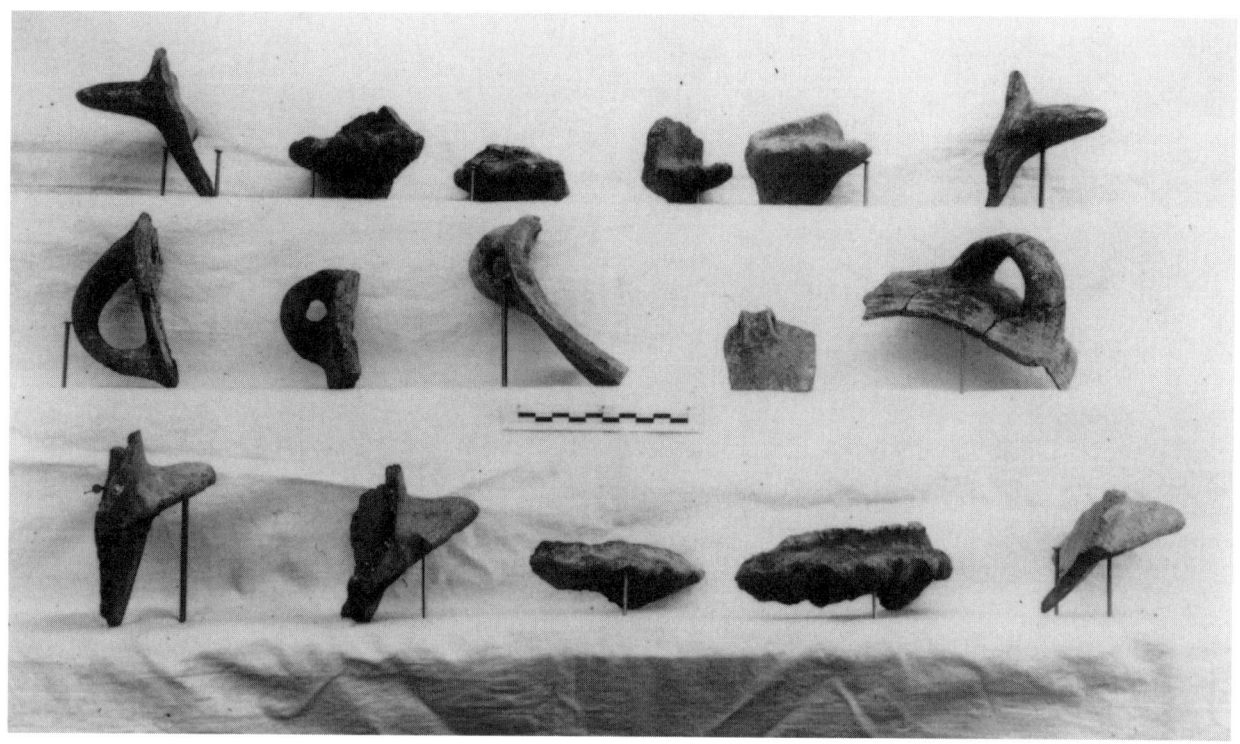

Figure 3.35 FitzGerald's photo of selected ceramics from Levels XIV and XIII (Field Neg. #2986).

Figure 3.36 FitzGerald's photo of selected ceramics from Levels XIV (lower row) and XIII (upper row) (Field Neg. #2943).

Figure 3.37 Small jar of Stratum XIV (Field Neg. #3003).

Figure 3.38 FitzGerald's photo of selected pottery from Level XIV (Field Neg. #2981).

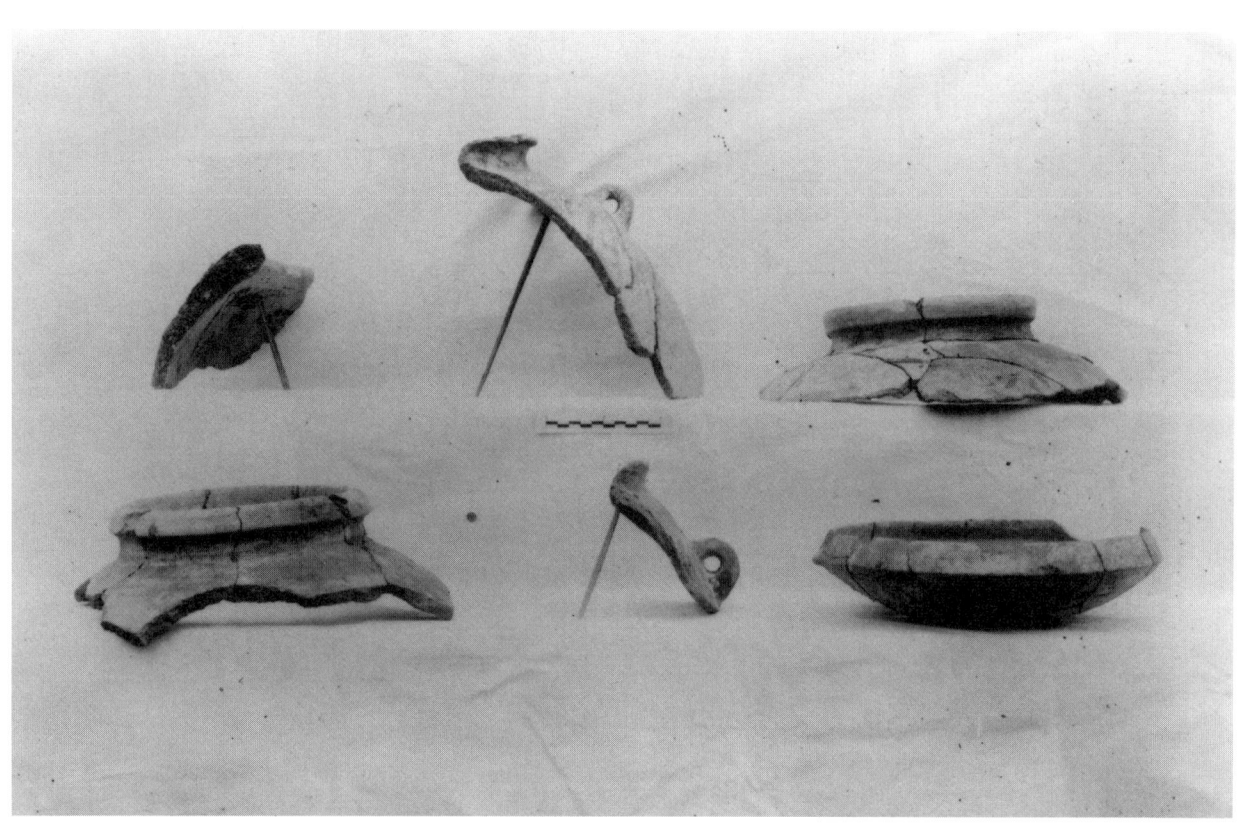

Figure 3.39 FitzGerald's photo of selected handles from Level XIII (Field Neg. #2980).

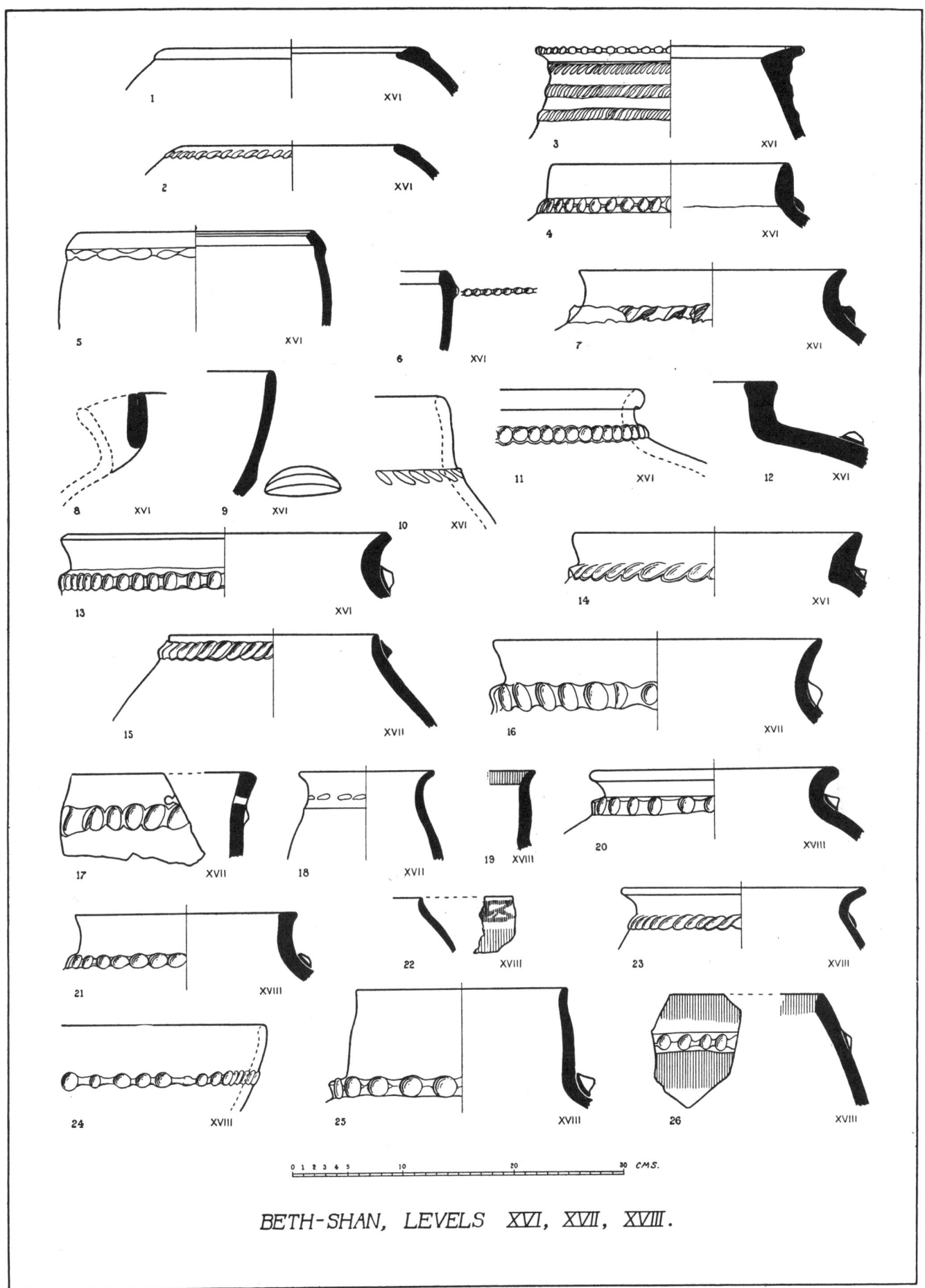

Plate I. Assorted ceramics, Levels XVI, XVII, XVIII.

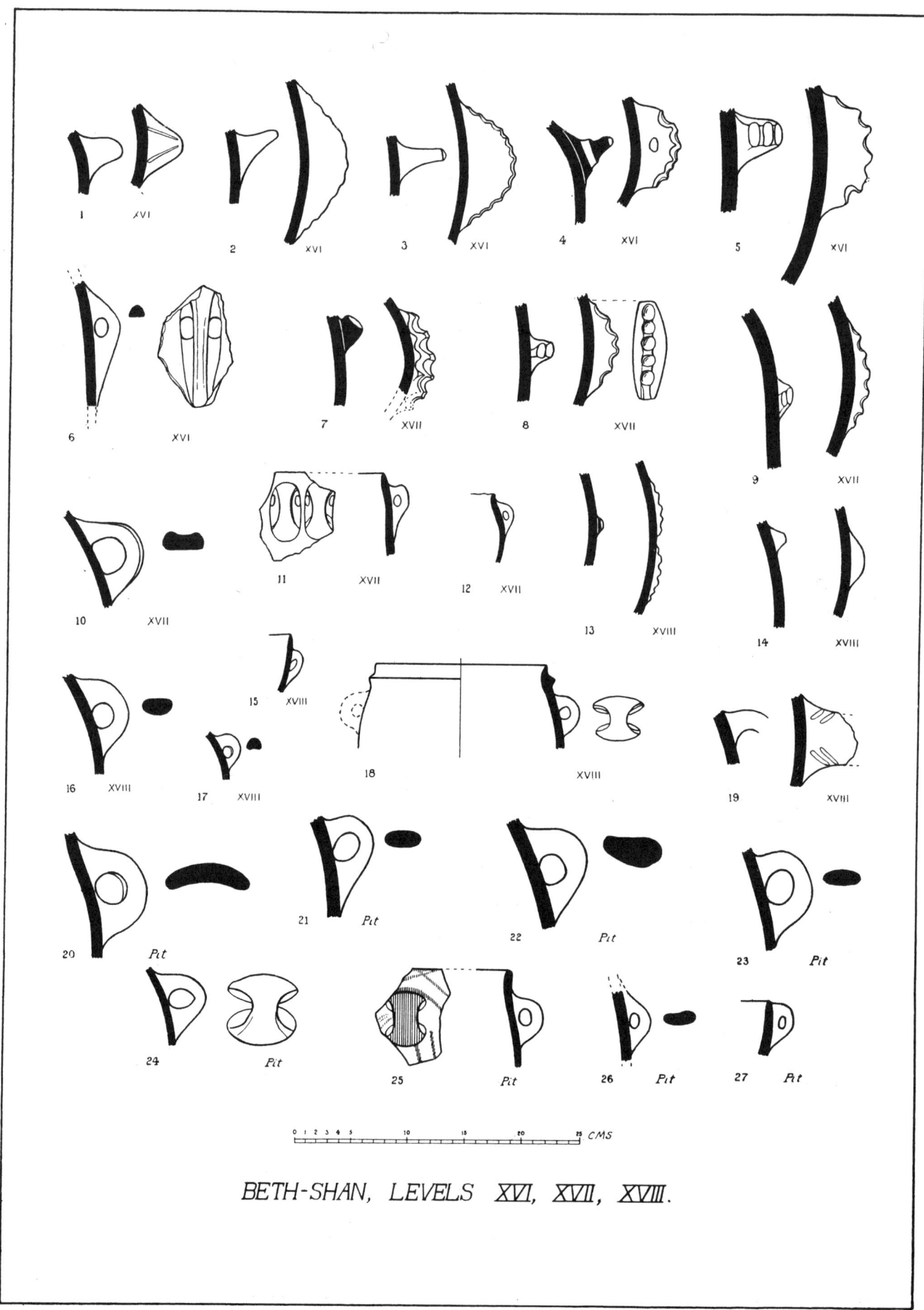

Plate II. Assorted ceramics, Levels XVI, XVII, XVIII.

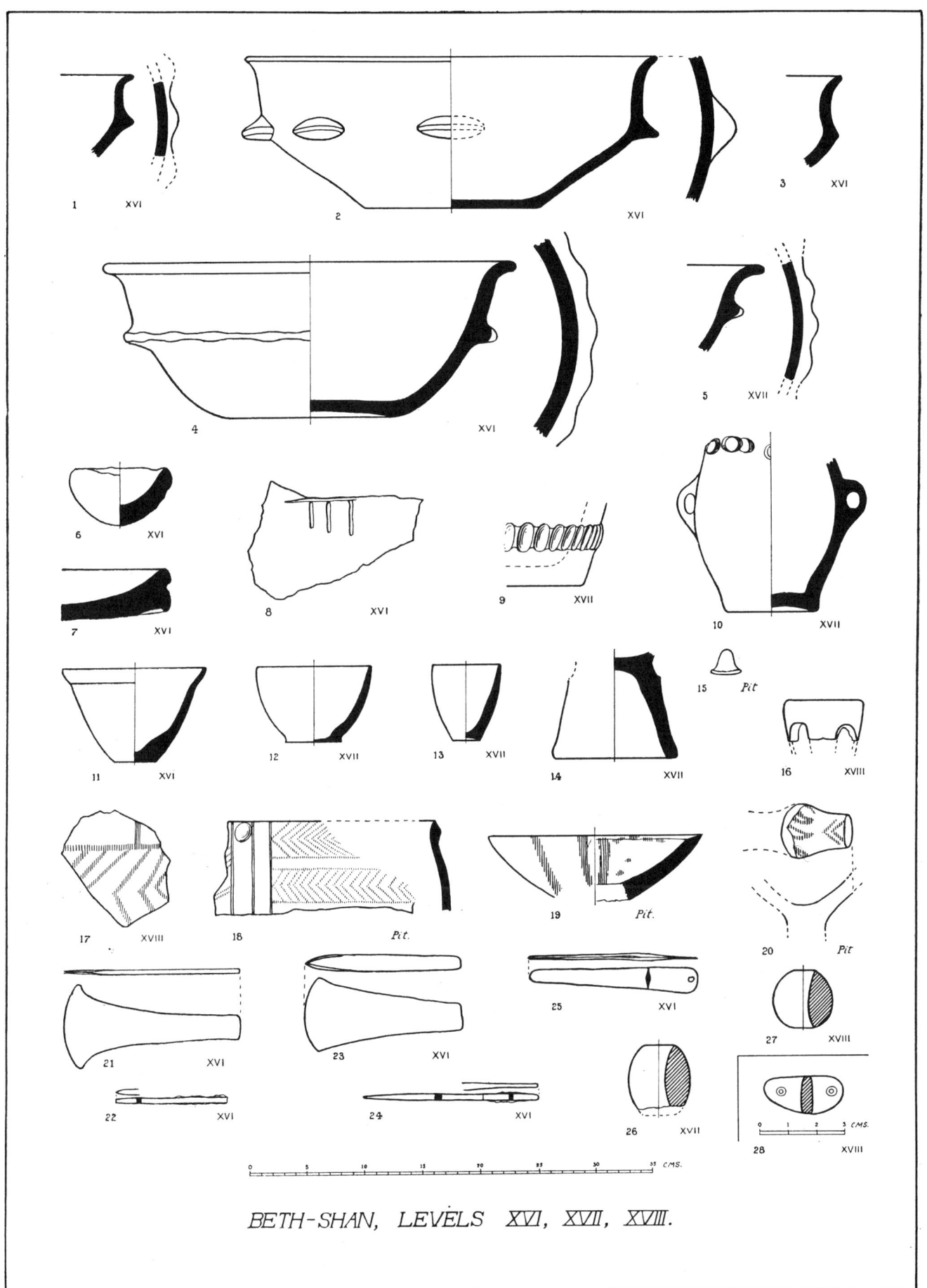

Plate III. Assorted ceramics, Levels XVI, XVII, XVIII.

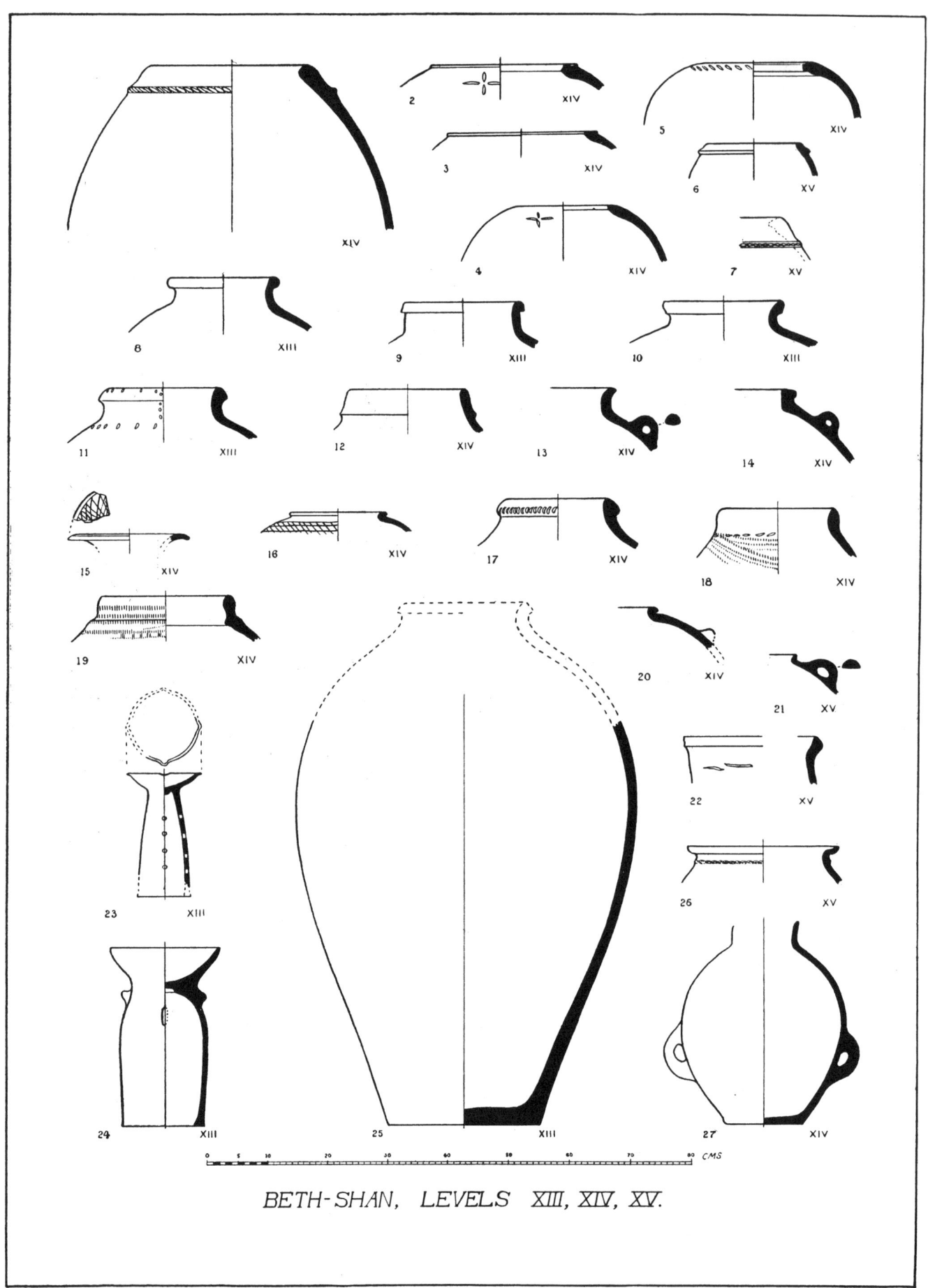

Plate IV. Assorted ceramics, Levels XIII, XIV, XV.

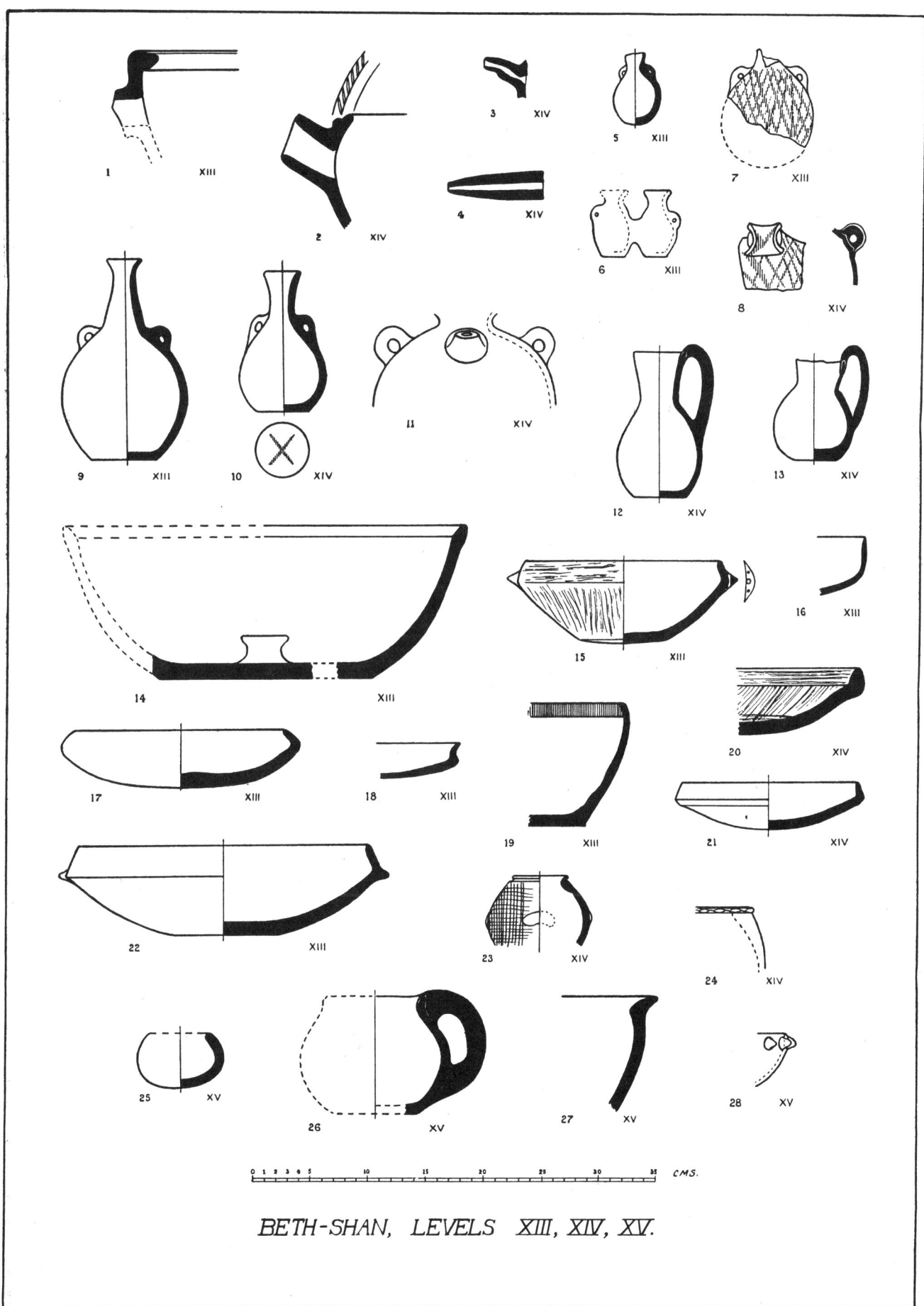

Plate V. Assorted ceramics, Levels XIII, XIV, XV.

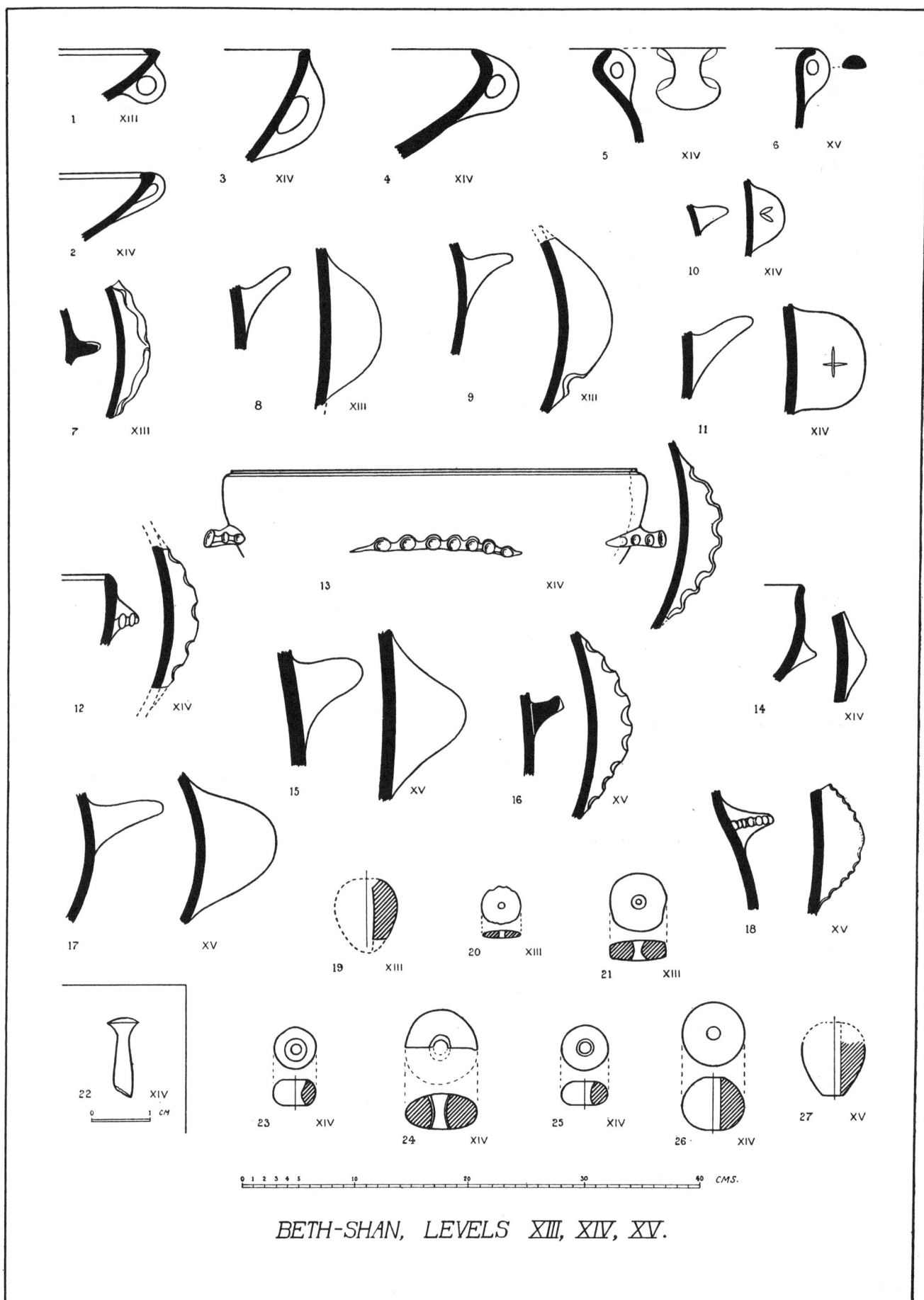

Plate VI. Assorted ceramics, Levels XIII, XIV, XV.

Figure 4.1 Metal (copper?) objects from Stratum XVI.

Figure 4.2 EB I Basalt Bowls. *a*, Museum #29-107-373.

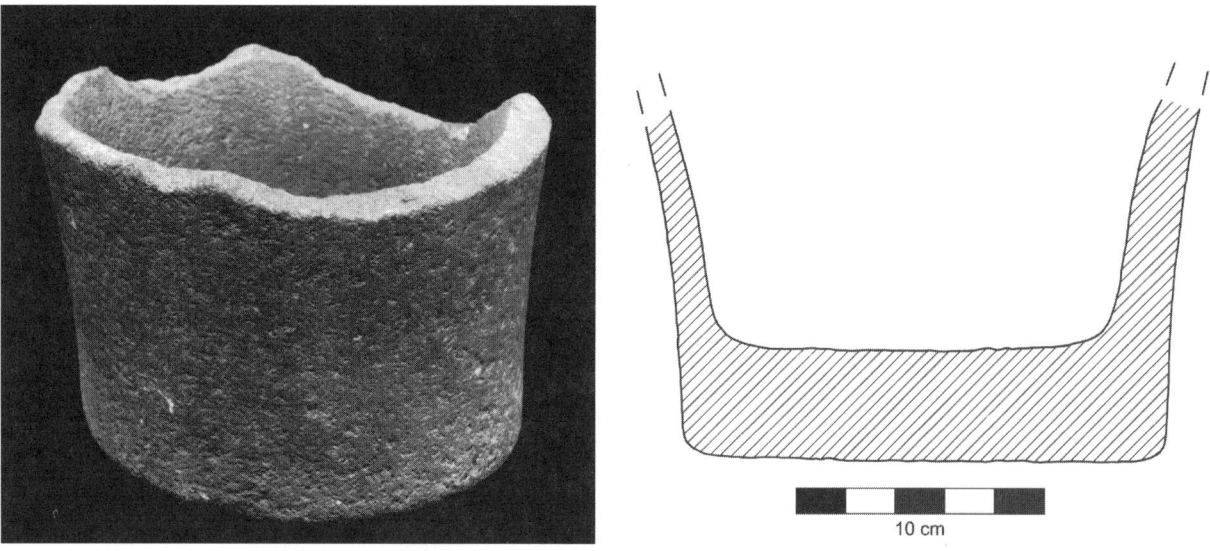

Figure 4.2 cont. *b*, Museum #34-21-45.

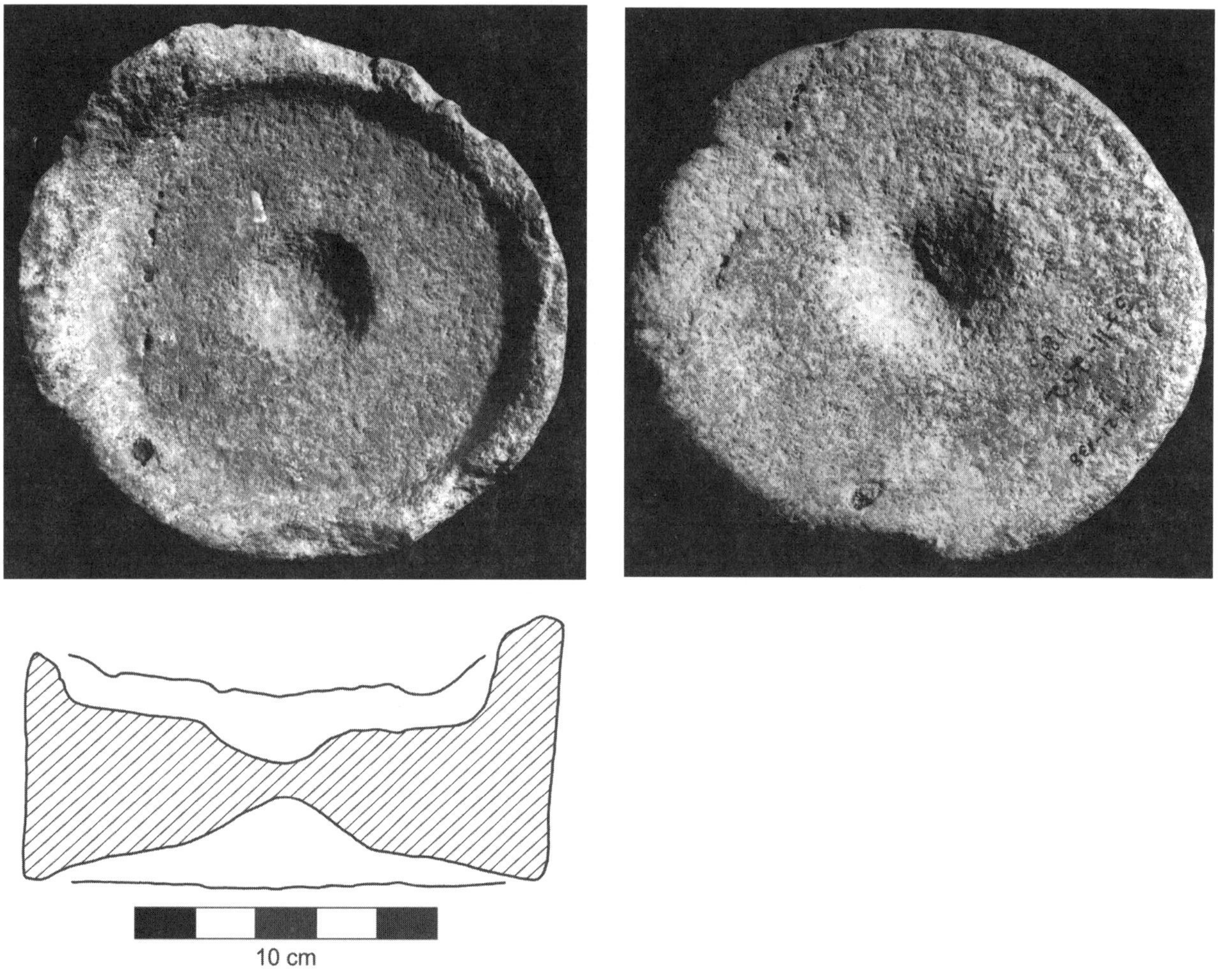

Figure 4.2 cont. *c*, Museum #34-21-138.

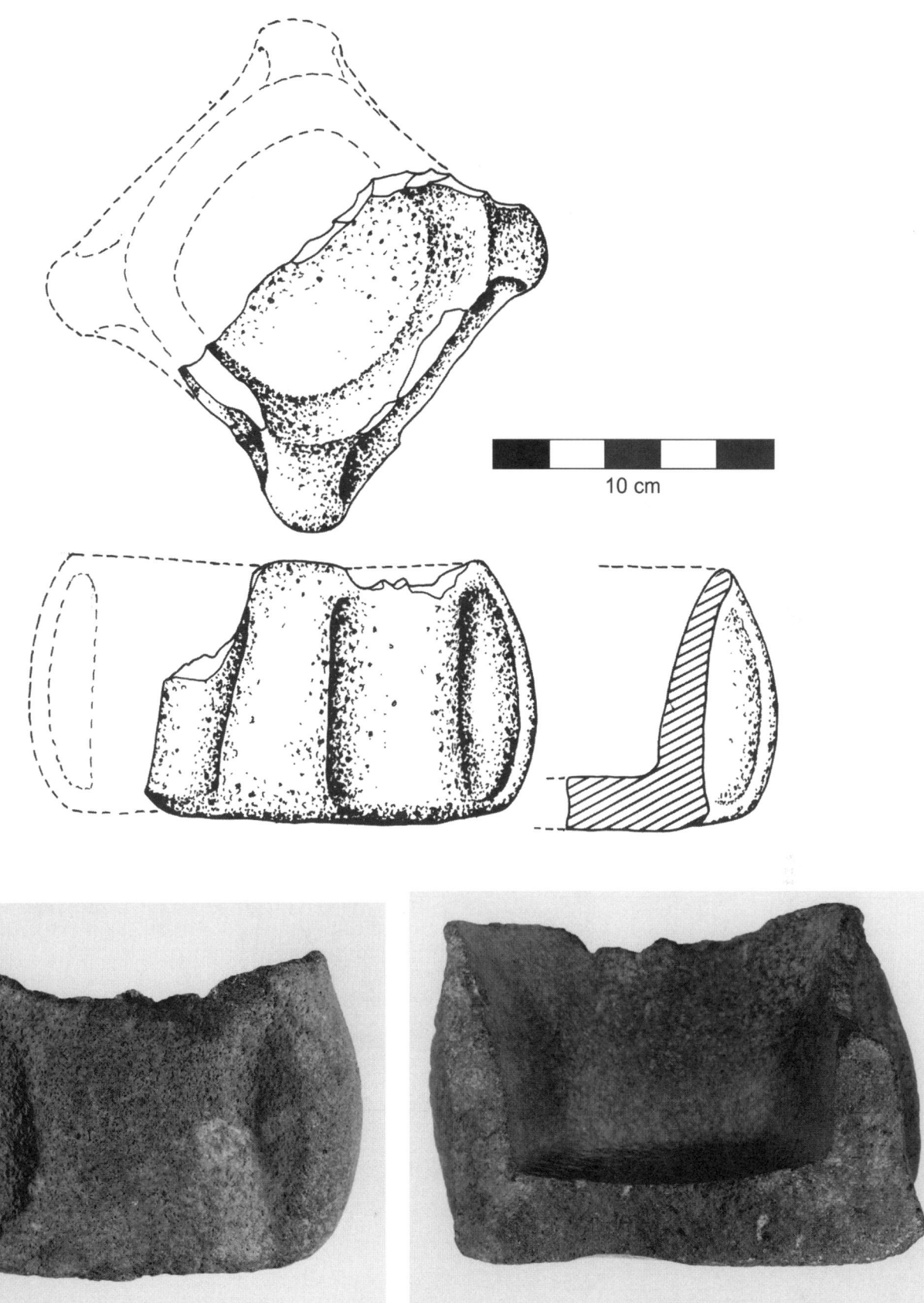

Figure 4.3 Large fragment of an unfinished, EB I Type III basalt bowl.

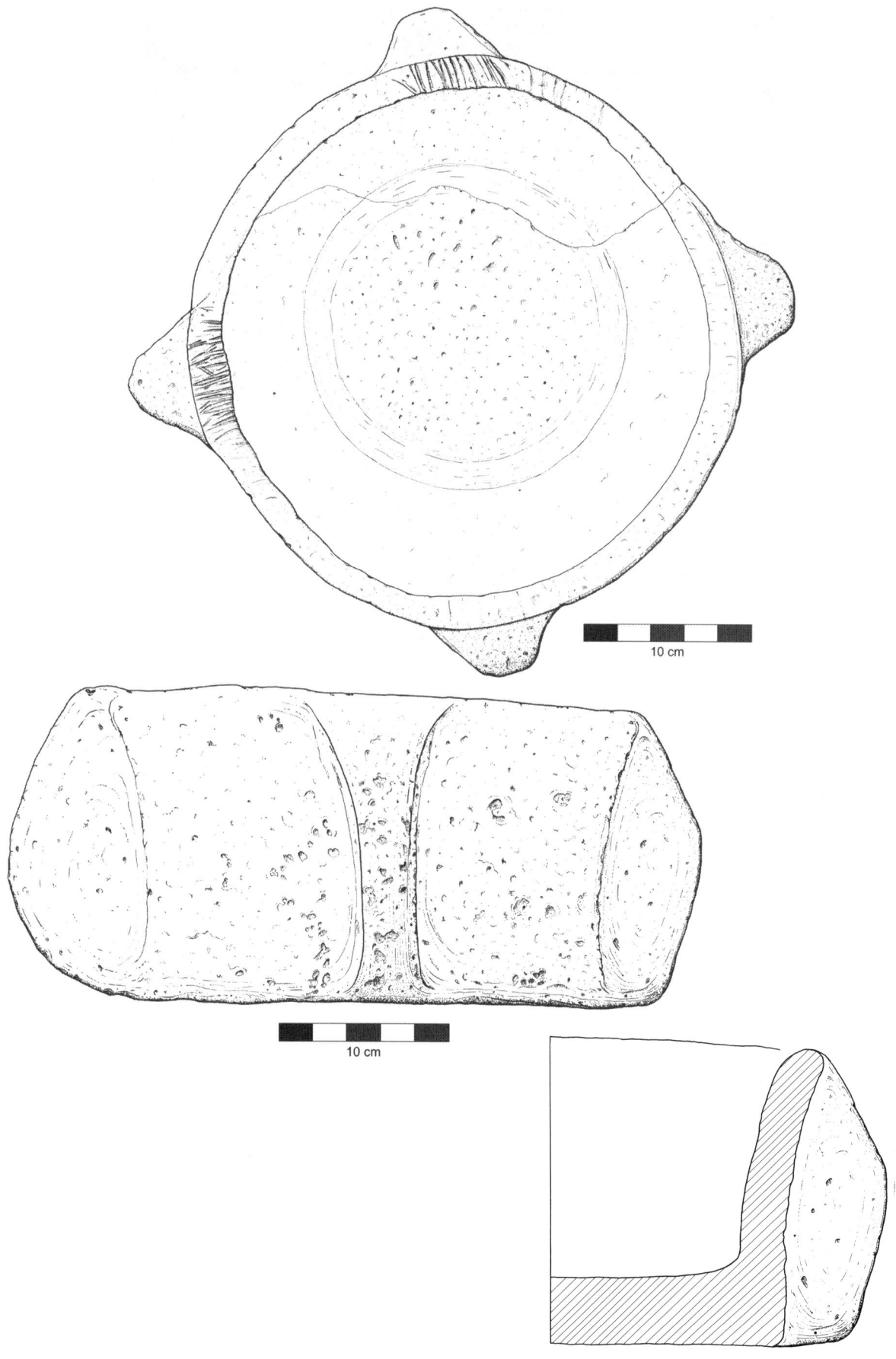

Figure 4.4 Type EB I basalt bowl from Stratum V (Mus #29-107-451).

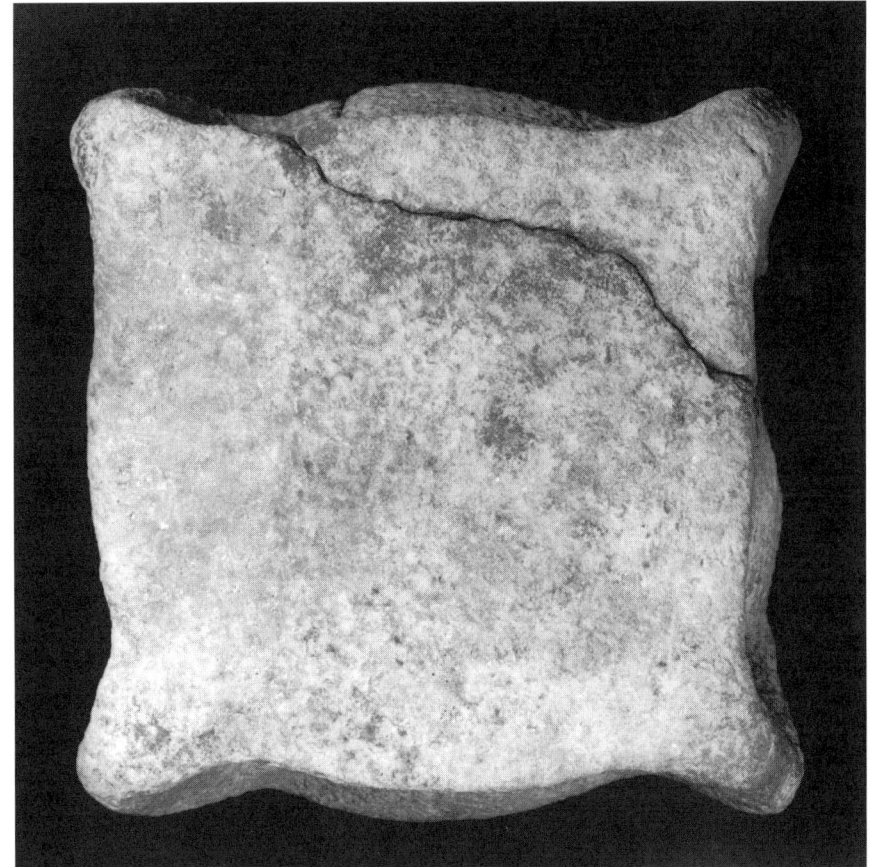

Figure 4.5 Photos of bowl in Figure 4.4.

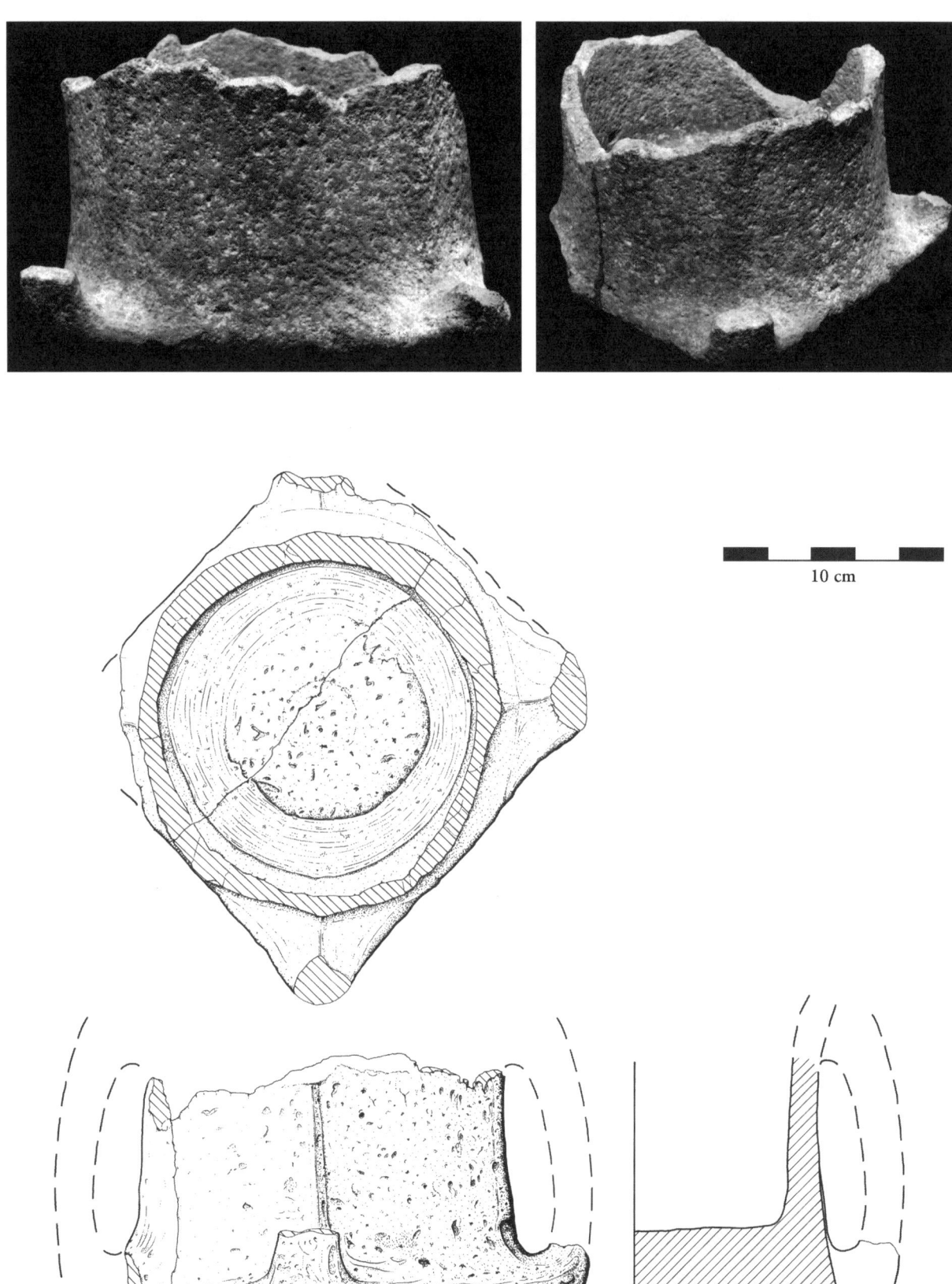

Figure 4.6 Large fragment of an EB I basalt bowl from Room 1897. Museum #34-20-702.

Figure 4.7 Example of 4-handled basalt bowl from an unknown, looted context. Courtesy of Israel Antiquities Authority.

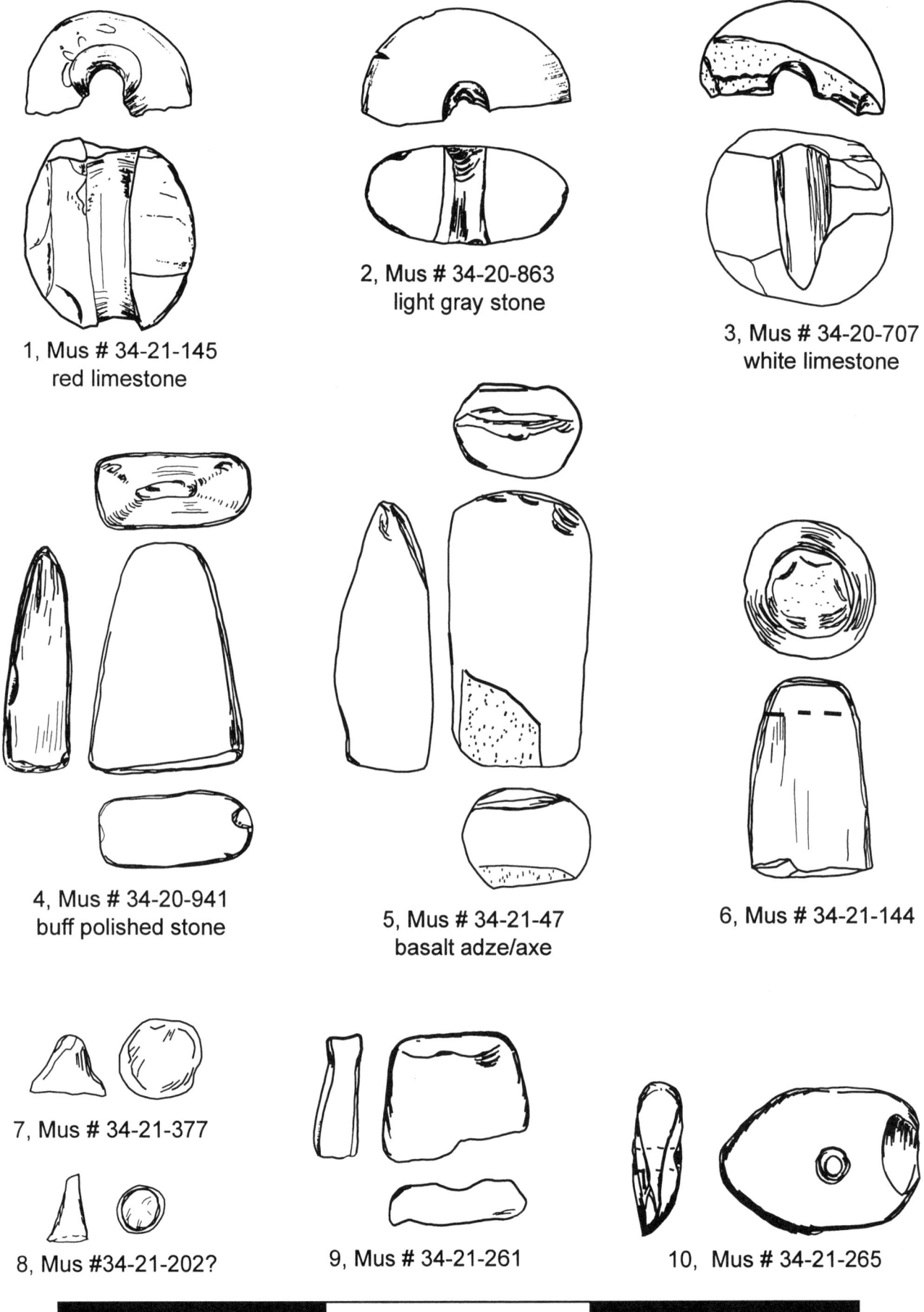

Figure 4.8 Small stone objects.

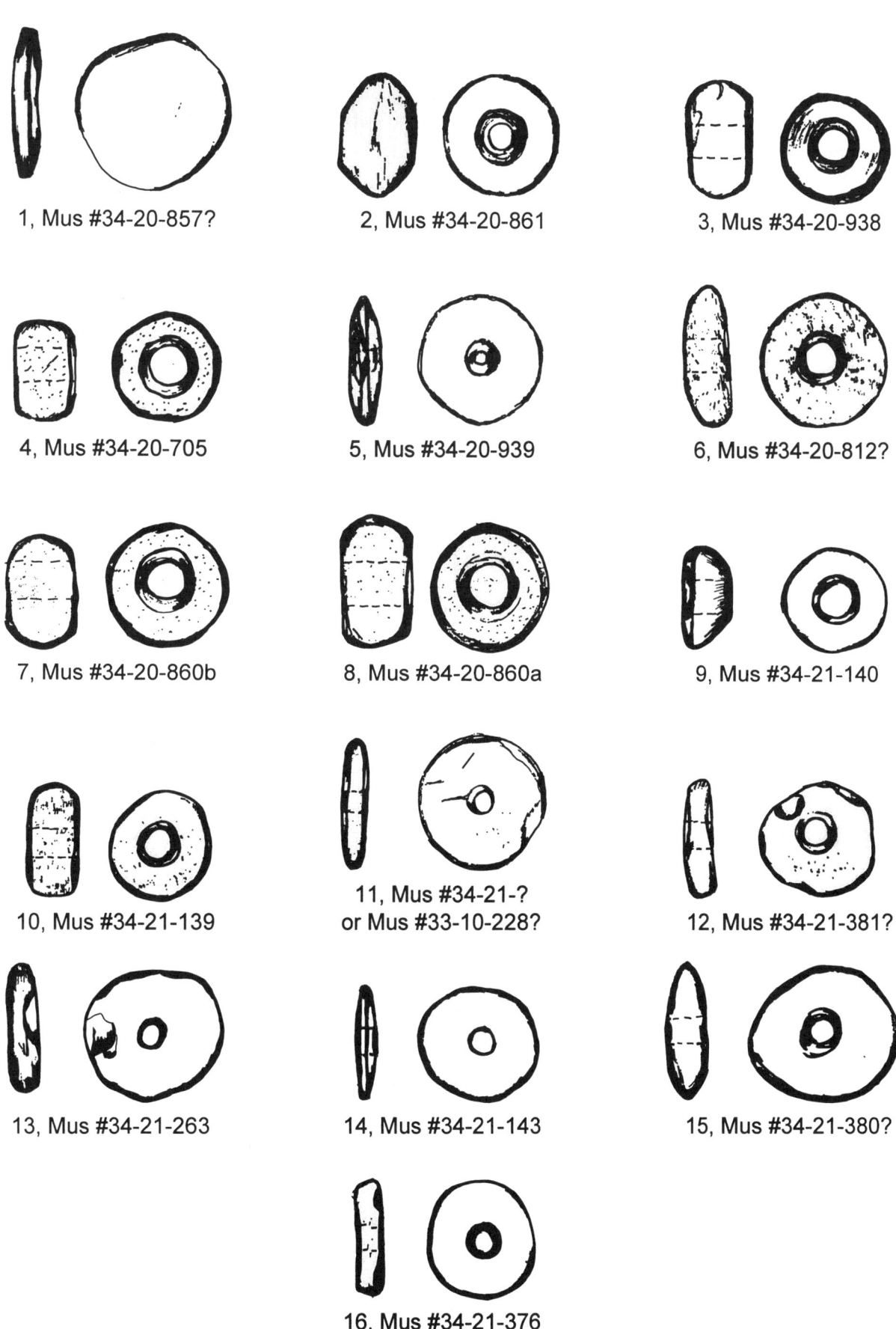

Figure 4.9 Small stone objects.

Figure 4.10 Assorted flint tools from Below Level XVIII (Stratum XIX) (Field Neg. #2939).

Figure 4.11 Assorted flint tools from Level XVIII (Field Neg. #2938).

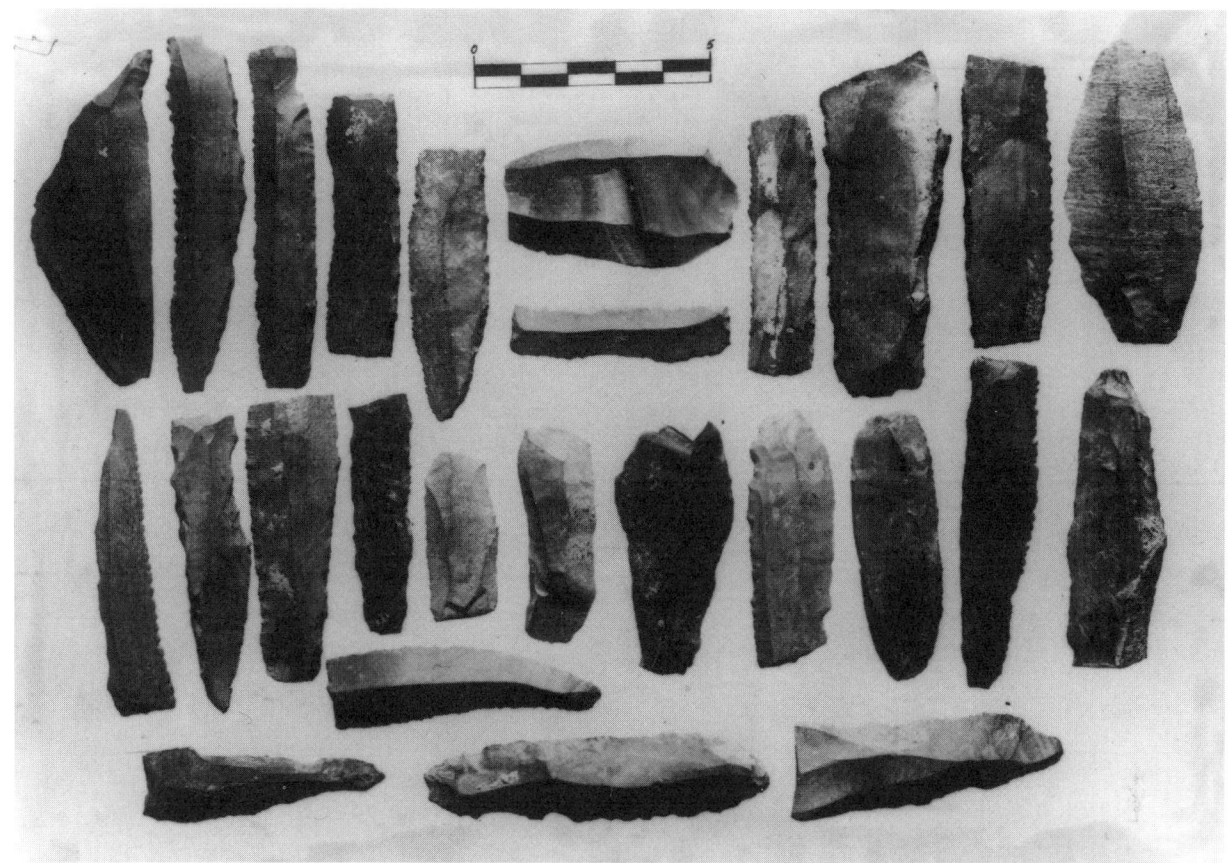

Figure 4.12 Assorted flint tools from Level XVIII (Field Neg. #2937).

Figure 4.13 Assorted flint tools from Level XVII (Field Neg. #2936).

Figure 4.14 Assorted flint tools from Level XVI (Field Neg. #2935).

Figure 4.15 Assorted flint tools from Level XV (Field Neg. #2934).

Figure 4.16 Assorted flint tools from Level XIV (Field Neg. #2933).

Figure 4.17 Assorted flint tools from Level XIII (Field Neg. #2932).

Figure 4.18 Assorted flint tools from Level XIII (Field Neg. #2892).

Figure 4.19 Assorted flint tools from Level XIII (Field Neg. #2891).

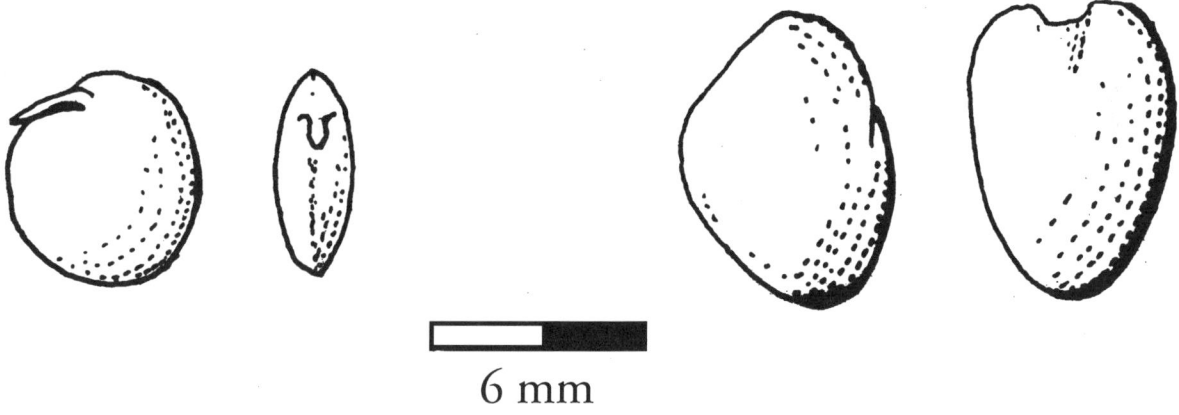

Figure A1.1 Seed of Beth Shan lentils.

Figure A1.2 Seed of Beth Shan common beans.

Index

Abu al-Kharaz, Tell, 29, 55
Abu Hamid, 33-34, 37, 47
Abydos Ware, 39
Afula, 46
Ain Ghazal, 12
Albright, W. F., 66
Aphek, Tel, 29
apsidal (apse, apsoidal, absidiale) architecture, 11-12, 14-16, 63, definition of, 11
Arad, 41, 60
architecture, 7-23, architectural traditions, (see apsidal, circular, curvilinear rectilinear)
Asia Minor, 66

band slip (see grain-wash)
Banning, E. B. M., 40
Bar-Yosef, O., 40
basalt, 41, 44, 57-60, 176, 178, 180, 182-183
beans, 66-67, 191
Beck, P., 53, 55
Beisân, 1
Beisân Expedition, 1, 3-5
bench, 17, 22, 25-26
Beth Shean Ware (BSW), 39-40
Beth Yerah, Tel, 29
Beth Yerah Ware (Khirbet Kerak Ware), 29, 64
bin (see storage facility)
black burnished, 16
bricks (see mudbricks)
Bronze Age, 66-67
Byblos, 12, 34, 41

Canaanean (blades), 60
Cavedweller-Ware, 2
ceramics (see pottery)
Chalcolithic, 5, 34-50, 56-58, 60-61, 162-163, Early Chalcolithic (EC), 12-13, 15, 28, 33,-34, 36, 40, 61-62
chipped stone (flint) artifacts, xiii-xiv, 60
circular (architecture), 14-15, 17, 19, 26, 69
Commenge, C., xiii, 47
copper, 56-57, 177
Crete, 66-67
curvilinear, curving, curved (architecture), 11-12, 14-20, 23, 28-29, 63, 68-70

Department of Antiquities of the British Mandate of Palestine, 2, 4, 32, 56
door socket, 27, 57
doorway (see also entranceway, threshold), 12, 21, 24, 26-27
Droop, J. P (wrote Jericho pottery report 1935), 38

Early Bronze Age (EBA), 4, 66, Early Bronze I (EB I), 12, 14-20, 28-29, 32-35, 37-38, 40, 42-58, 60-65, 132, 164, 177, 179-180, 182, Early Bronze II (EB II), 41, 50-55, 64, Early Bronze III (EB III), 29, 51, 62, Early EB I, 14-15, 17, 28, 34, 37-38, 42-44, 46, 48-50, 52, 56, 61-63, 133, Early Bronze IV (see Intermediate Bronze)
Egypt, 2, 5, 40, 66-67
Egyptian, 29, 53-54
Egyptianized, 53, 164

Ein el Jarba, 45
Eisenberg, E., 41, 52
ellipse (architecture), 14
Enéolithique Récent (see also Chalcolithic), 41
entranceway (see doorway)
En Shadud, 19, 28, 32, 37, 46, 48-50, 52-54
Epipaleolithic, 9
erosion, 9, 20, 26, 30
es-Sakan, Tel, 29
es-Sayidiyeh, Tell, 29

Fendi, Tall, 42
FitzGerald, G. M., xiii-xiv, 1-5, 7-10, 14-18, 20, 22-24, 26-29, 31-35, 39-40, 42-44, 49, 51-54, 56-59, 62-64, 66, 81, 85, 87, 90, 94, 98, 103, 107, 112, 164-70
flint, 4, 56, 58, 60, 186-90
floor (see pavement)
fortifications, 23, 29, 64

Garfinkel, 34, 37-43, 46
Ghassul, Teleilat, 33, 37-38, 40-42, 44
Ghassulian (post Rabah, late phase of Chalcolithic), 40-42
Ghrubba, 34
Gilboa, Mt., 3
Gilead, 3
grain, 26, 64, 66
grain-wash (band slip), 50, 52, 54
Gray Burnished Ware (GBW; Esdraelon Ware), 16, 39, 42, 46, 48-49
Greece, 66
ground stone artifacts, xiii, 56-57, 60

Harod Valley, 2-3
Hebrew University, 29, 44, 63-66, 83
Husn, el Tell, 1

Illin Tahtit, Horvat, 41, 59
infant jar burials, 41
Initial EB I, 38
Intermediate Bronze period (Middle Bronze I, Early Bronze IV), 55, 57
Irano-Turanian, 67
Israel Antiquities Authority (IAA), 3-4, 32-33, 56, 183
Issachar, Heights of, 3
Istaba, Tell, 64

Jalud (Nahal Harod), 2
James, Frances, 3
Jawa, 29
Jayne, Horace H. F. (Museum Director, 1929-40), 1-2, 4
Jericho, 2, 29, 34-35, 38, 41-42
Jordan Valley, 1-3, 33-34, 37-38, 43, 47-48, 50, 52-55
Judaean Desert, 59

Kabri, 28
Khirbet Kerak Ware (see also Beth Yerah Ware), 29
Kittan, Tell, 52

lane (path, passageway, thoroughfare), 17-18, 20, 22-24, 26-28, 117
Late EB I, 17, 19, 29, 41, 44, 46, 48-55, 63-65, 164
Late Neolithic (LN), 11-13, 15-16, 28, 32-33, 35-37, 41, 45, 60-62
Late Chalcolithic, 41, 45
Late Chalcolithic/Pottery Neolithic B (LN/PNB), 42
Late Neolithic/Early Chalcolithic (LN/EC), 12-13, 15-16, 31-37, 39-40, 42-51, 59-61, 63-65
ledge handle, 5, 16, 35, 38-39, 42-43, 46, 48, 50-54
legumes, 26
lentils, 66-67, 191
level books (Beisân Expedition notebooks with elevations of architecture), 3-4
limestone, 58-59
locus ("L"), 3, 8, 12, 16-17, 21-22, 24, 26, 28, 68
Lod, Tel, 17
long room, 16
loop handles (strap handles), 16, 33-34, 44-45, 47, 50, 52, 54
lost horizon, the, 42
Lovell, J., 39, 41
Lower Galilee, 34

Mazar, A., 25, 28, 40, 44, 50, 54, 64, 83
Mefjar, Tell el, 43
Megiddo (Mutesellim, Tell el), 1, 19, 29, 51, 63
Me'ona, 60
Meser, 48
metal, 54, 56-57, 60, 177
Middle Bronze Age, 2, Middle Bronze Age I (see Intermediate Bronze Age)
Middle Chalcolithic, 31, 34, 37-43, 61
Middle Europe, 66-67

mudbrick (bricks), 7, 9, 12, 14, 16, 18, 20, 24-26, 28, 30-31, 116
Munhatta, 33-34, 38, 45, 47
Museum (University of Pennsylvania Museum of Archaeology and Anthropology), xiii, 1-4, 32-33, 56, 58, 81
Mutesellim, Tell el (Megiddo), 1
Nahal Harod, 2
Nahal Mishmar, 56
Nahal Qanah, 37
Naharon, Tel, 4
Negev, 47, 54
Neolithic (Neolithique), xiii, 2, 5, 9-15, 19, 33-45, 47, 55, 61, 66-67
Neolithique Moyen, 34
Neolithique Rècent, 34
Northern EB I, 16, 50, 53, 63

oval (architecture), 14

Palestine, 1-2, 4, 56, 66-67
Palmahim Quarry, 19, 59
pavement (floor of stone, potsherds or mudbrick), 14, 17, 20, 23, 26-27, 30
Pella, 52
Petrie, W. F. M., 2
pilaster, 21-23
pillars, 28
pit dwellings (semi-subterranean dwellings), 7, 9-10, 61
pits, 7-10, 14, 30-31, 34-36, 40, 43, 61-62, 92-93, 164
plano-convex bricks, 9, 13-15, 97
plants, 66-67
post holes, 26
pot stands, 12
potter's wheel, 57
pottery, xiii-xiv, 2, 4-6, 8, 10, 12, 15-16, 24, 28-55, 61, 63-64, 120-61, 169
Pre-Pottery Neolithic, 41
Proto-Urban (pre-urbain), 48

Qatifian Ware, 39

Rabah, Wadi (LN phase/stage, post Sha'ar Hagolan), 33-35, 38, 40, 45
rectangular (architecture), 12, 24, 26, 28, 53, 58

rectilinear (architecture), 11-20, 23-24, 26-29, 45, 53, 63-64
Rockefeller Museum, 4
roof, 9-10, 22, 26
rotary motion, 45, 57-60
rounded corner (see also rectilinear architecture), 27

Sartaba, Jebel, 42
sausage-shaped, 14, 16, 18, 28
Sayidiyeh, Tell es-(et Tahta), 29
seeds, 66-67
Sha'ar Hagolan phase/stage (LN, pre-Rabah), 33-35, 37
Shalem, Tel, 29, 51, 54, 64
Shuna, Tell es-, 34, 42
silo (see storage facility)
social organization, 20, 23, 29, 63
South Temple, 58
square (architecture) (see rectangular)
squatters, 17
stone wall foundations/architecture, 13-14, 16, 18-20, 24, 26, 28, 30
storage facility (bin, silo), 14, 17, 19, 22, 26, 68-69
stratigraphy, 3-4, 6-30, 40

Teo, Tel, 41
Thawwab, Jebel Abu el-, 43
Thotmes Temple, 58
threshold (see doorway)
tournette, 33, 35, 37
Troy, 66-67
Tsaf, Tel, 34, 36
tubular handles, 34, 39

Umm Hammad, Tell, 51
Umm Hammad Ware (ceramique proto-urbain D; Proto-Urban D Ware), 48, 55

virgin soil (natural deposit free of artifacts), 1-2, 7-8, 57
Vitto, Fanny, 4

weeds, 66-67
white ware (vaiselles blanches), 33, 35
Wright, G. E., 2, 5

Yadin, Y., 25
Yarmukian (earliest LN phase), 35
Yiftah'el, 28, 32, 37-38, 41-46, 48-49, 57, 63, 132